EXPEDITION
BACKYARD

EXPLORING NATURE FROM COUNTRY TO CITY

ALSO BY
ROSEMARY MOSCO

BIRDING IS MY FAVORITE VIDEO GAME

SOLAR SYSTEM: OUR PLACE IN SPACE
(WITH JON CHAD)

THE ATLAS OBSCURA EXPLORER'S GUIDE FOR THE WORLD'S MOST ADVENTUROUS KID
(WITH DYLAN THURAS AND JOY ANG)

BUTTERFLIES ARE PRETTY . . . GROSS!
(WITH JACOB SOUVA)

A POCKET GUIDE TO PIGEON WATCHING: GETTING TO KNOW THE WORLD'S MOST MISUNDERSTOOD BIRD

EXPEDITION BACKYARD

EXPLORING NATURE FROM COUNTRY TO CITY

ROSEMARY MOSCO

AND

BINGLIN HU

COLOR DESIGN BY ASHANTI FORTSON
FLATTING ASSISTANCE BY DESOLINA FLETCHER

RH GRAPHIC

NEW YORK

Expedition Backyard was drawn using fountain pen–friendly India ink in a .35mm nib fountain pen on 110lb paper, then digitally colored with Photoshop. It was lettered with Zemke Hand.

Text copyright © 2022 by Rosemary Mosco
Cover and interior illustrations copyright © 2022 by Binglin Hu

All rights reserved. Published in the United States by RH Graphic, an imprint of Random House Children's Books, a division of Penguin Random House LLC, New York.

RH Graphic with the book design is a trademark of Penguin Random House LLC.

Visit us on the web! RHKidsGraphic.com • @RHKidsGraphic

Educators and librarians, for a variety of teaching tools, visit us at RHTeachersLibrarians.com

Library of Congress Cataloging-in-Publication Data is available upon request.
ISBN 978-0-593-12734-6 (hardcover) — ISBN 978-0-593-12735-3 (lib. bdg.)
ISBN 978-0-593-12736-0 (ebook)

Design by Patrick Crotty
Color design by Ashanti Fortson
Flatting assistance by Desolina Fletcher

MANUFACTURED IN CHINA
10 9 8 7 6 5 4 3 2 1
First Edition

A comic on every bookshelf.

To my heroes, the wildlife rehabilitators who work tirelessly to help all urban creatures, including the many that I've brought to you.
—R.M.

For Ethan.
—B.H.

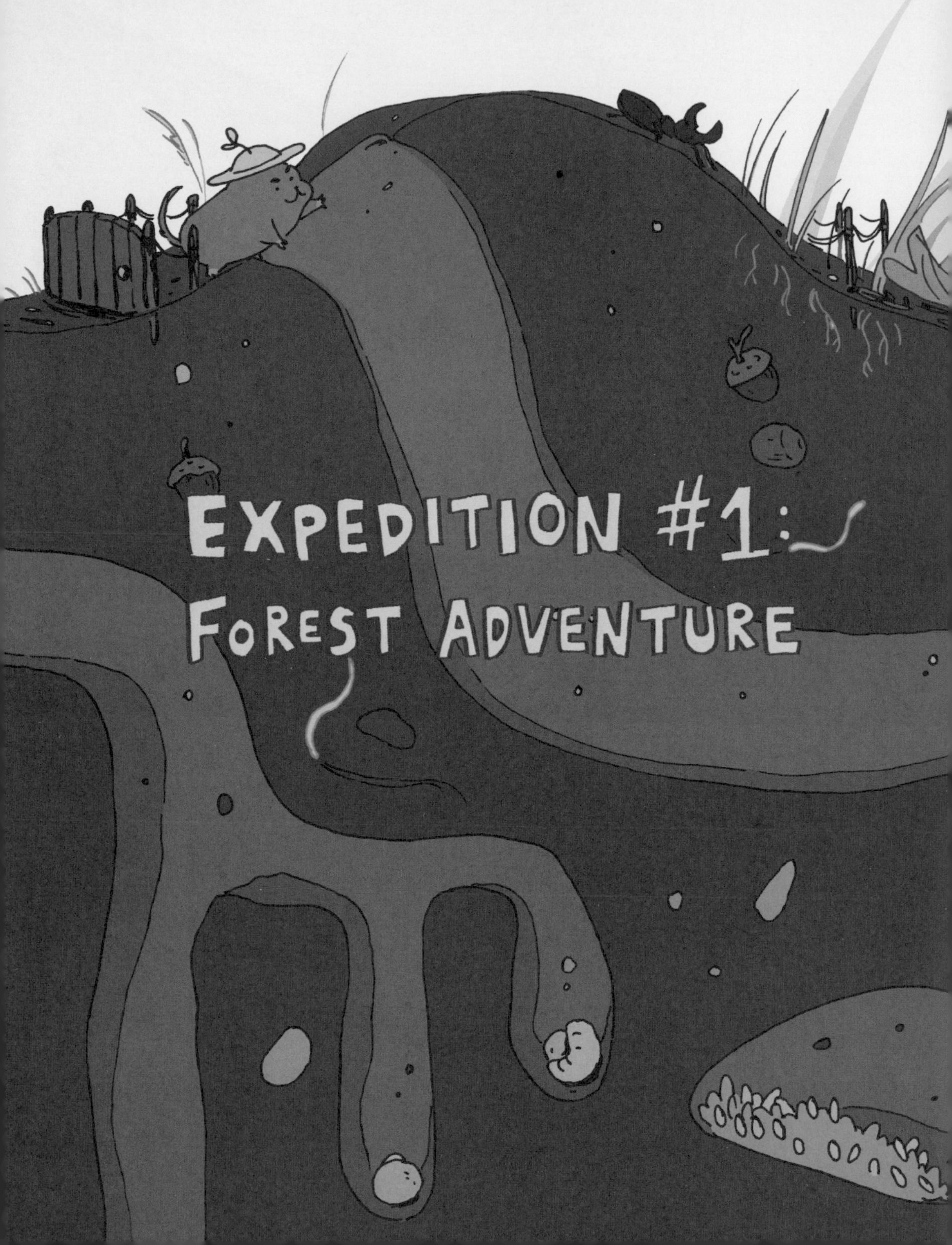
EXPEDITION #1:
FOREST ADVENTURE

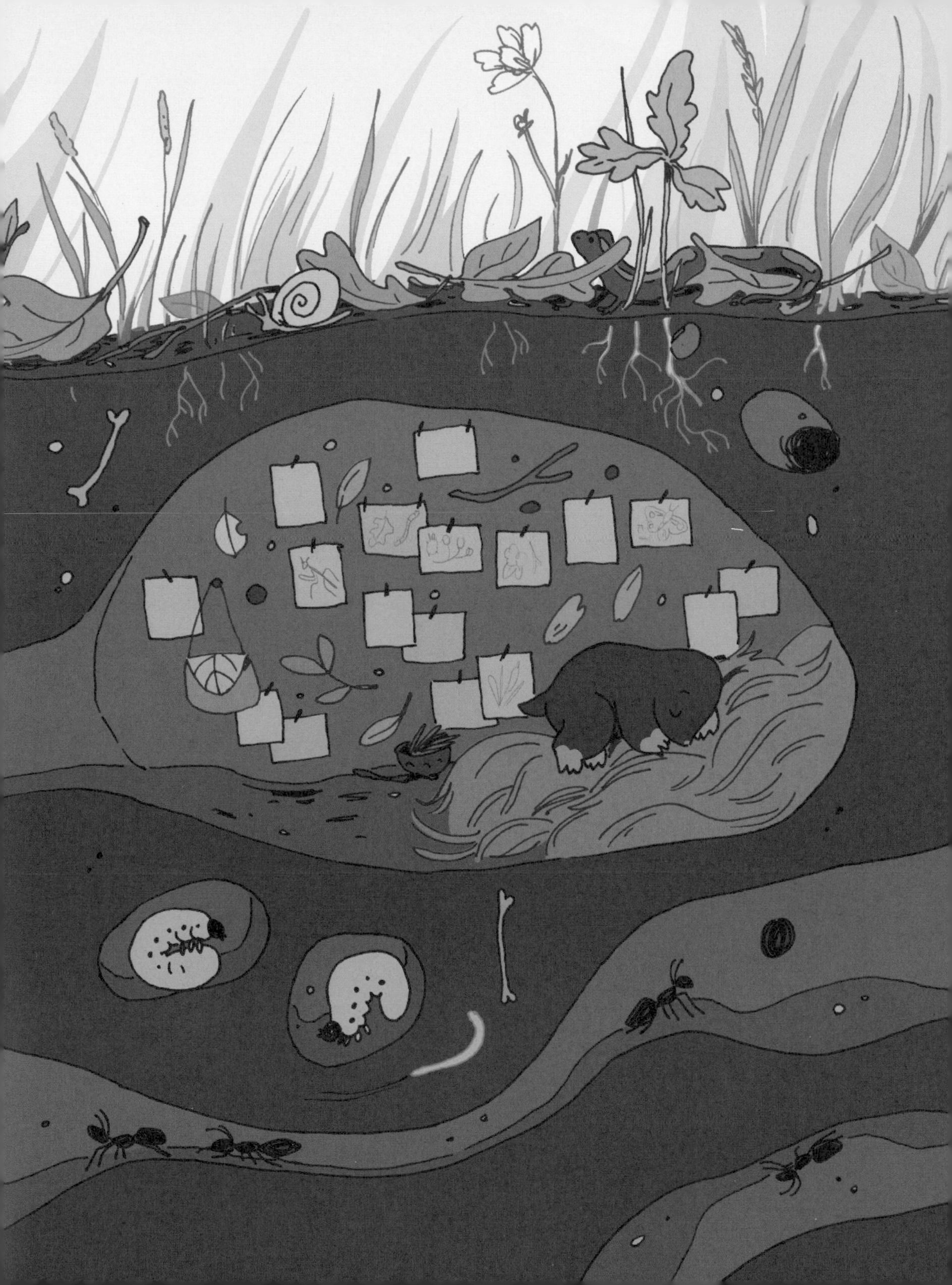

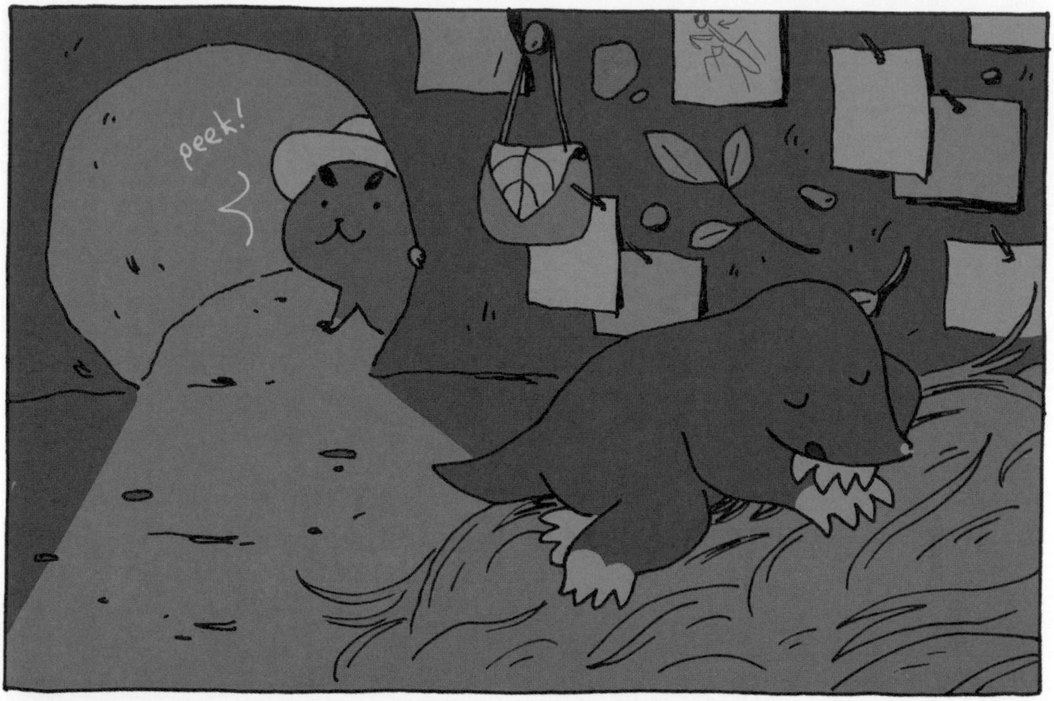
peek!

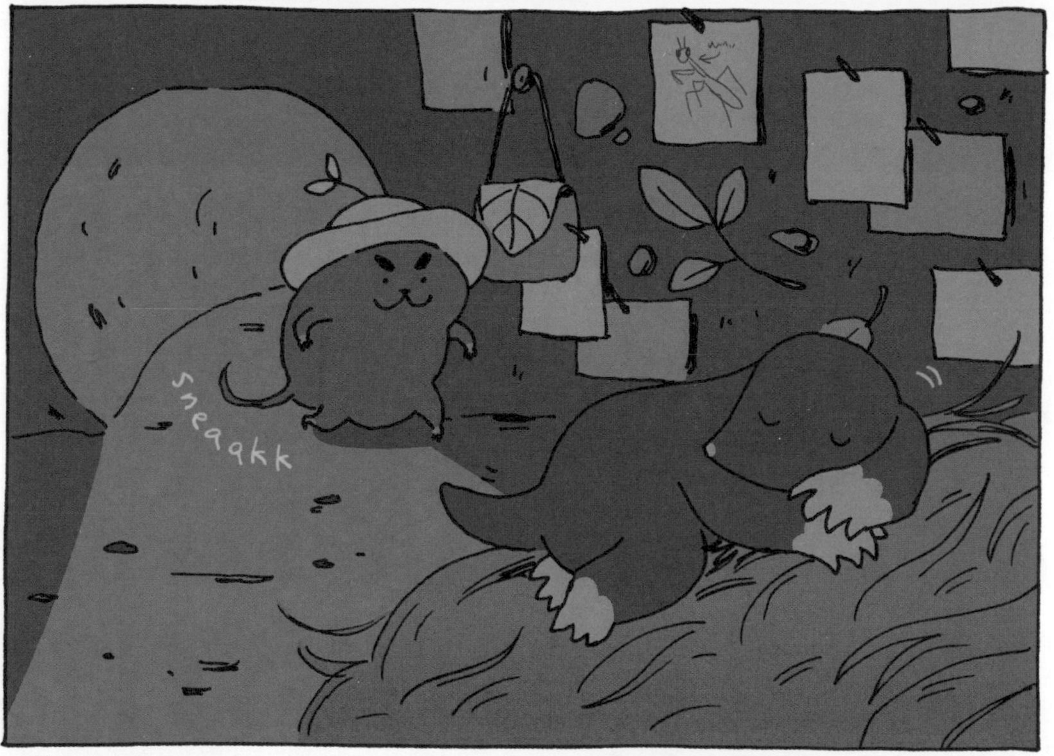
sneaakk

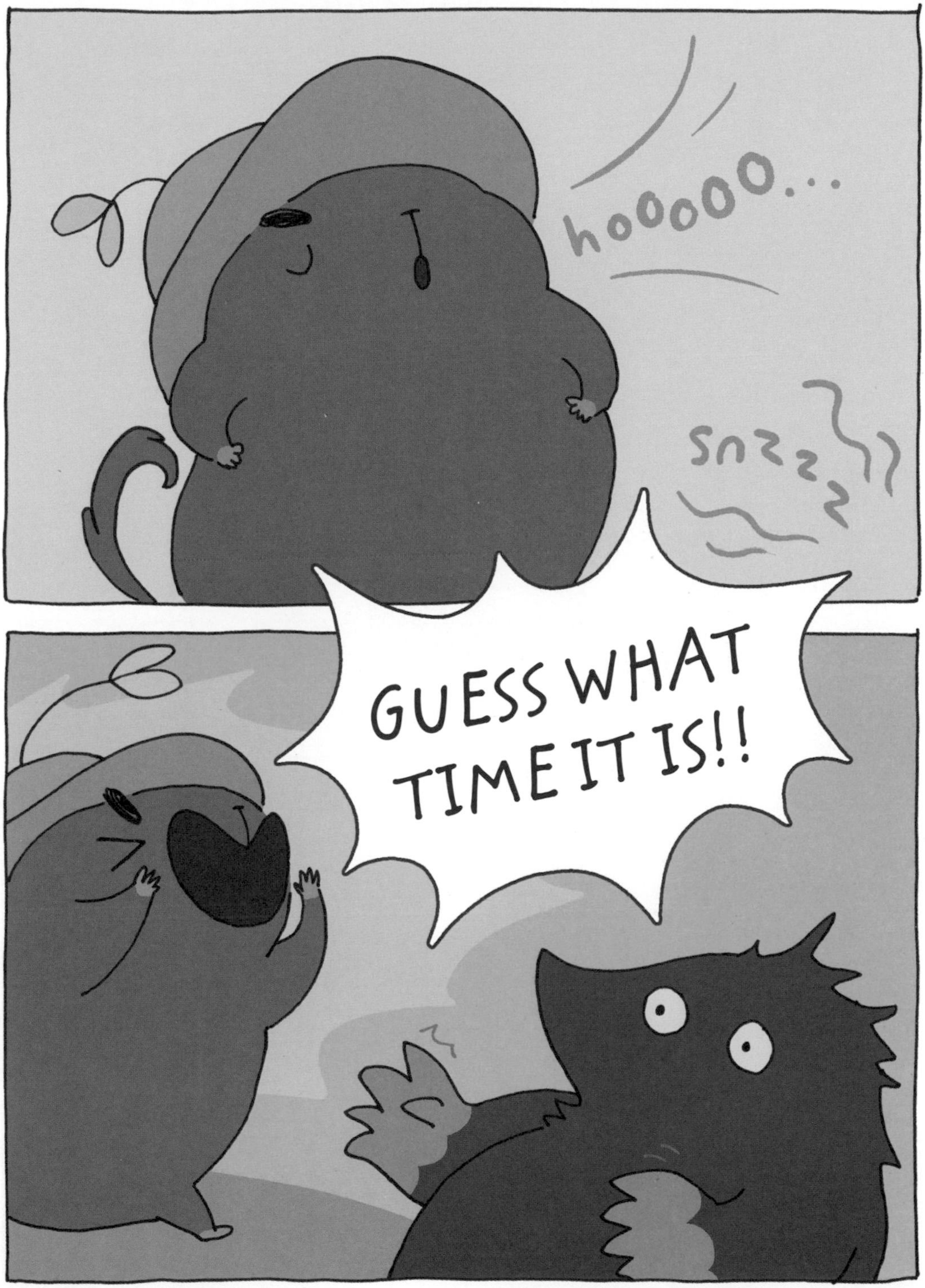
hoOoOO...
Snzzzz
GUESS WHAT TIME IT IS!!

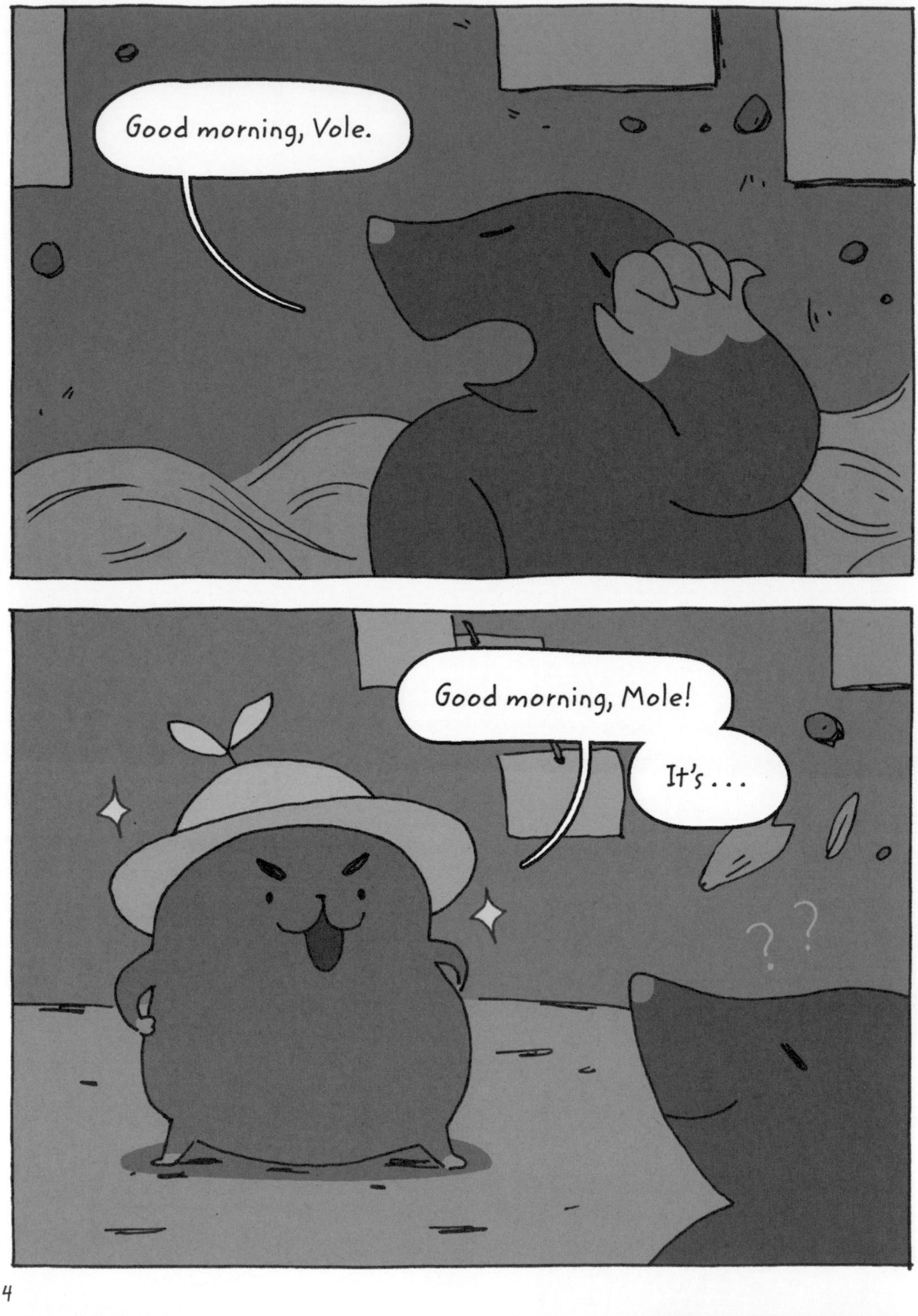
Good morning, Vole.
Good morning, Mole!
It's . . .
? ?

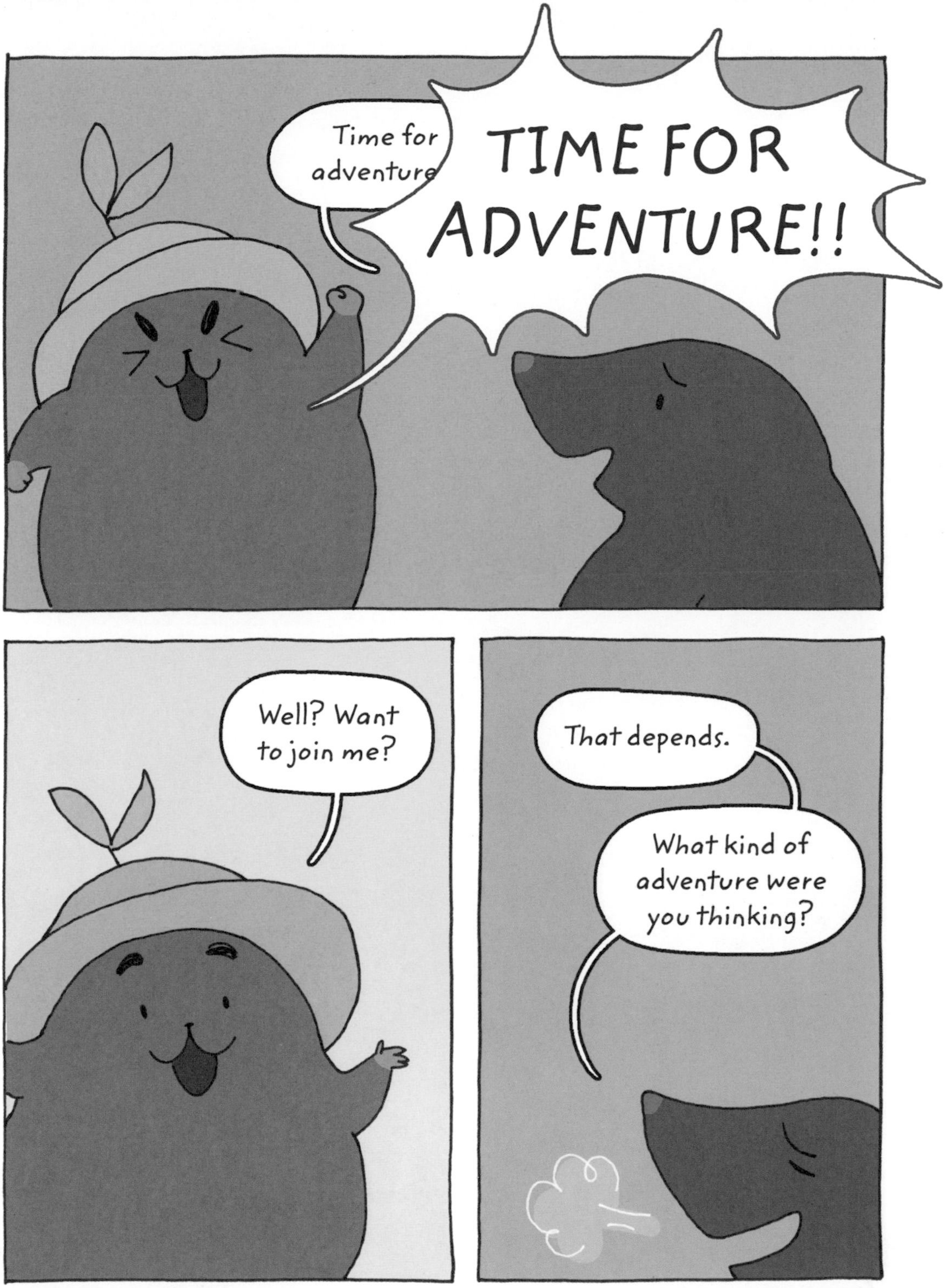
Time for adventure
TIME FOR ADVENTURE!!
Well? Want to join me?
That depends.
What kind of adventure were you thinking?

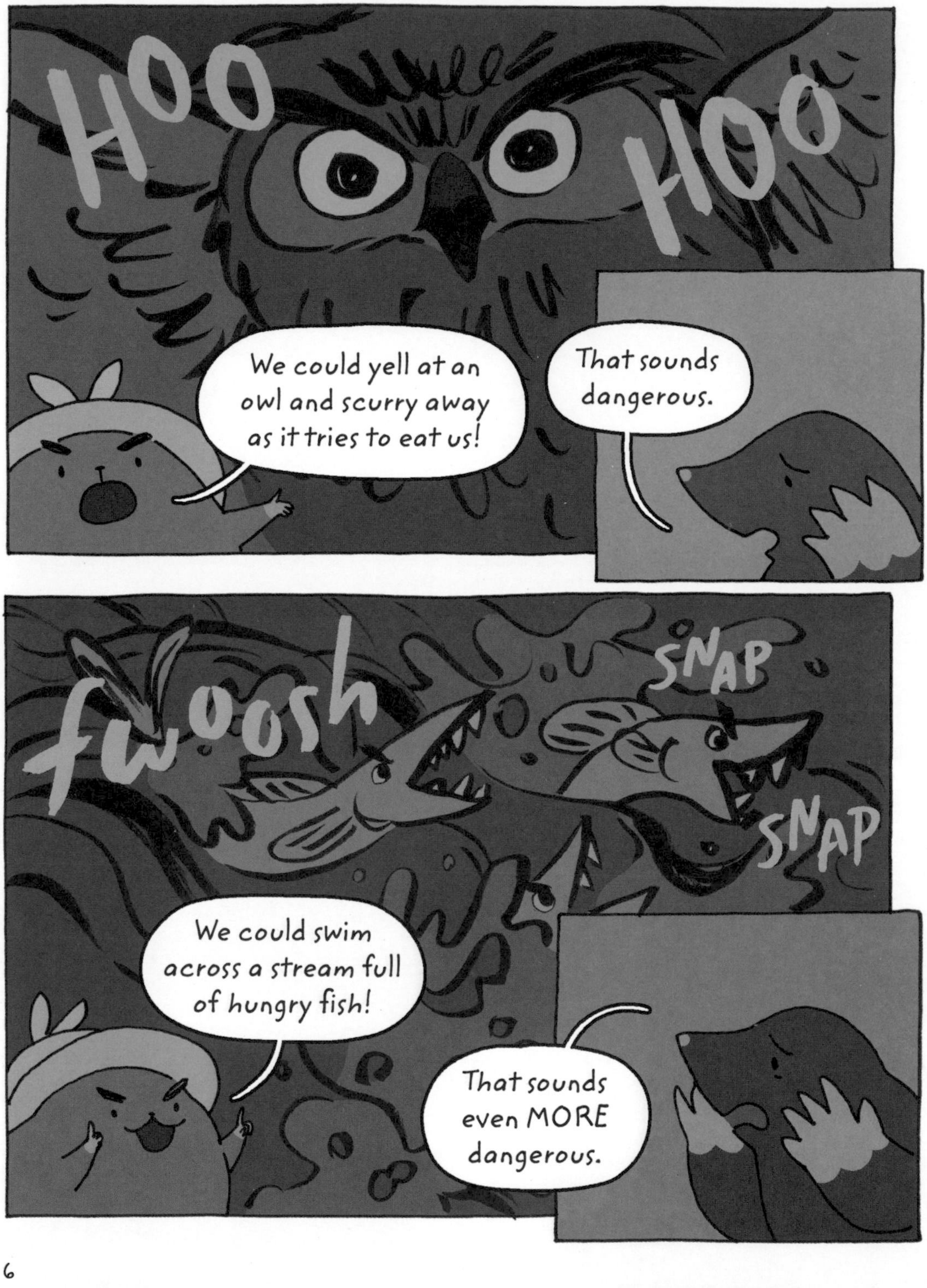
HOO
HOO
We could yell at an owl and scurry away as it tries to eat us!
That sounds dangerous.
fwoosh
SNAP
SNAP
We could swim across a stream full of hungry fish!
That sounds even MORE dangerous.

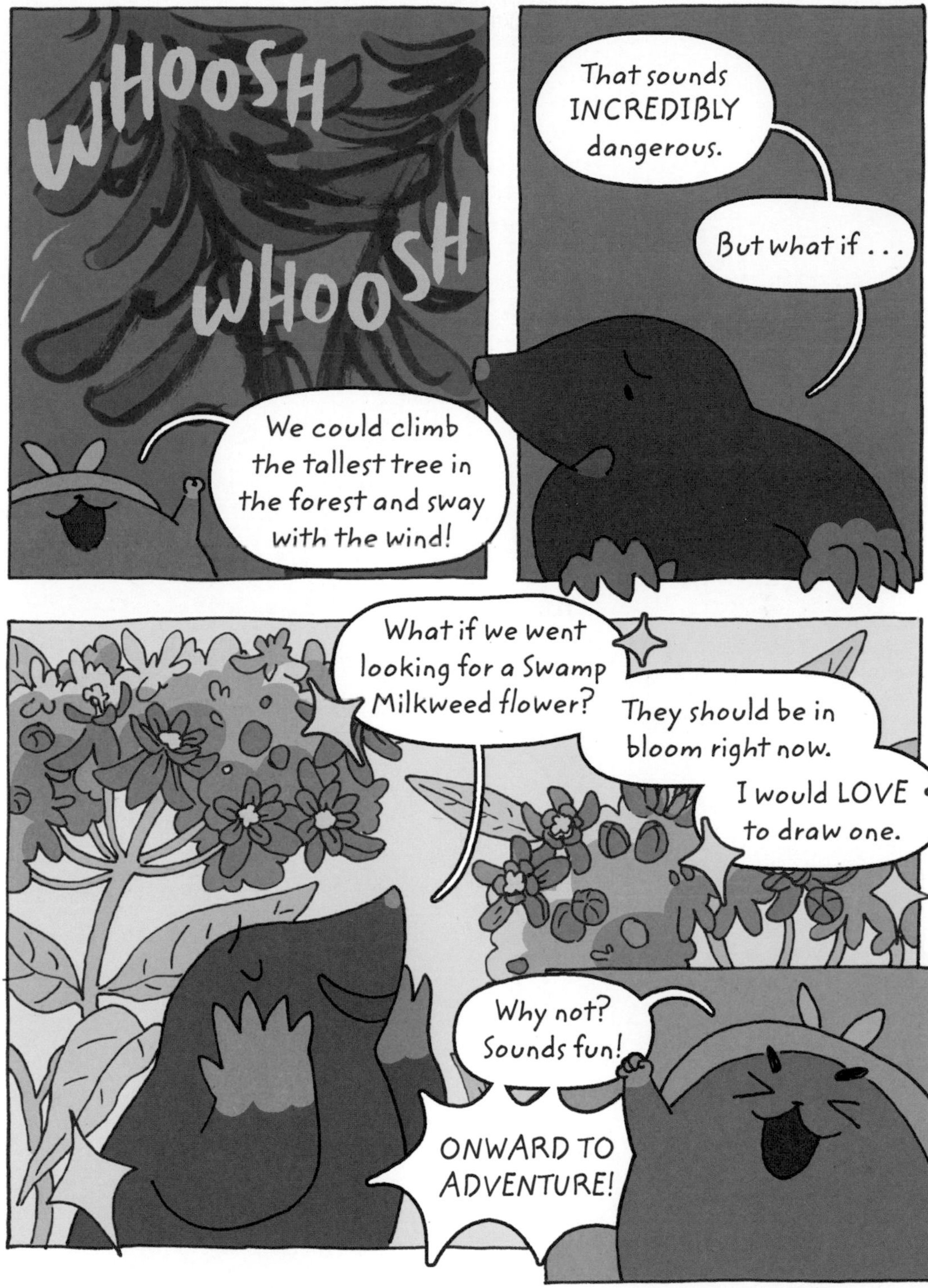
WHOOSH
WHOOSH
We could climb the tallest tree in the forest and sway with the wind!
That sounds INCREDIBLY dangerous.
But what if . . .
What if we went looking for a Swamp Milkweed flower?
They should be in bloom right now.
I would LOVE to draw one.
Why not? Sounds fun!
ONWARD TO ADVENTURE!

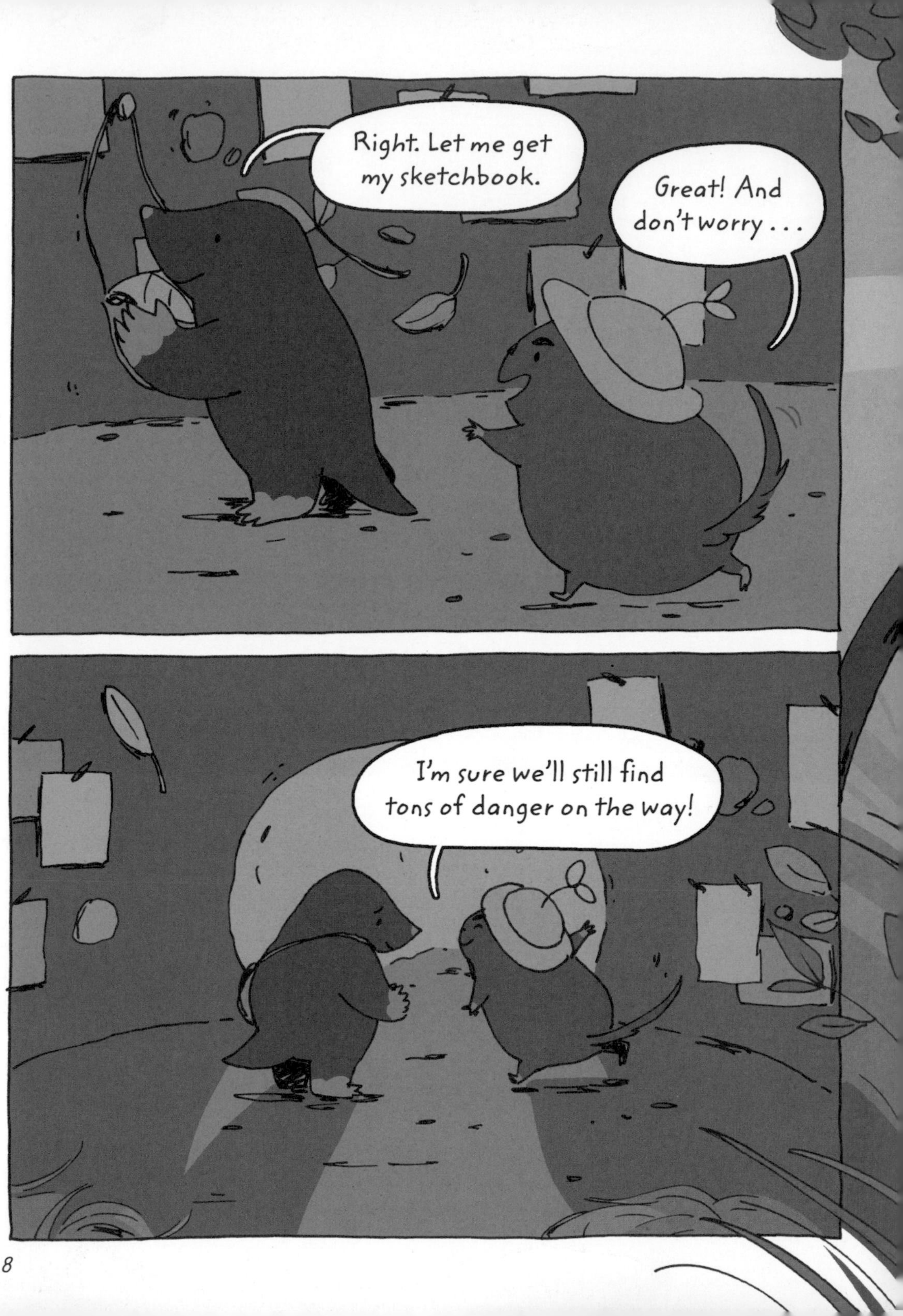
Right. Let me get my sketchbook.
Great! And don't worry . . .
I'm sure we'll still find tons of danger on the way!

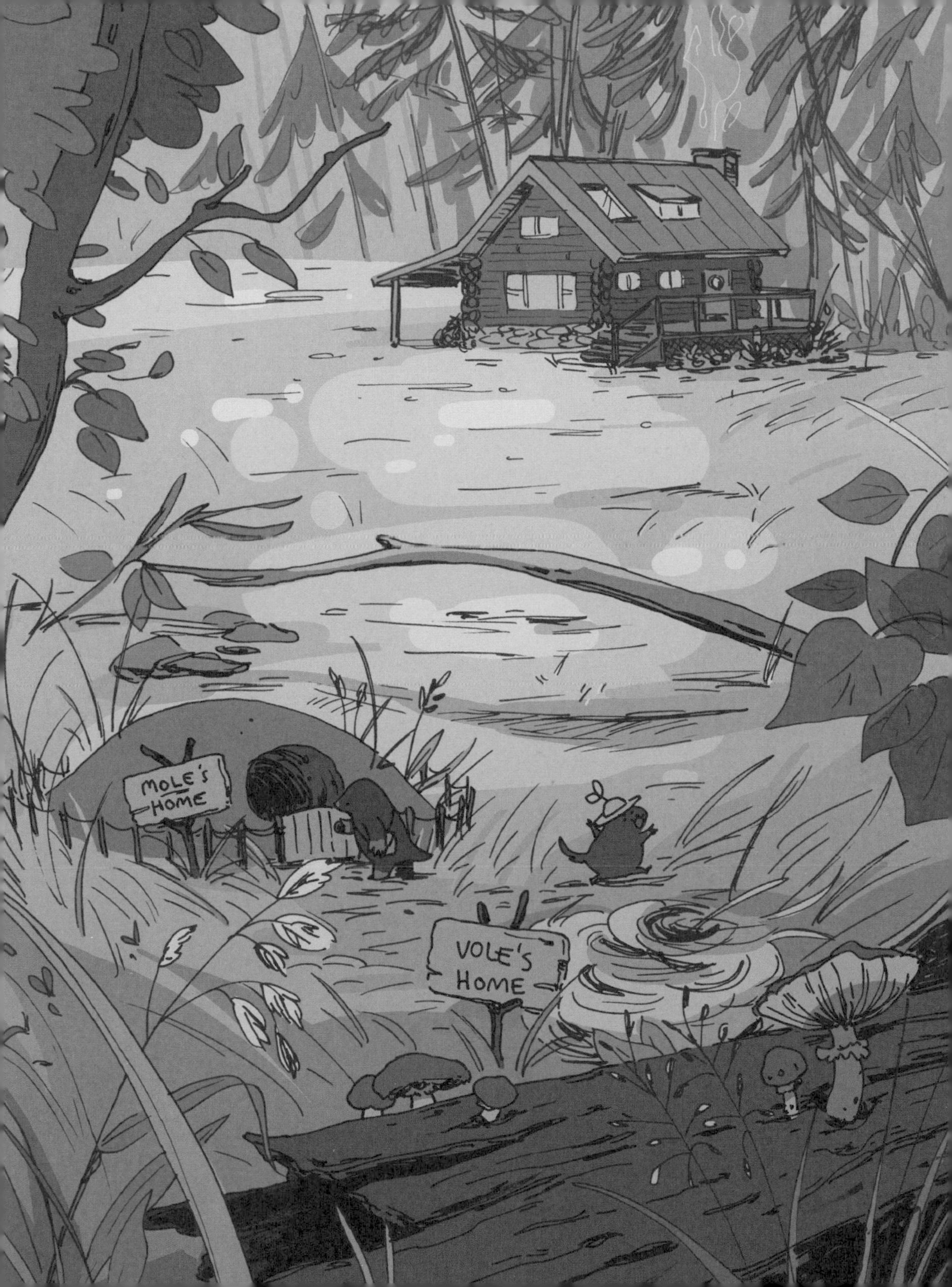
MOLE'S HOME
VOLE'S HOME

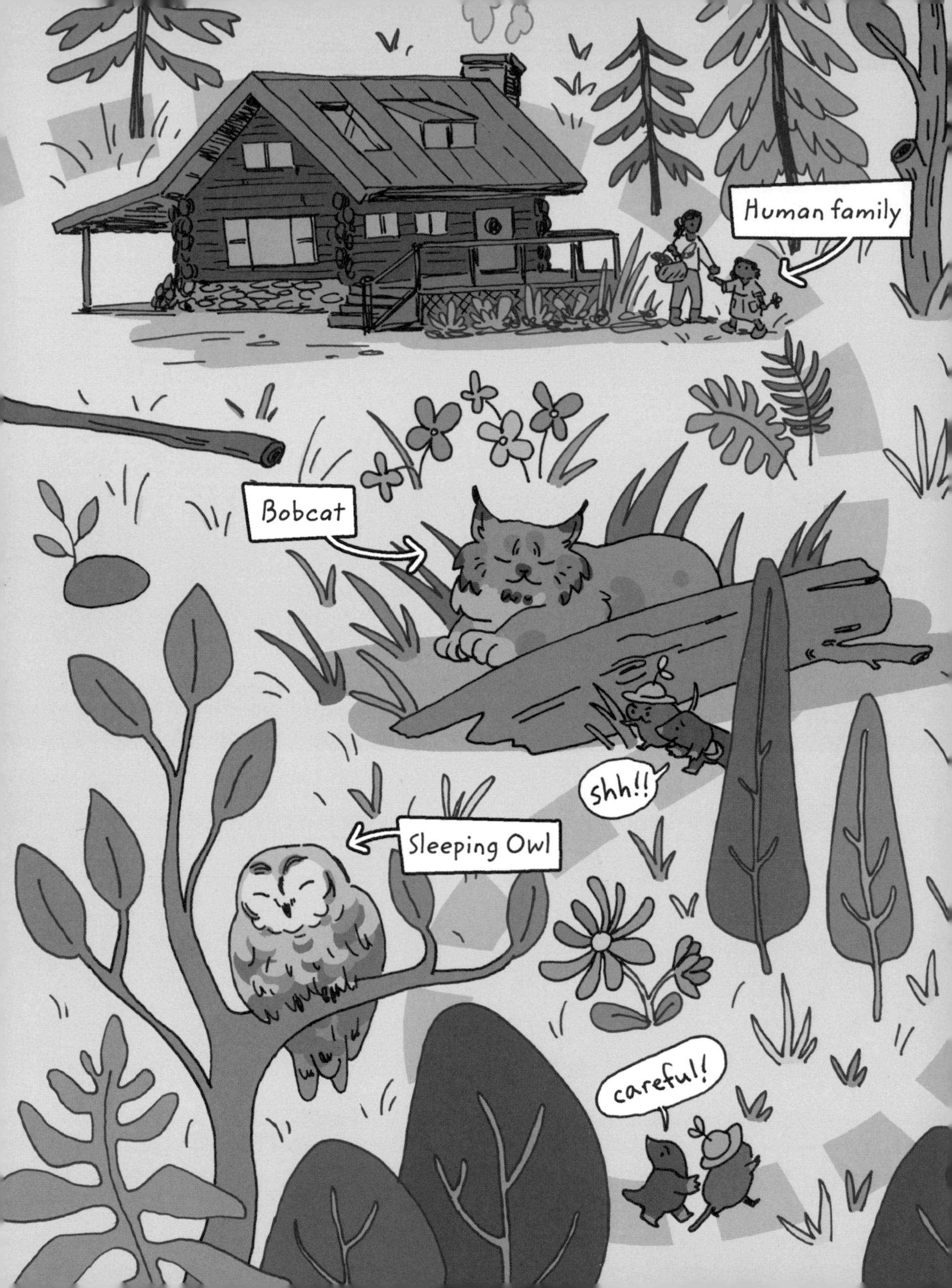
Human family
Bobcat
shh!!
Sleeping Owl
careful!

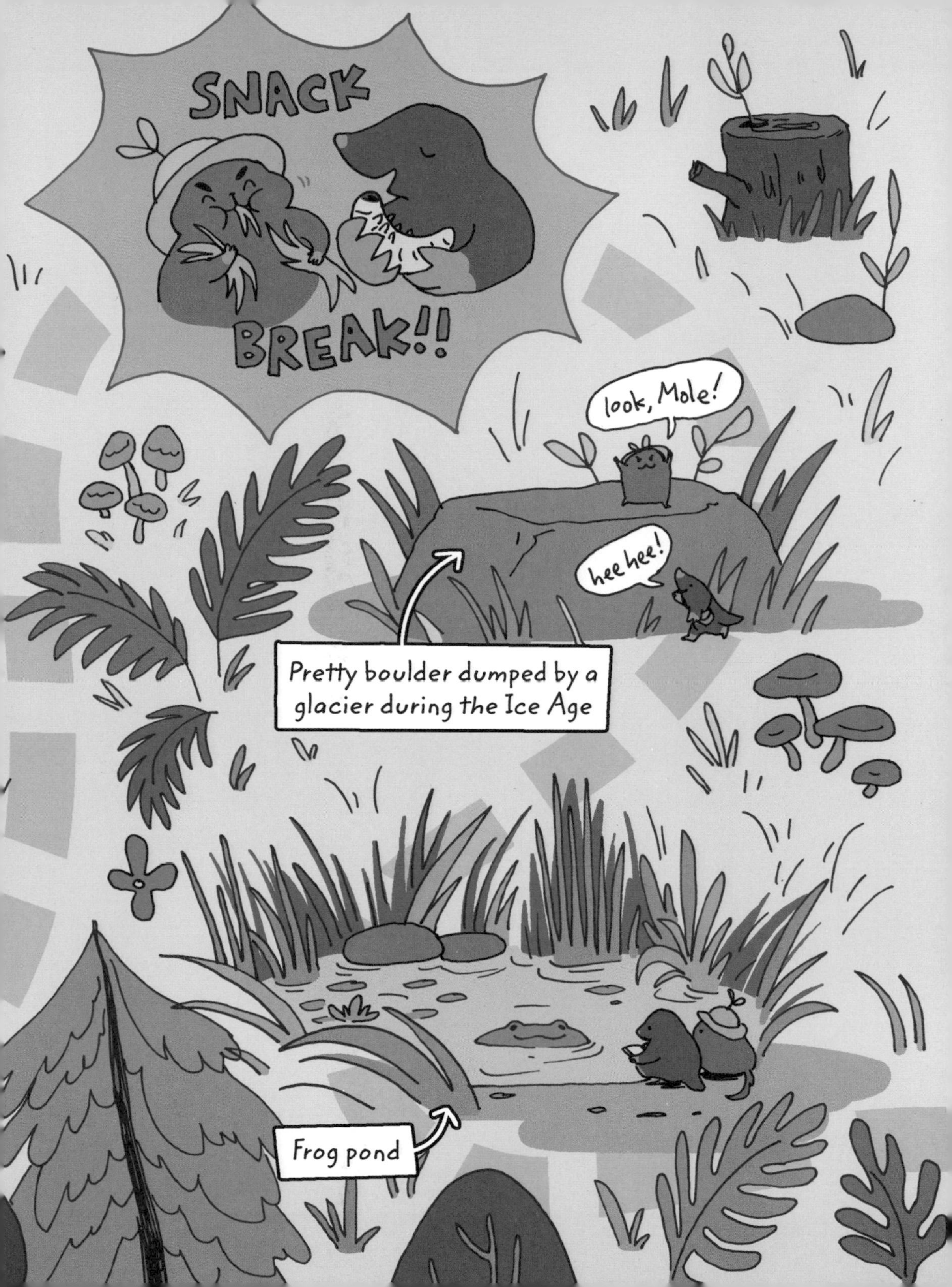
SNACK BREAK!!
look, Mole!
hee hee!
Pretty boulder dumped by a glacier during the Ice Age
Frog pond

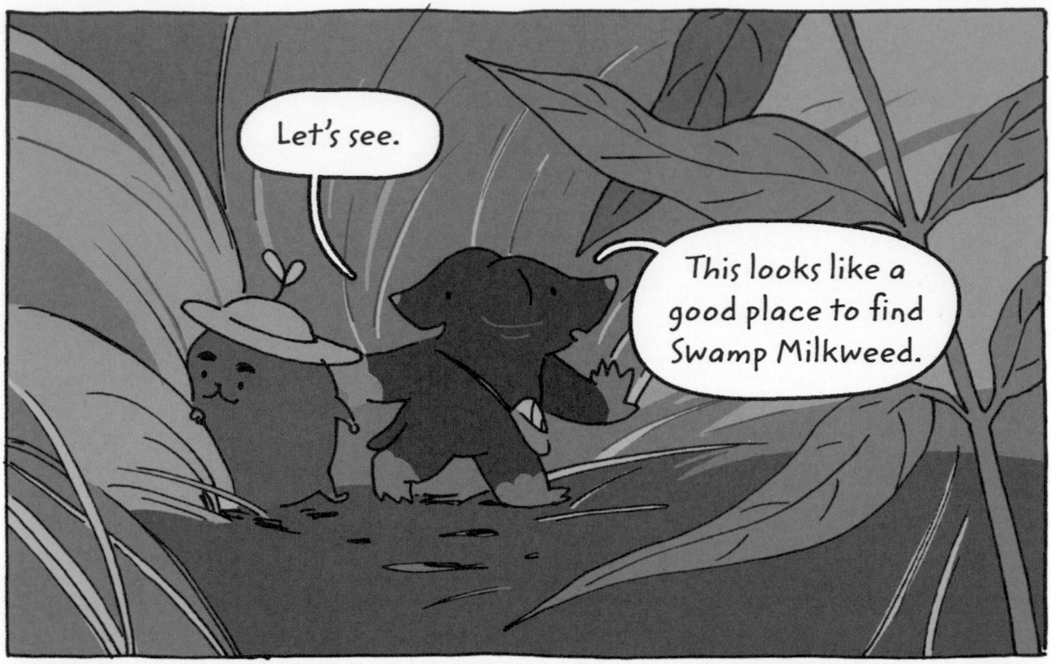
Let's see.
This looks like a good place to find Swamp Milkweed.

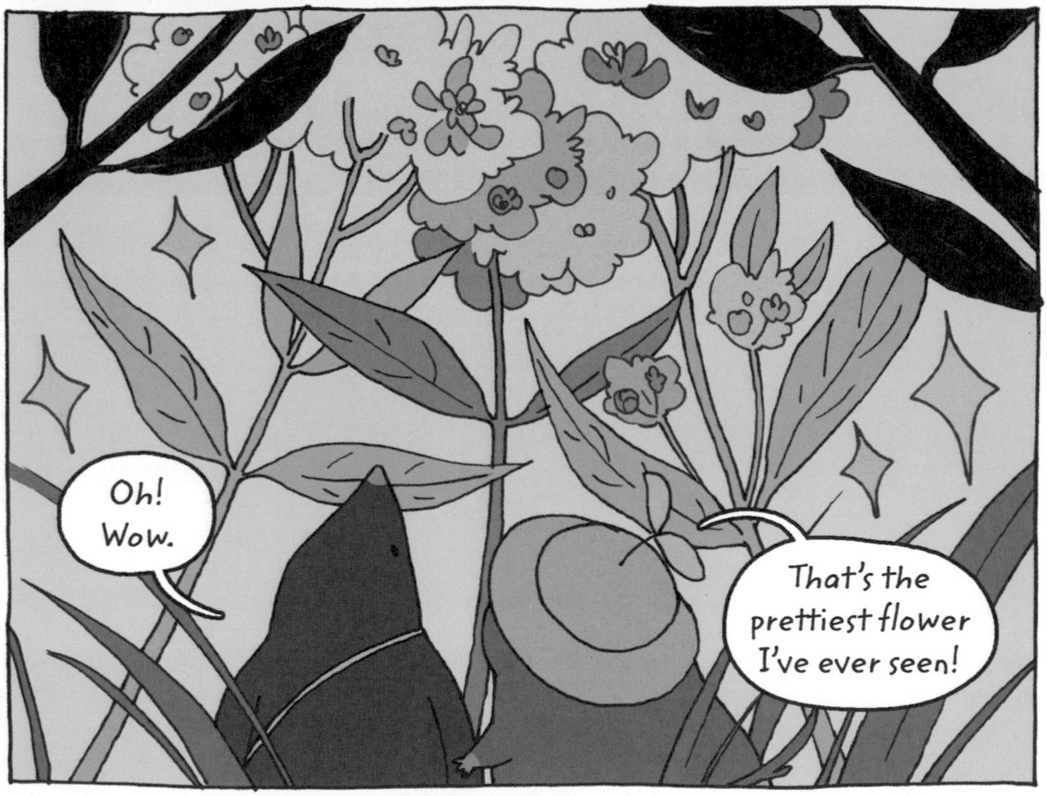
Oh! Wow.
That's the prettiest flower I've ever seen!

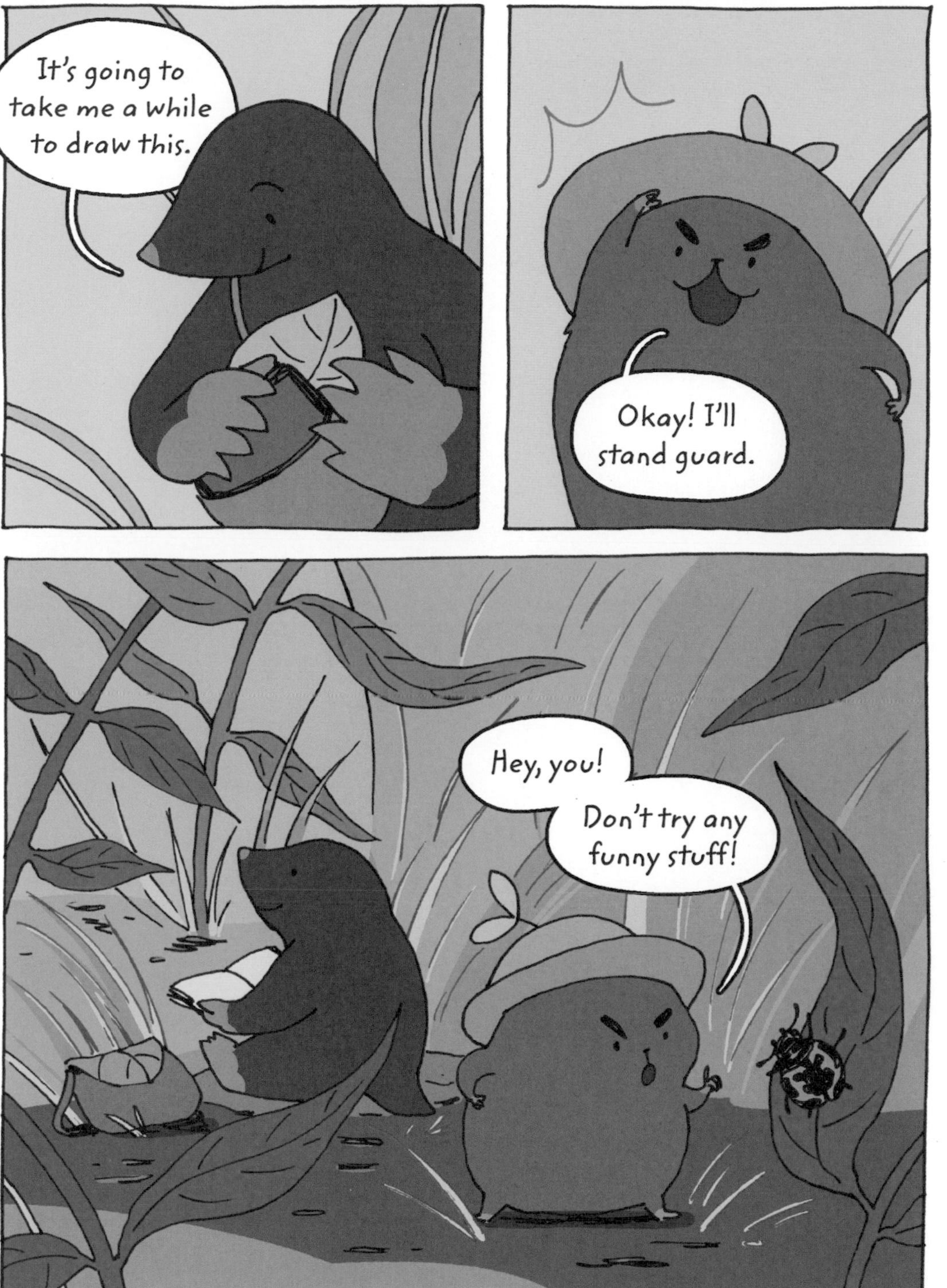
It's going to take me a while to draw this.
Okay! I'll stand guard.
Hey, you!
Don't try any funny stuff!

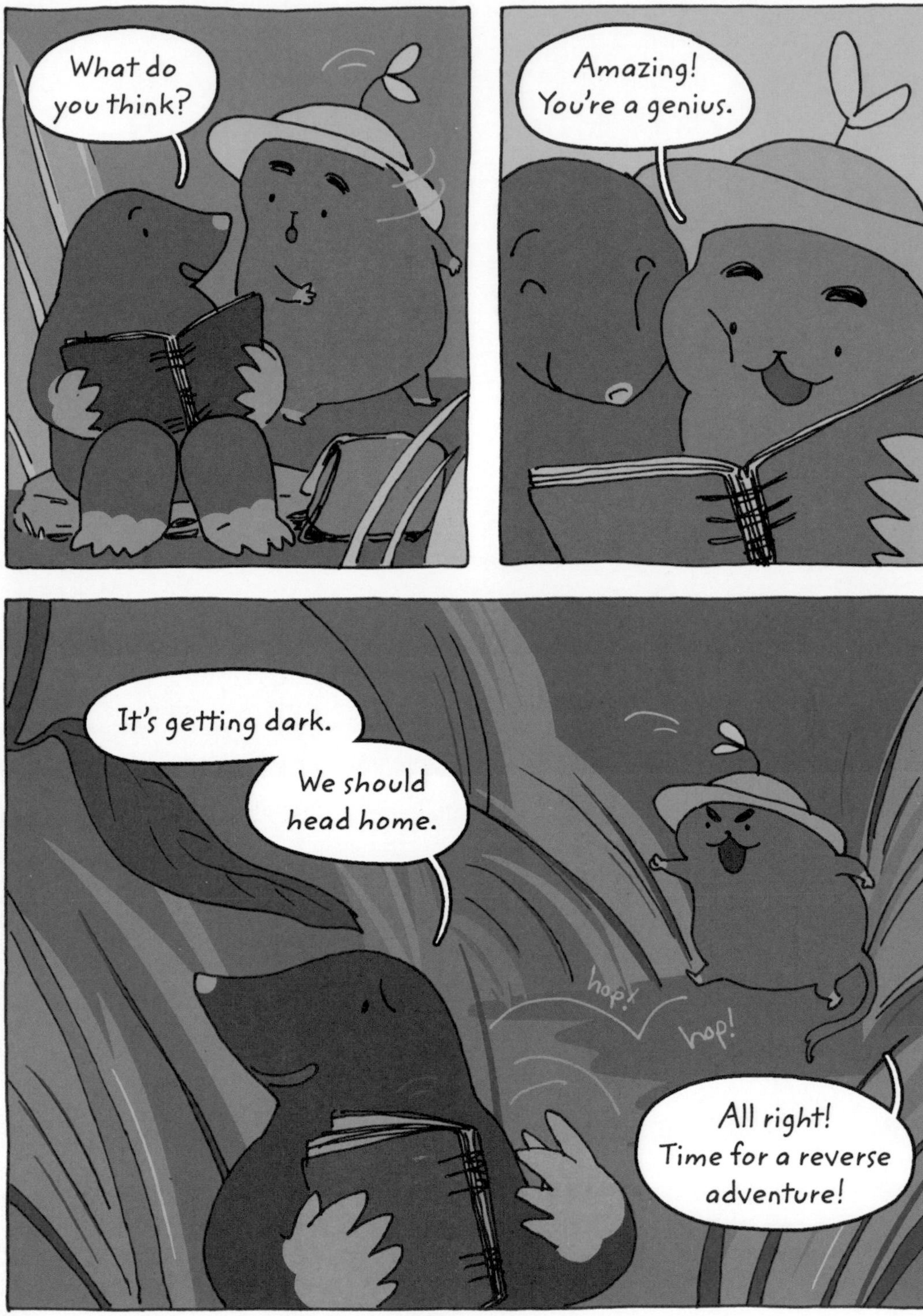
What do you think?
Amazing! You're a genius.
It's getting dark.
We should head home.
hop!
hop!
All right! Time for a reverse adventure!

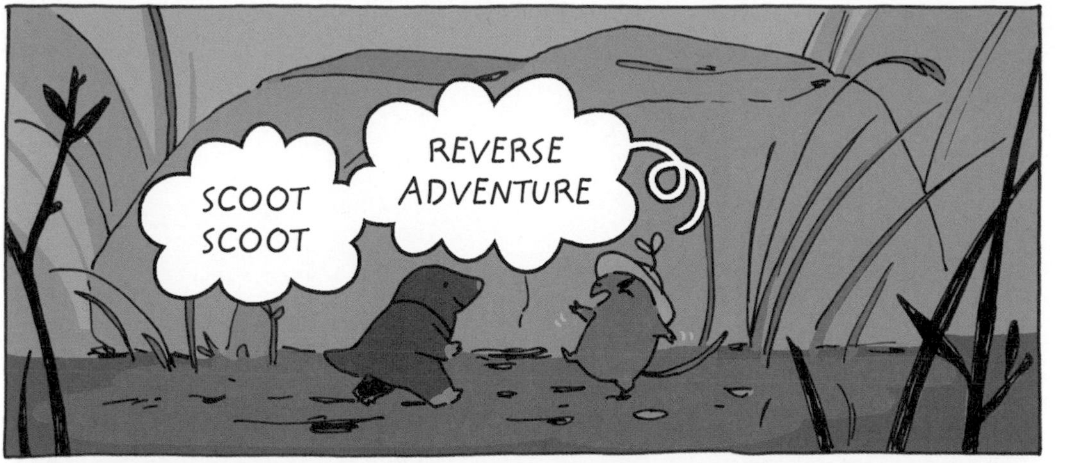
SCOOT
SCOOT
REVERSE
ADVENTURE
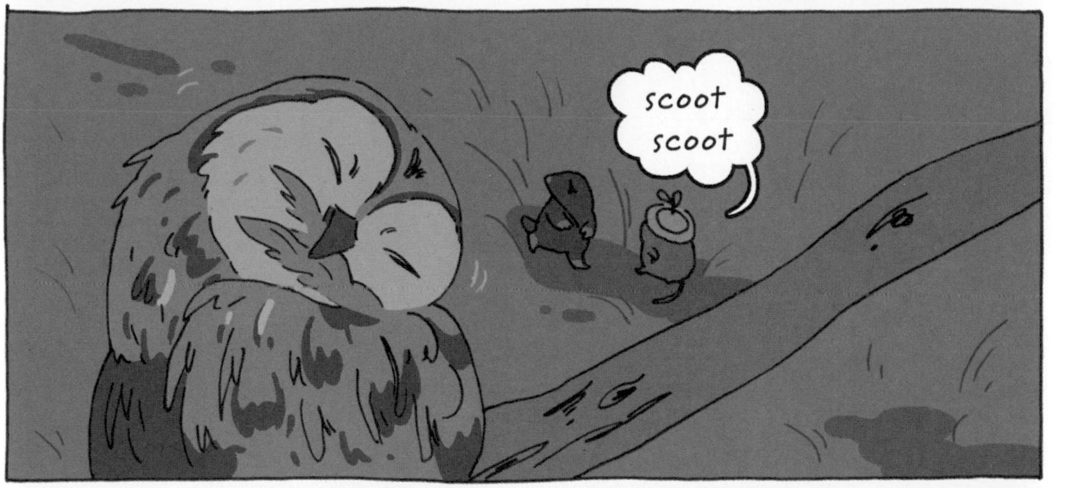
scoot
scoot
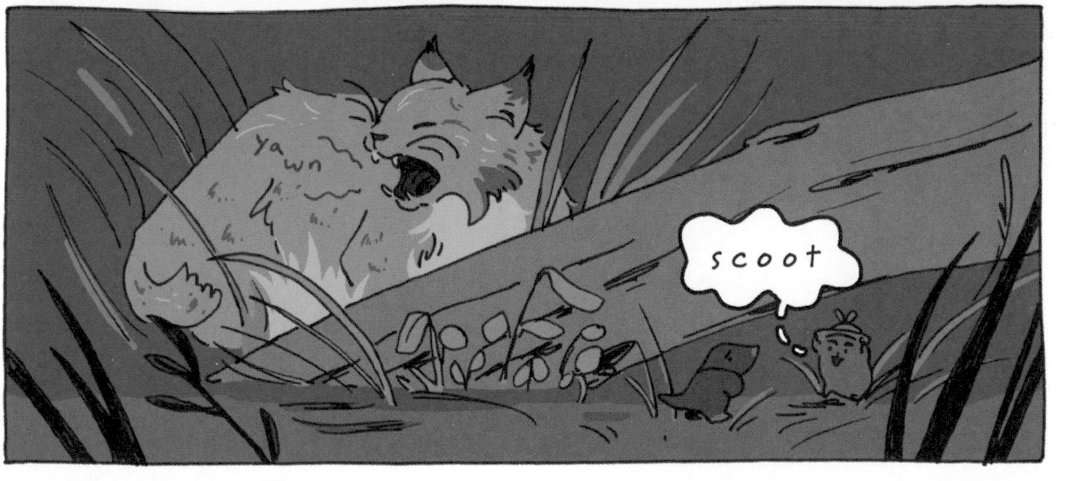
yawn
scoot

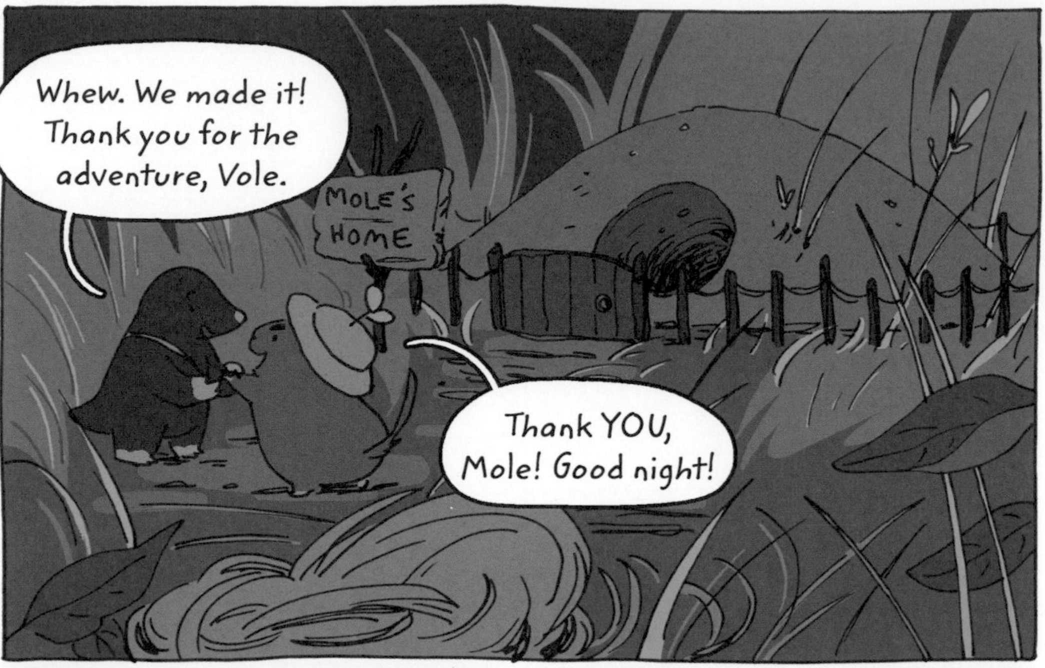
Whew. We made it! Thank you for the adventure, Vole.
MOLE'S HOME
Thank YOU, Mole! Good night!

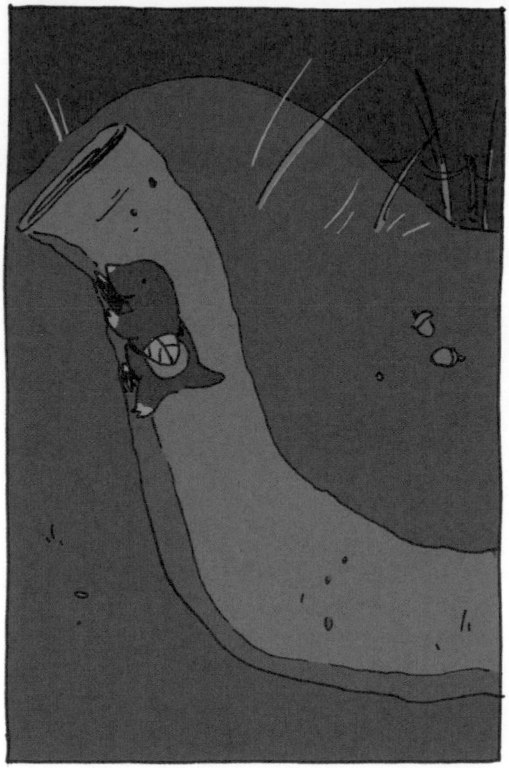

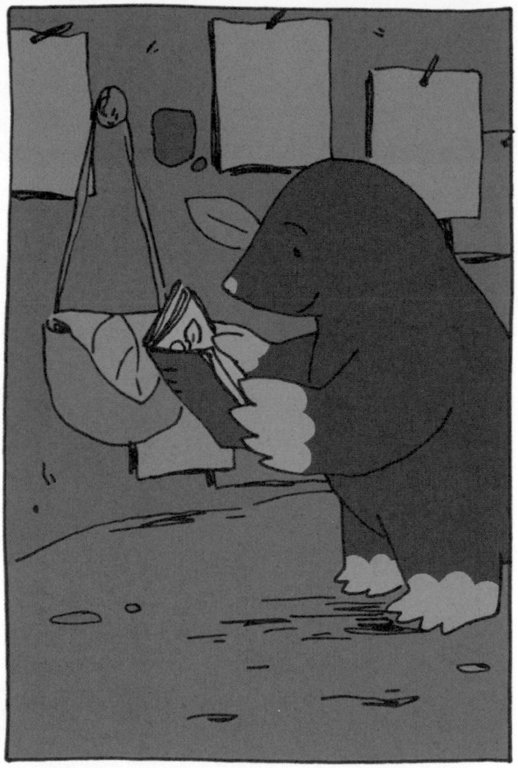

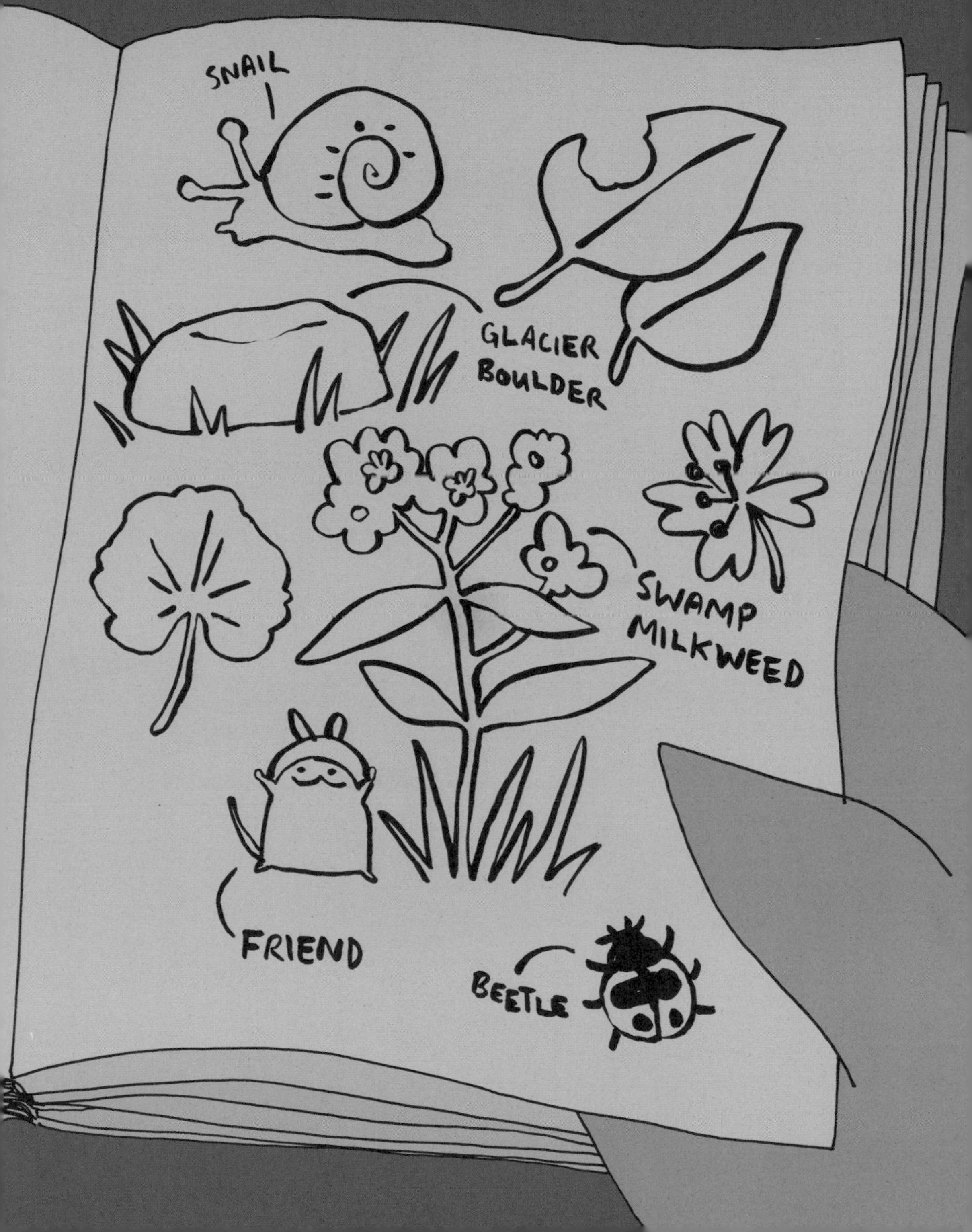
SNAIL
GLACIER BOULDER
SWAMP MILKWEED
FRIEND
BEETLE

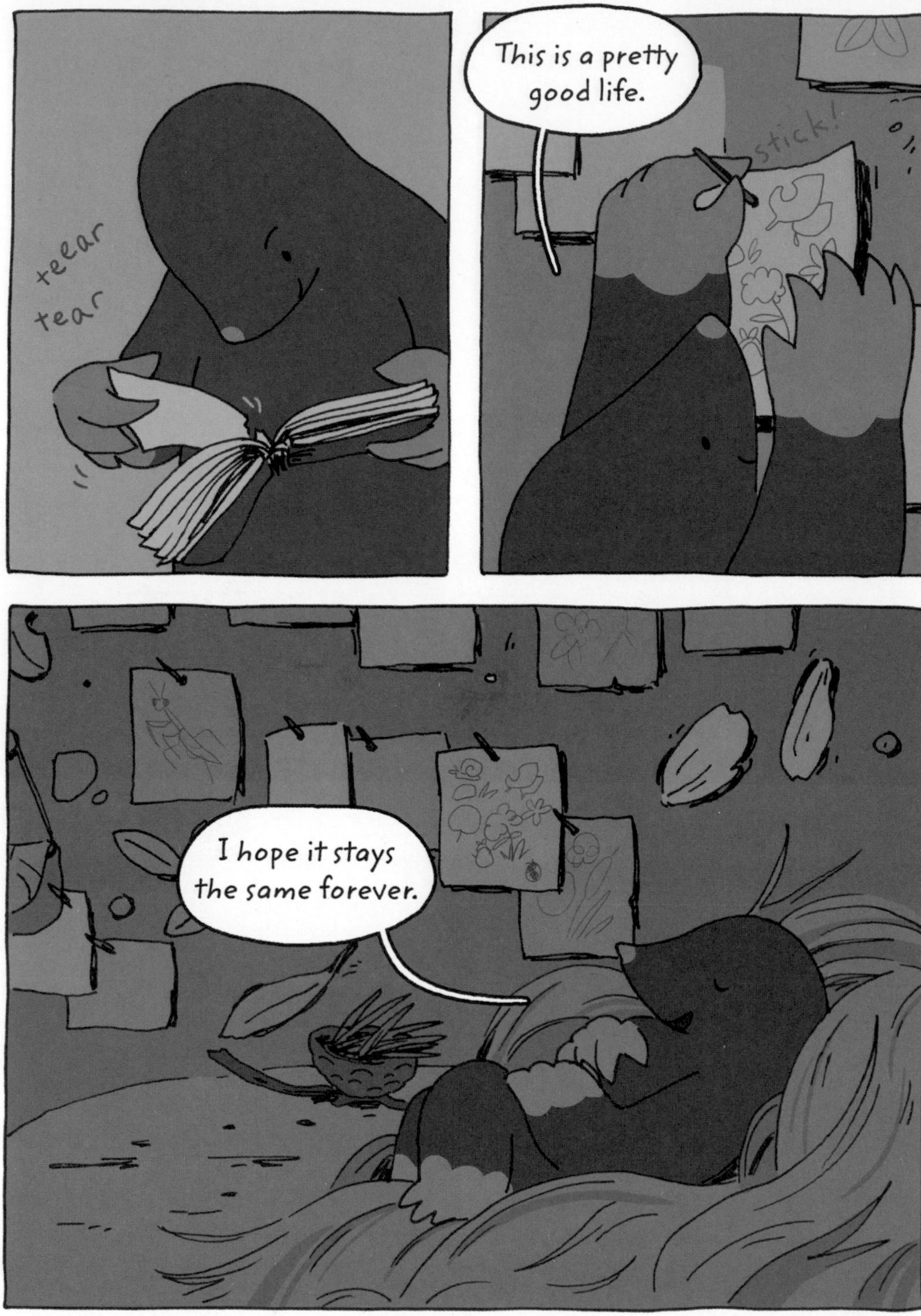
teear
tear
This is a pretty good life.
stick!
I hope it stays the same forever.

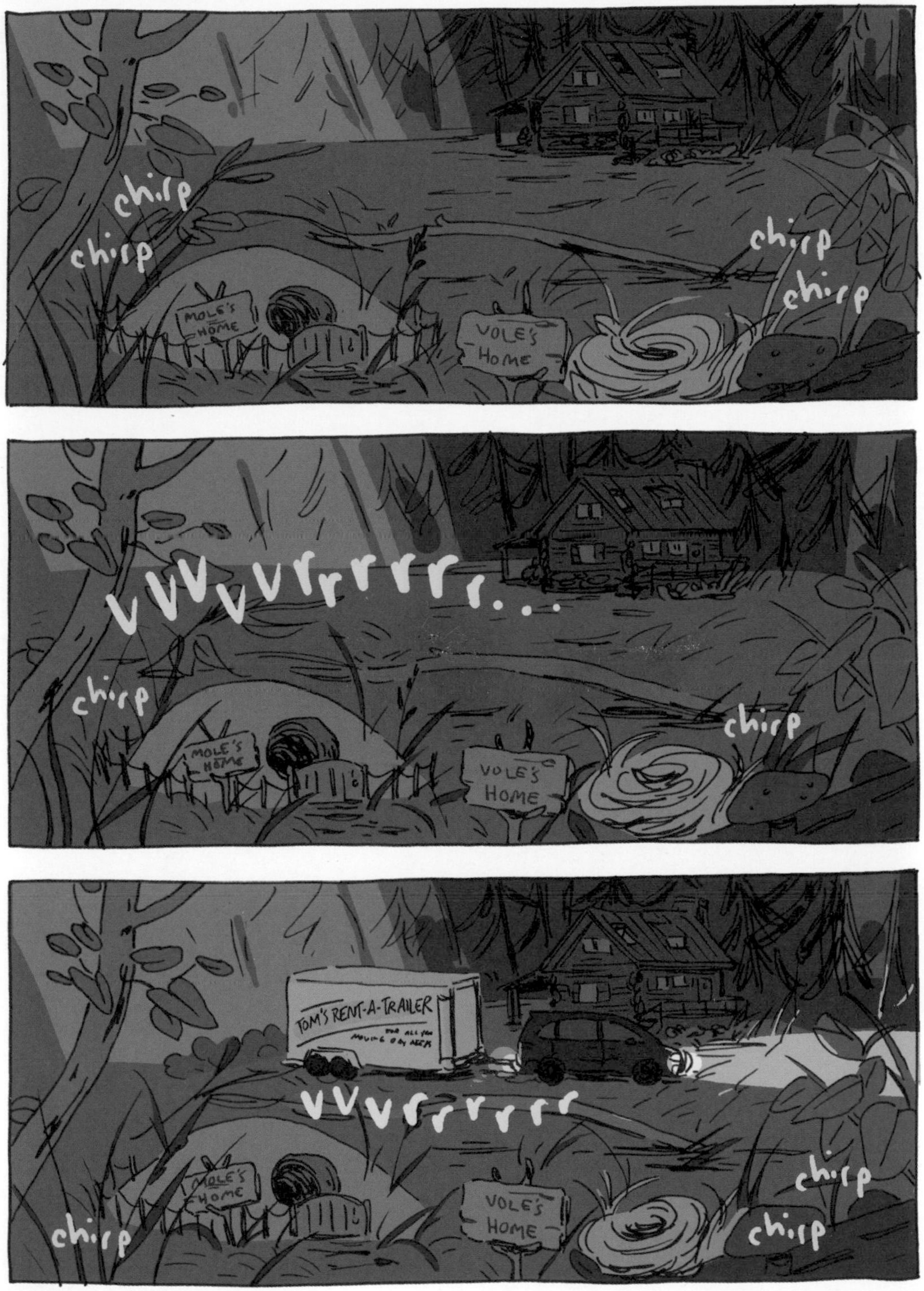
chirp
chirp
MOLE'S HOME
VOLE'S HOME
chirp
chirp
VVVVVrrrrrr...
chirp
MOLE'S HOME
VOLE'S HOME
chirp
TOM'S RENT-A-TRAILER
VVVVrrrrrrr
MOLE'S HOME
VOLE'S HOME
chirp
chirp
chirp

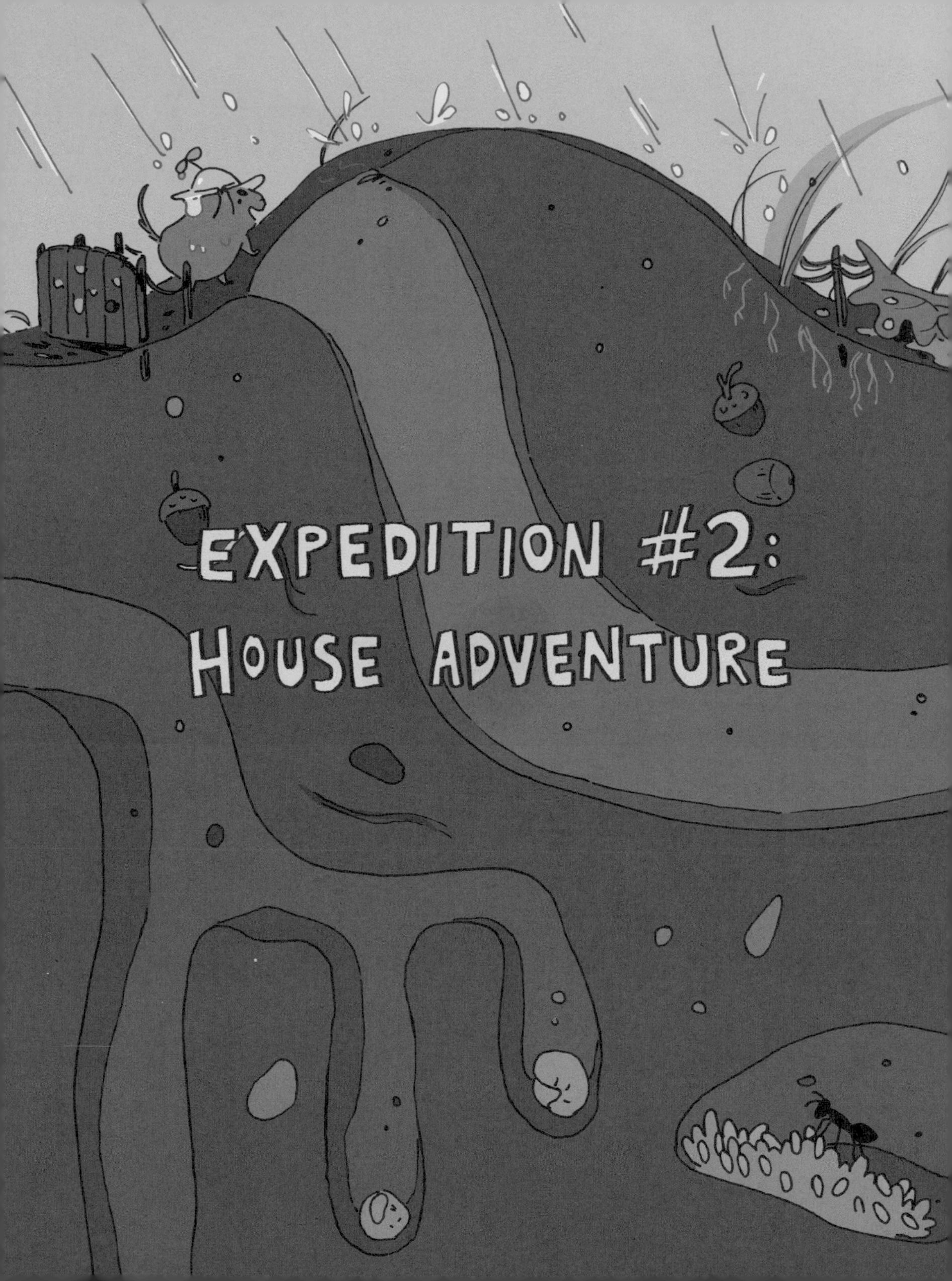
EXPEDITION #2:
HOUSE ADVENTURE

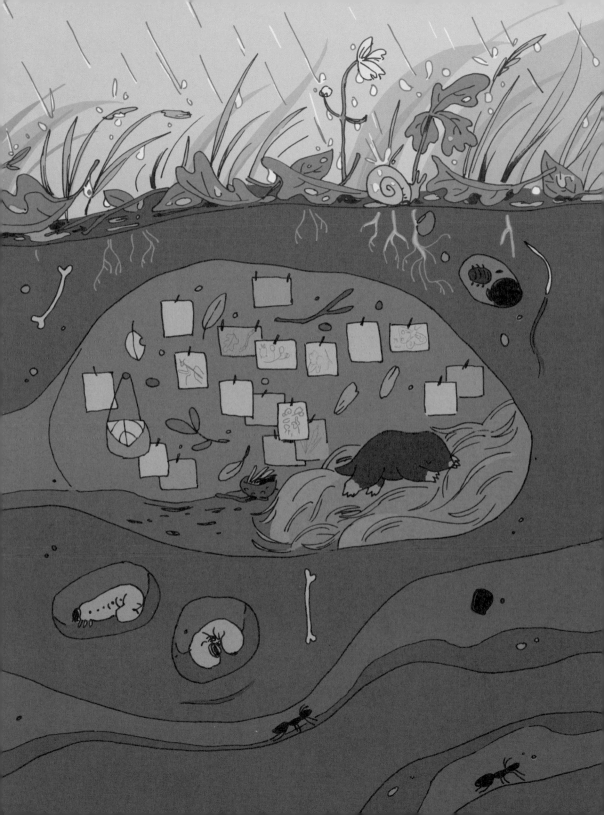

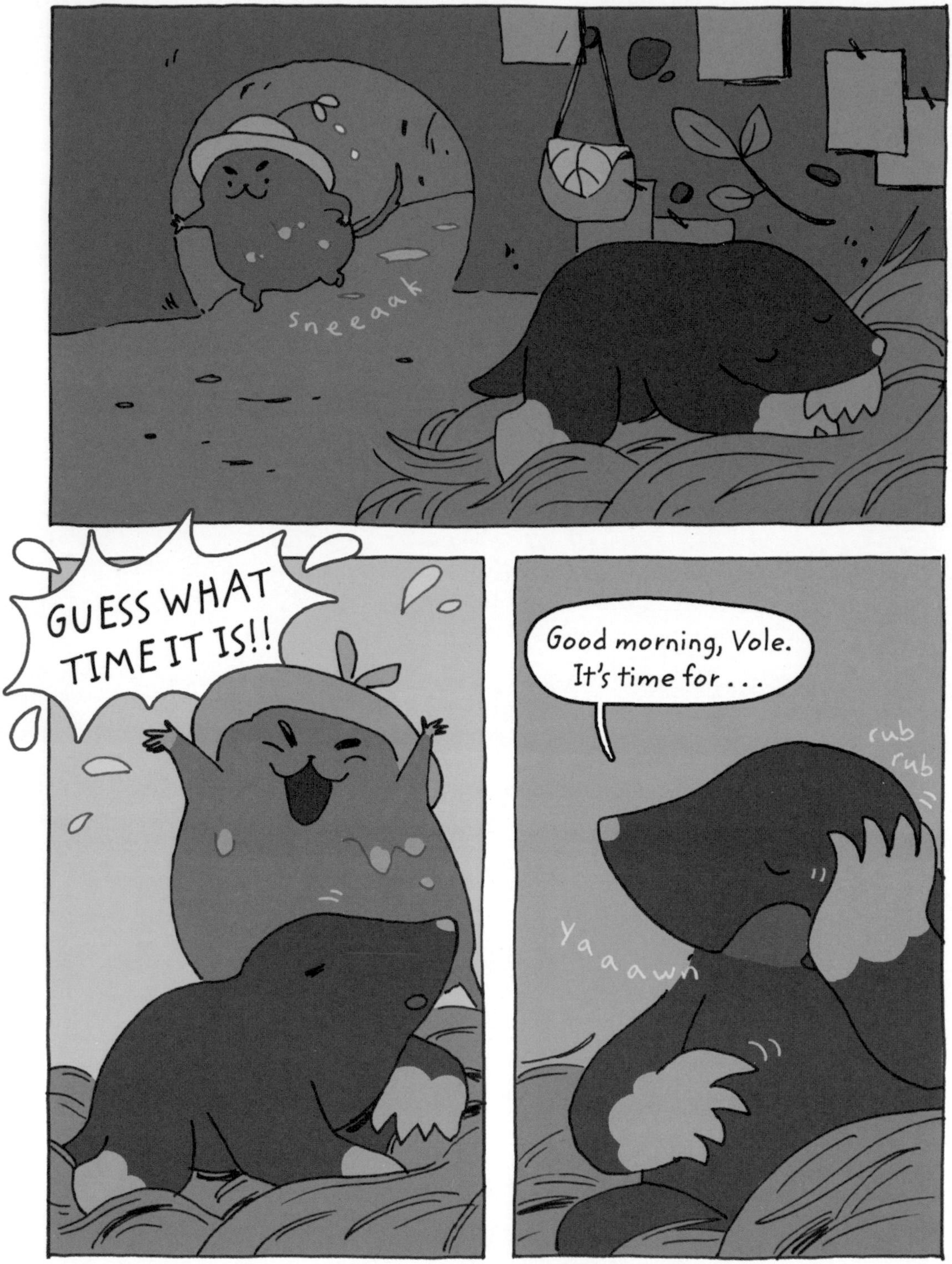
sneeaak
GUESS WHAT TIME IT IS!!
Good morning, Vole. It's time for . . .
rub rub
Yaaawn

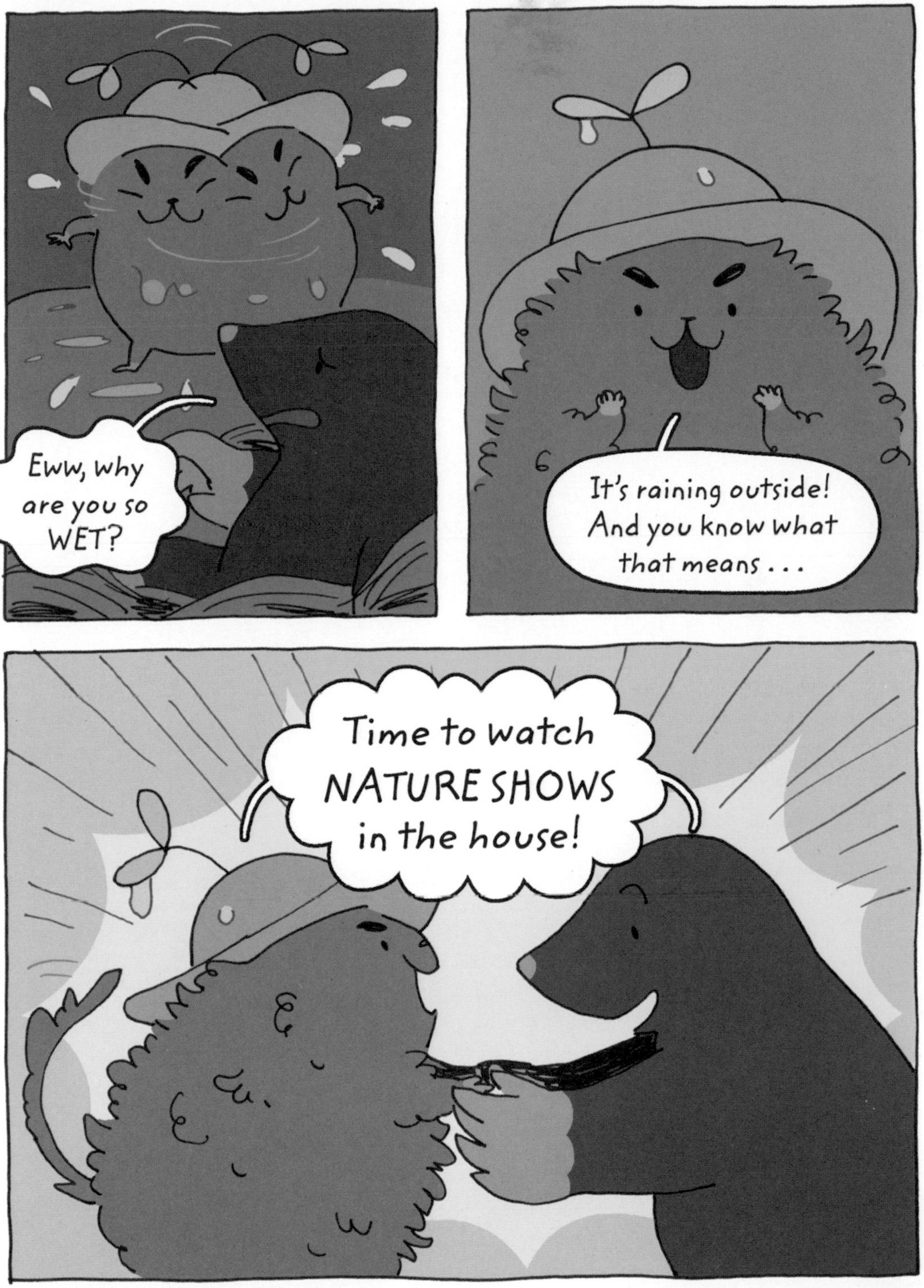
Eww, why are you so WET?
It's raining outside! And you know what that means . . .
Time to watch NATURE SHOWS in the house!

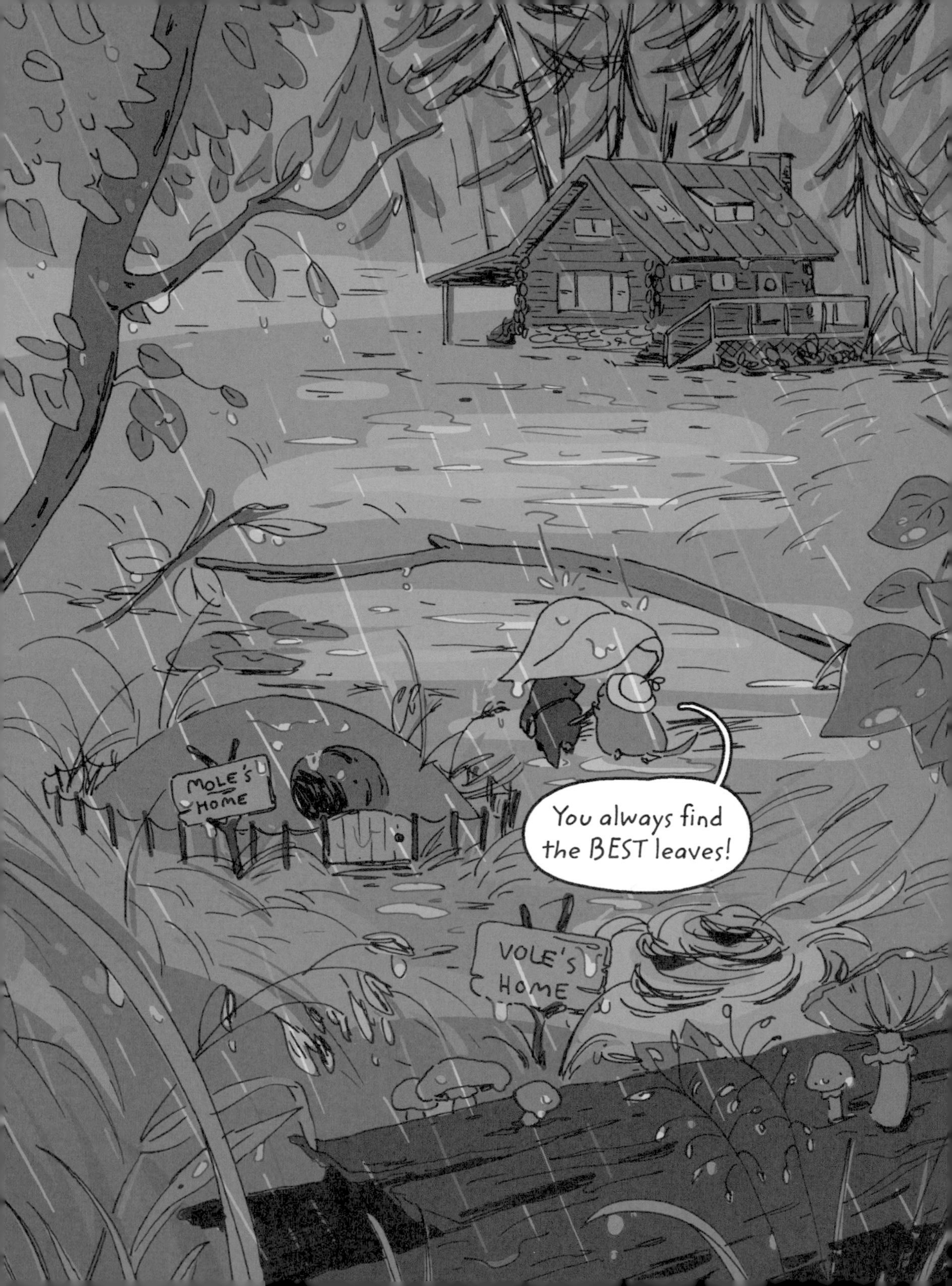
You always find the BEST leaves!
MOLE'S HOME
VOLE'S HOME

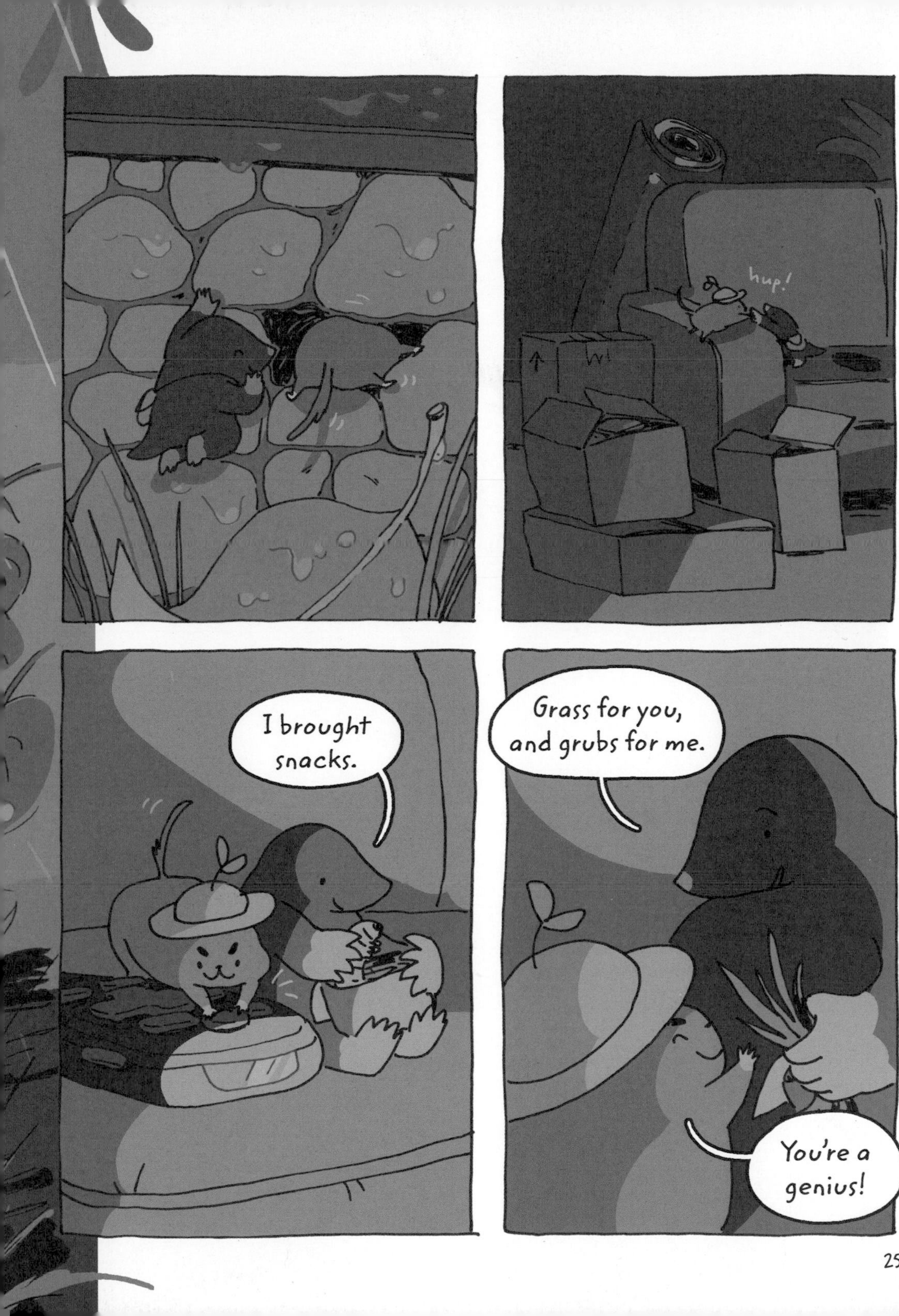
hup!
I brought snacks.
Grass for you, and grubs for me.
You're a genius!

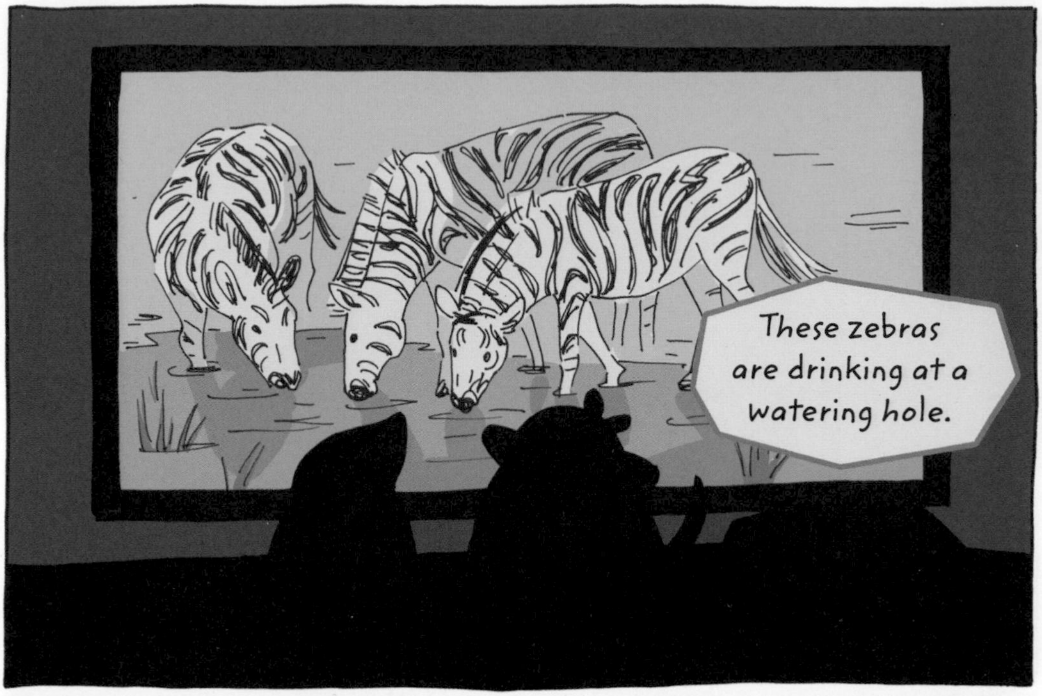
These zebras are drinking at a watering hole.

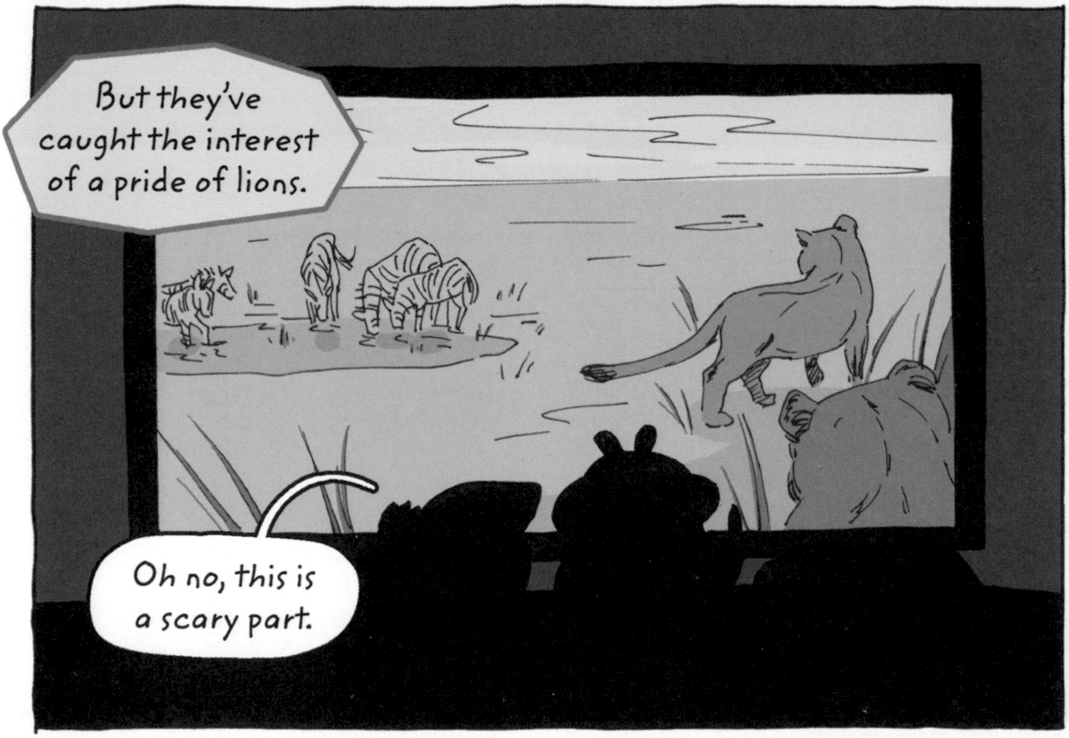
But they've caught the interest of a pride of lions.
Oh no, this is a scary part.

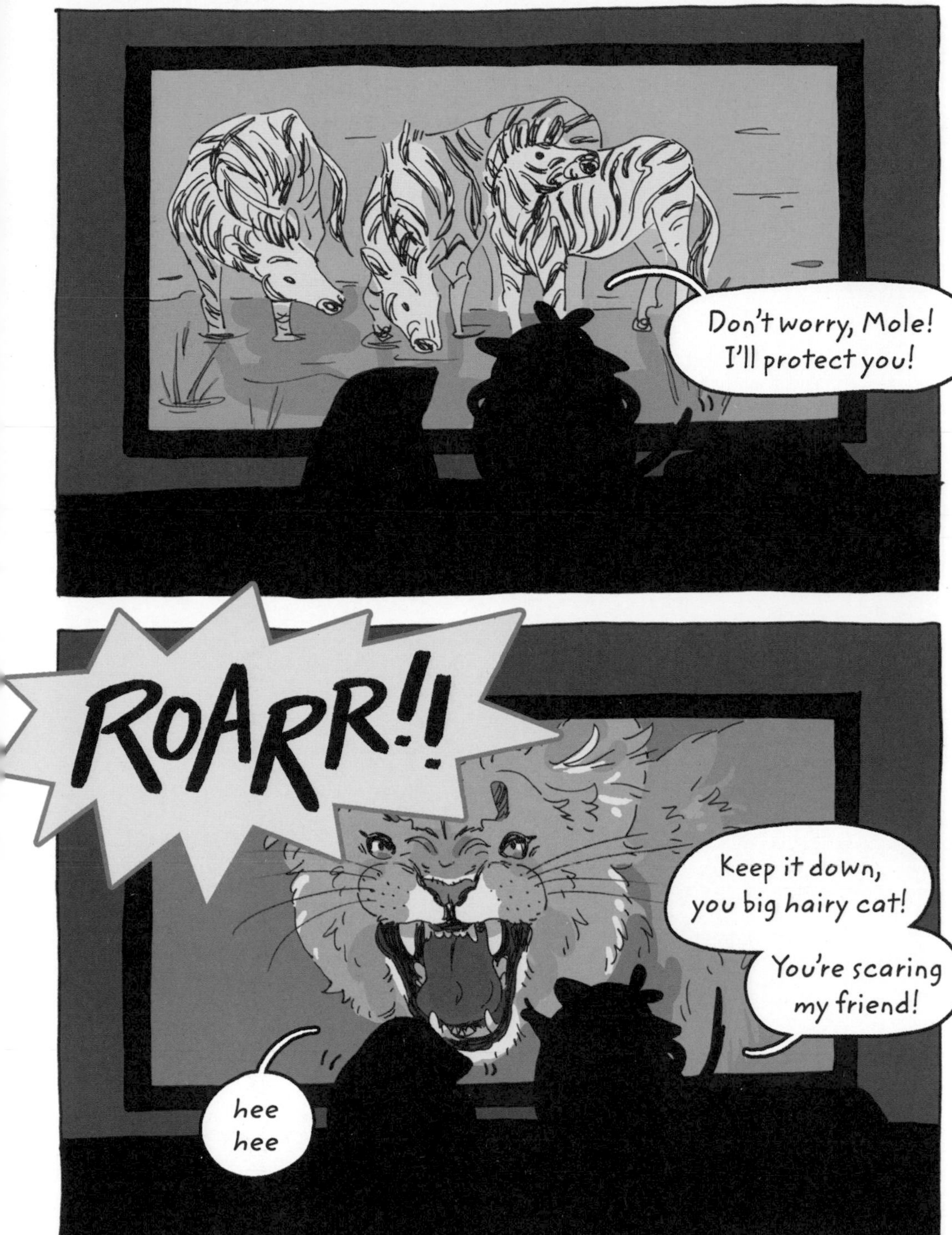
Don't worry, Mole! I'll protect you!
ROARR!!
Keep it down, you big hairy cat!
You're scaring my friend!
hee hee

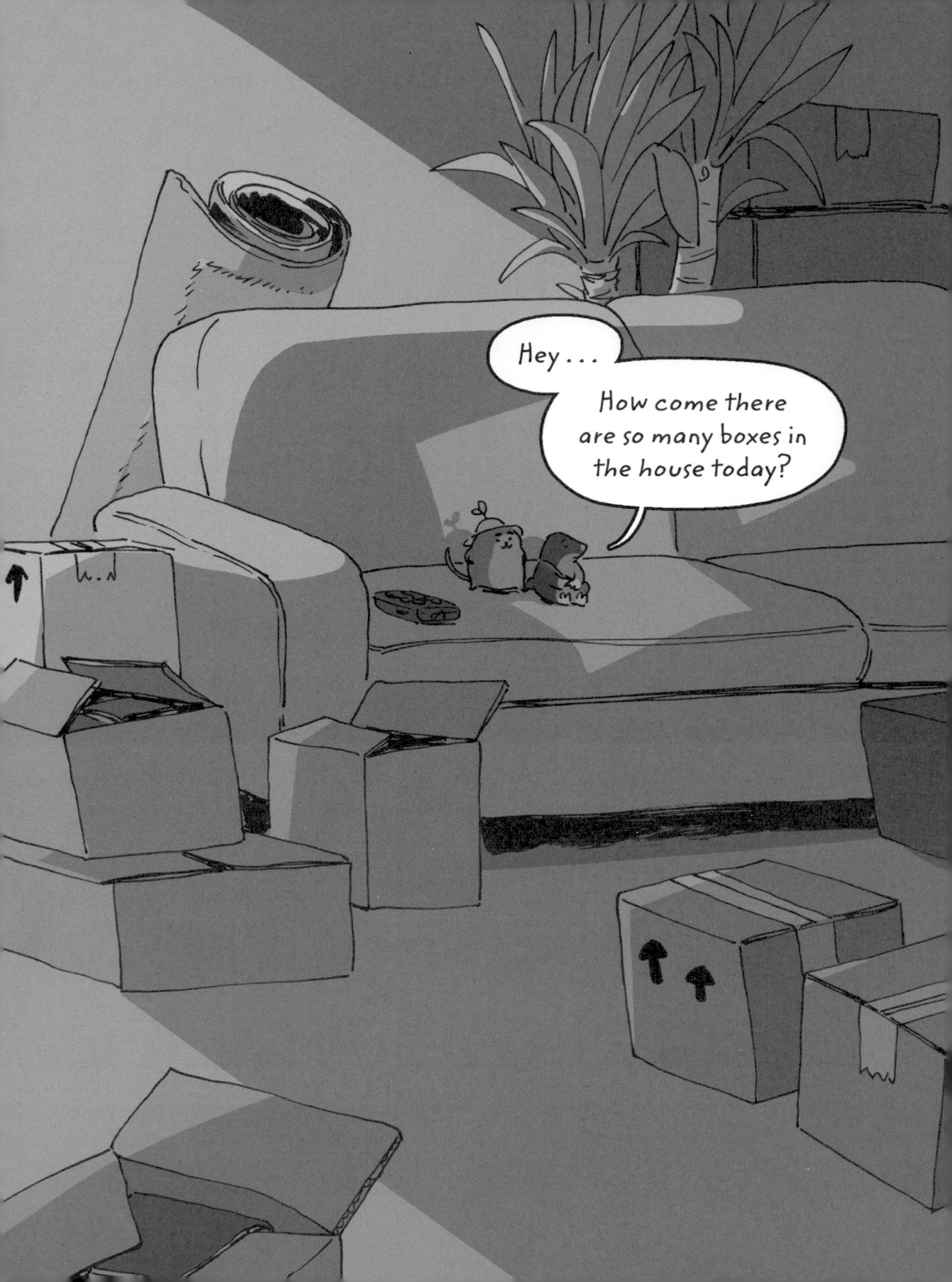
Hey...
How come there are so many boxes in the house today?

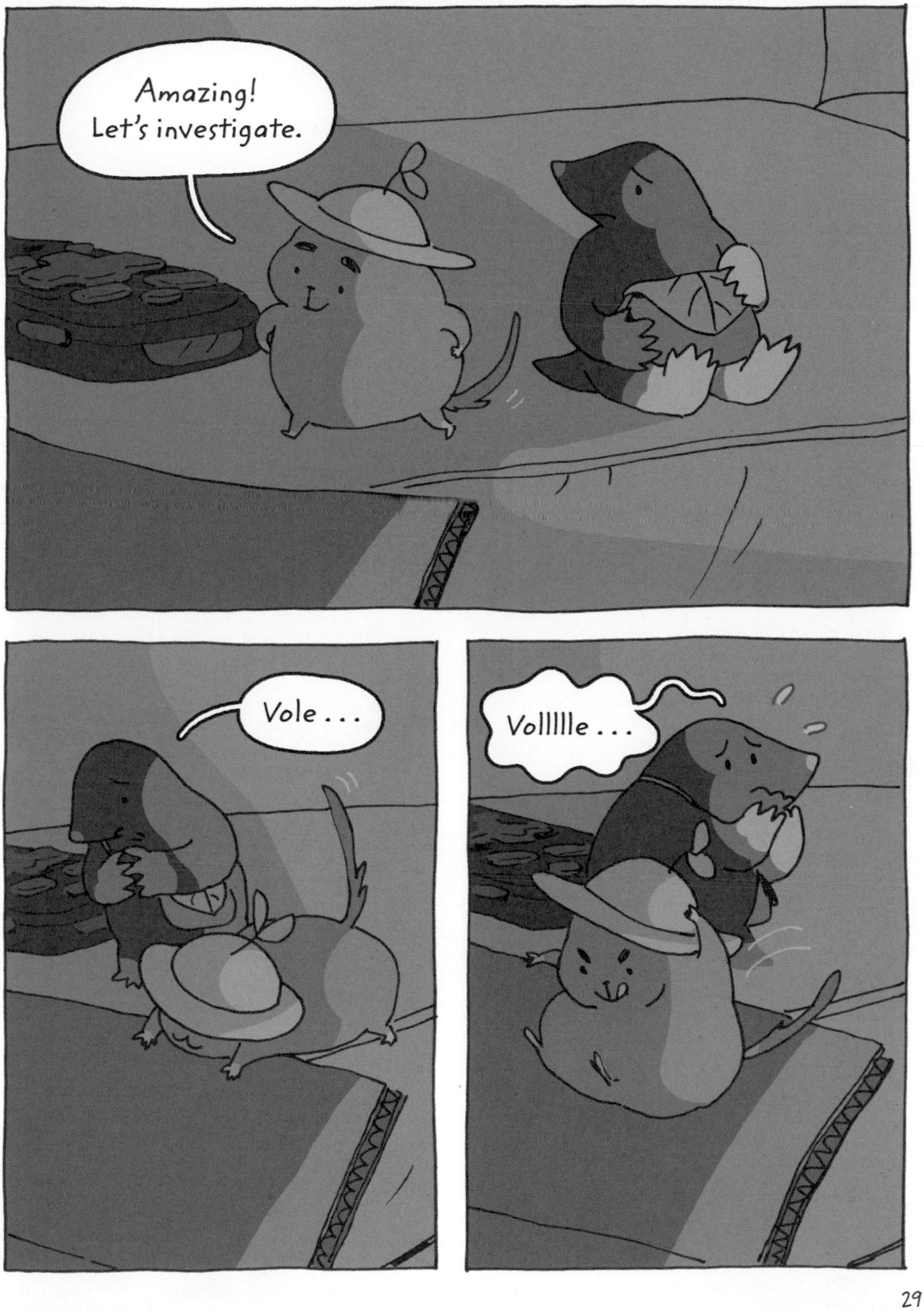
Amazing!
Let's investigate.
Vole . . .
Volllllle . . .

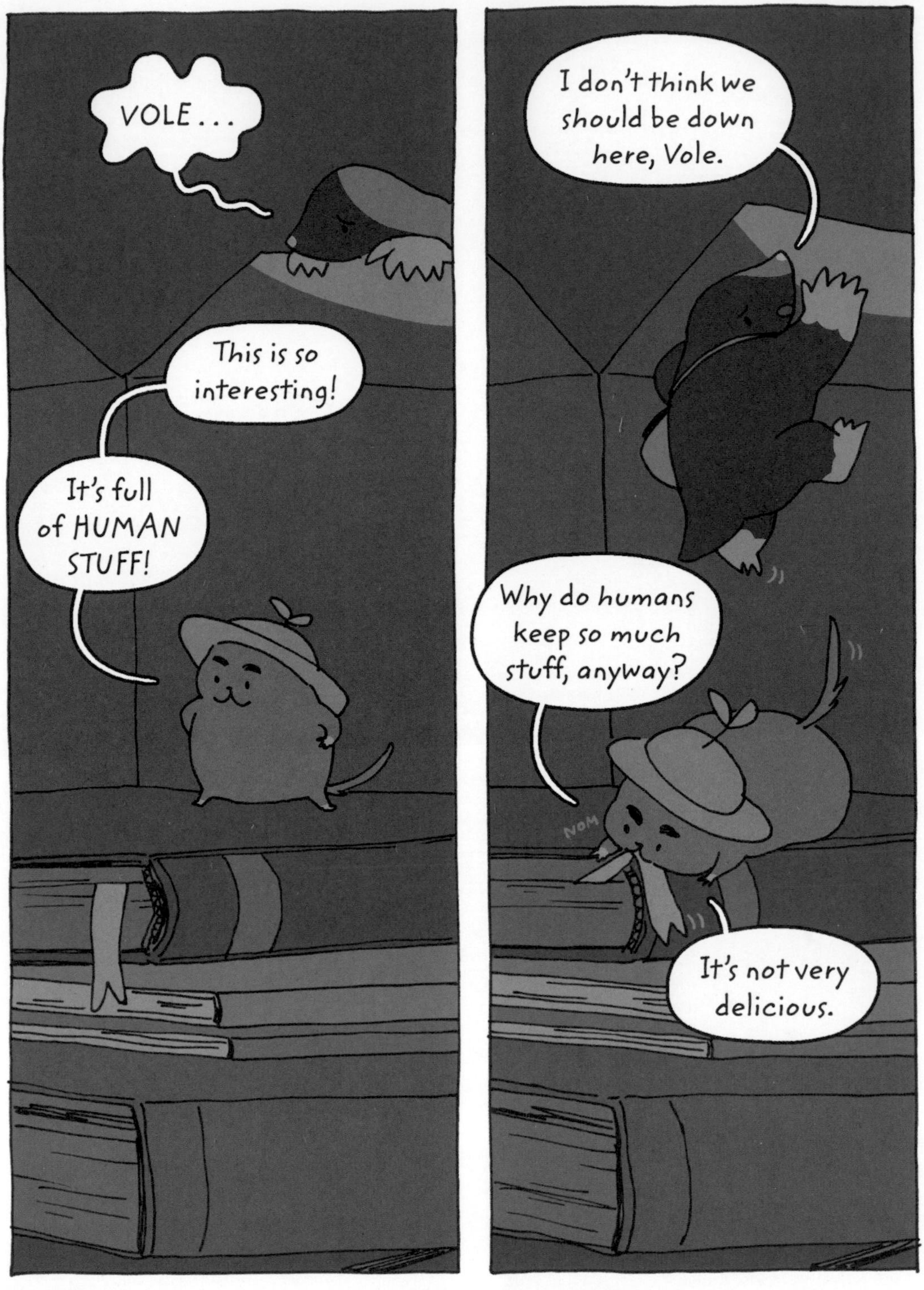
VOLE . . .
This is so interesting!
It's full of HUMAN STUFF!
I don't think we should be down here, Vole.
Why do humans keep so much stuff, anyway?
NOM
It's not very delicious.

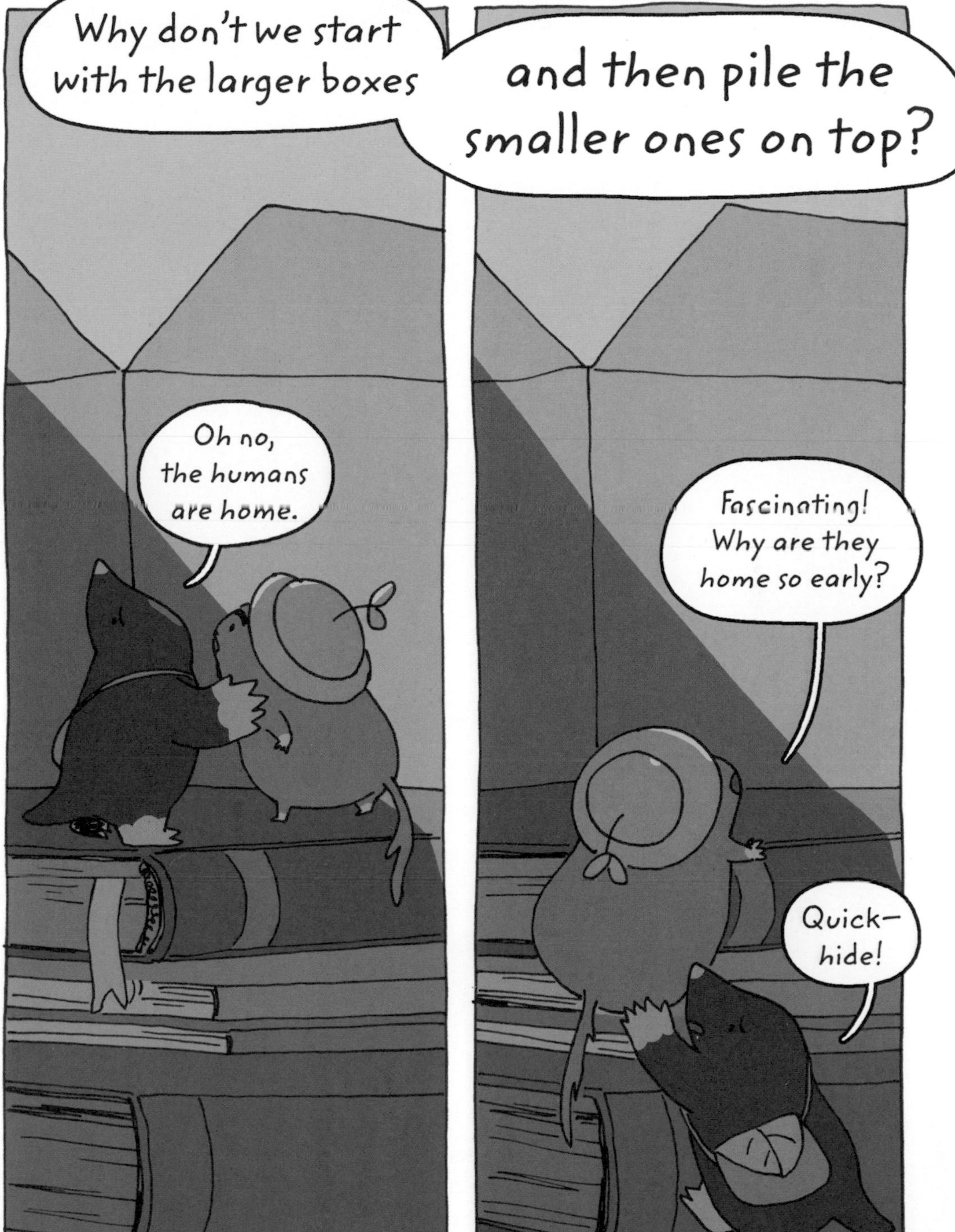
Why don't we start with the larger boxes
and then pile the smaller ones on top?
Oh no, the humans are home.
Fascinating! Why are they home so early?
Quick— hide!

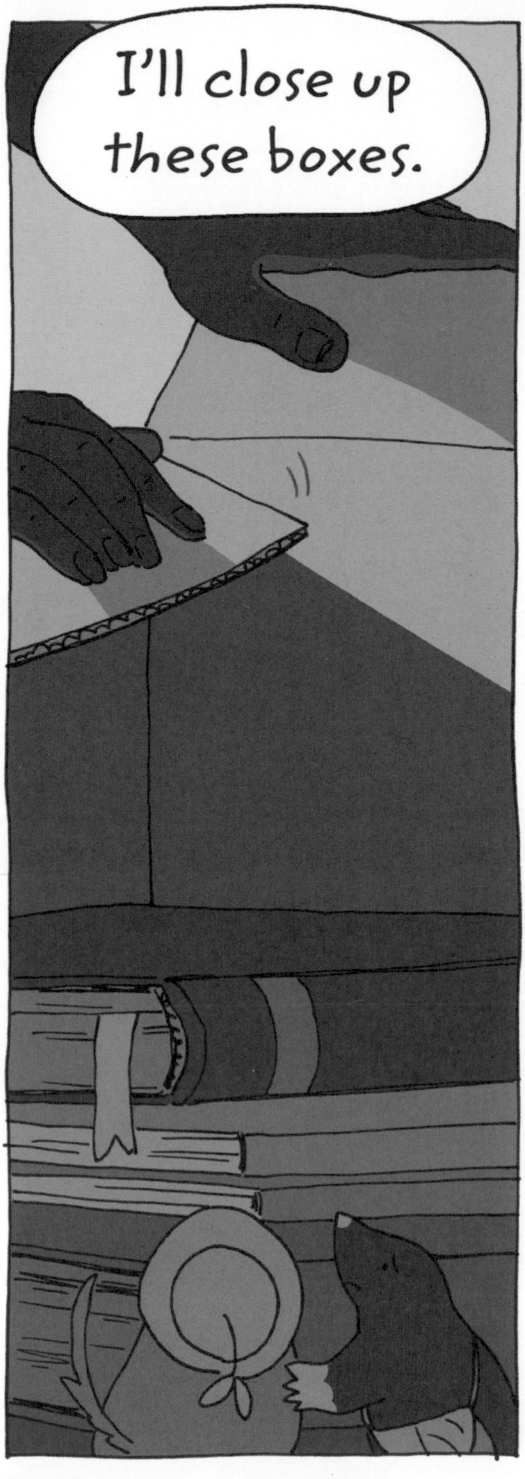
I'll close up these boxes.

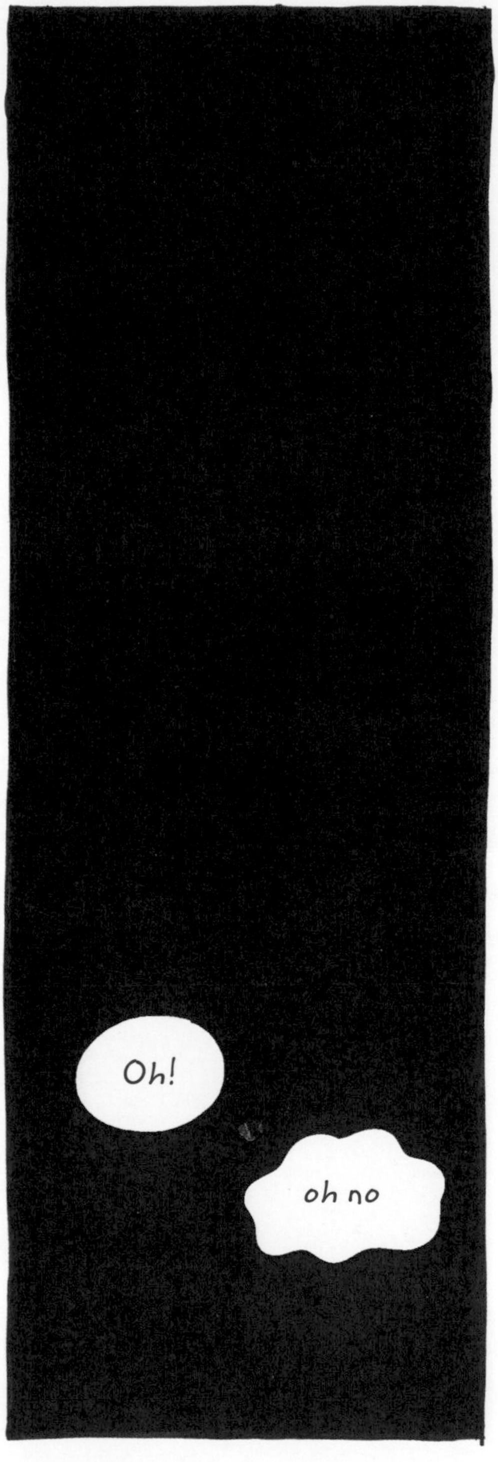
Oh!
oh no

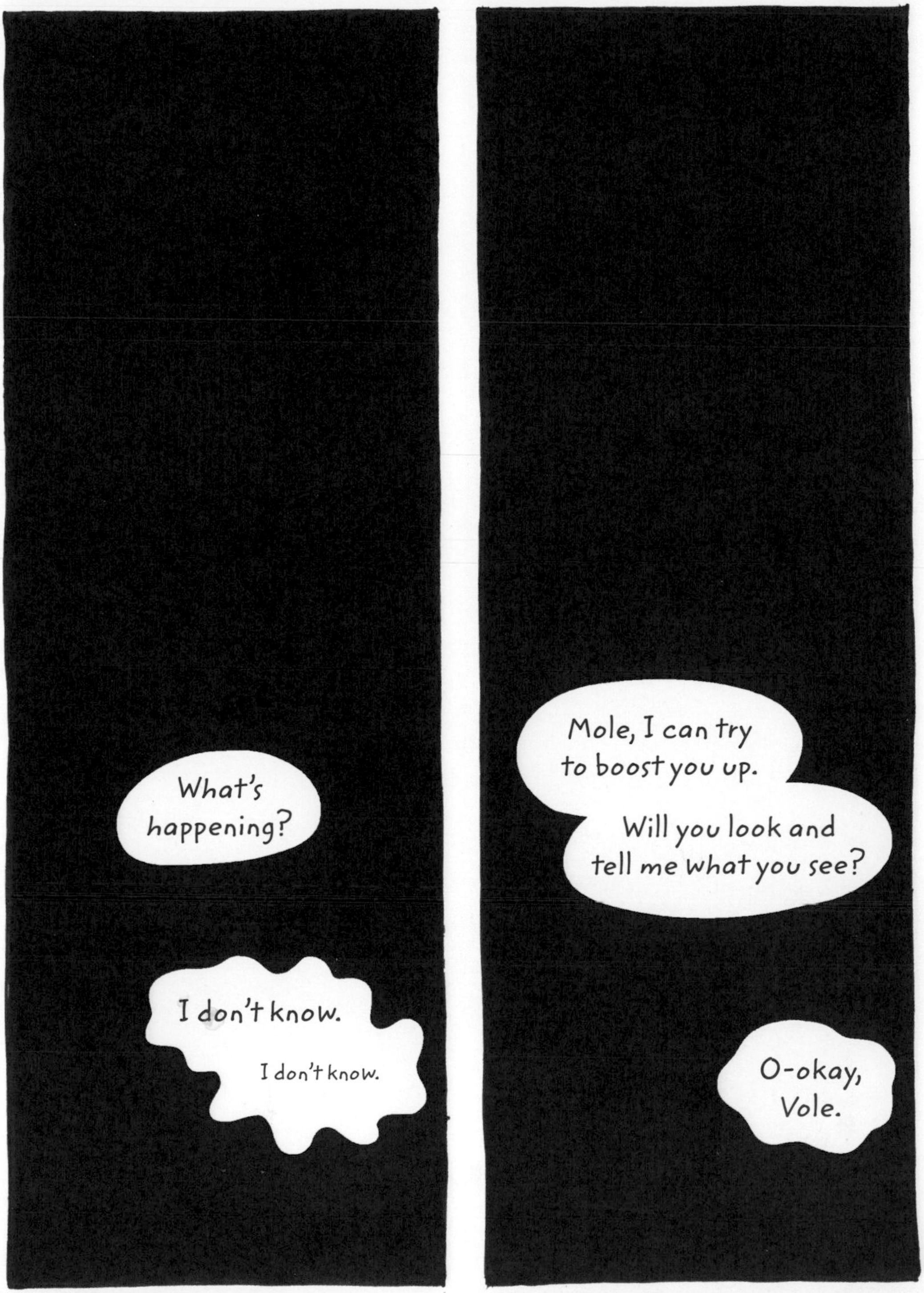
What's happening?
I don't know.
I don't know.
Mole, I can try to boost you up.
Will you look and tell me what you see?
O-okay, Vole.

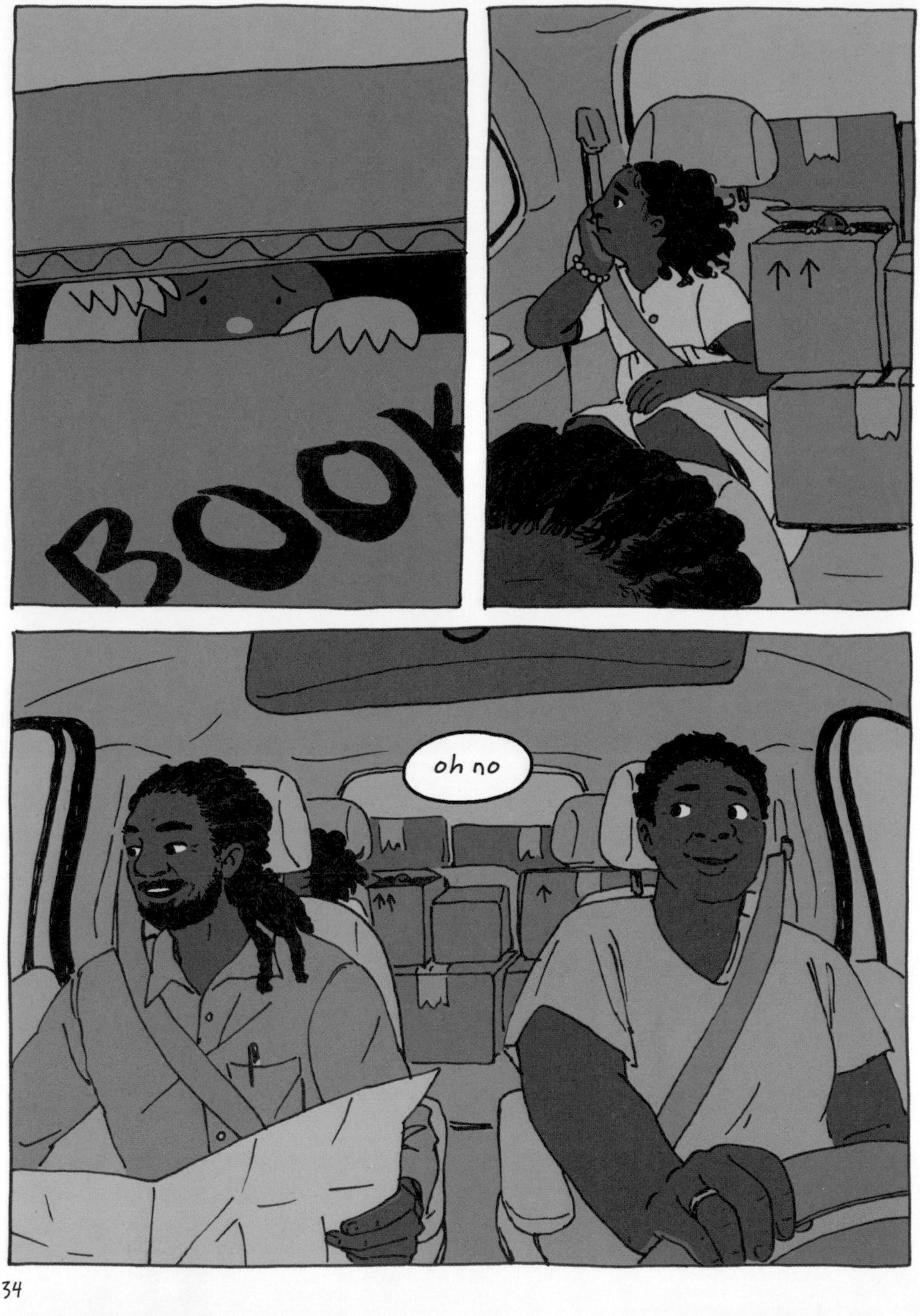
BOOK
oh no

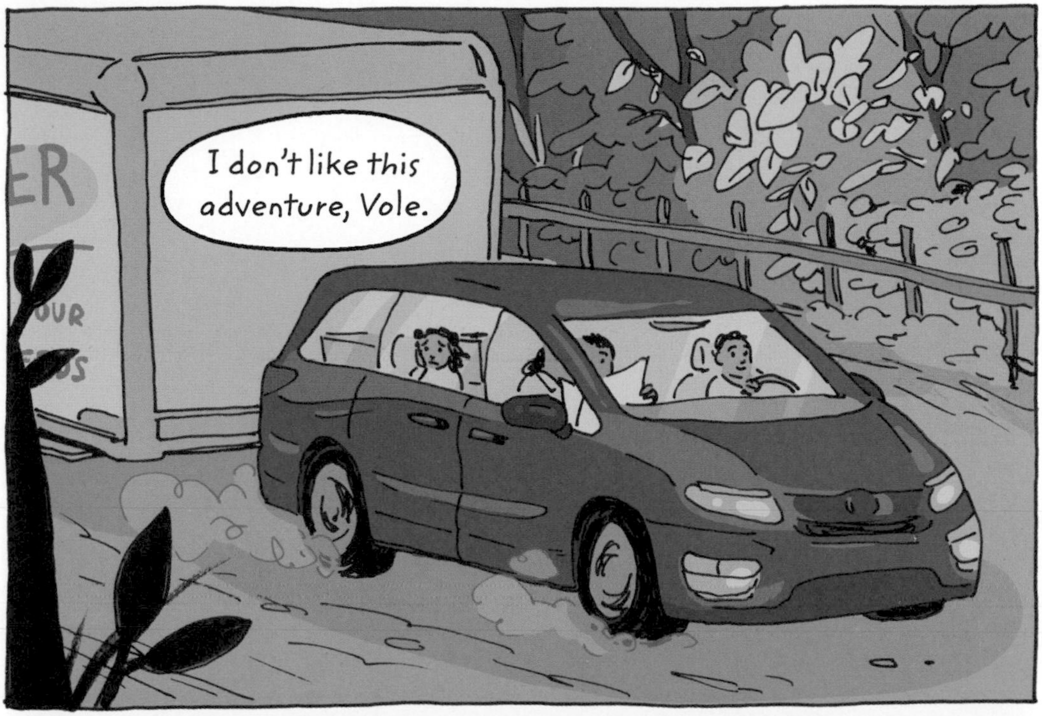
I don't like this adventure, Vole.

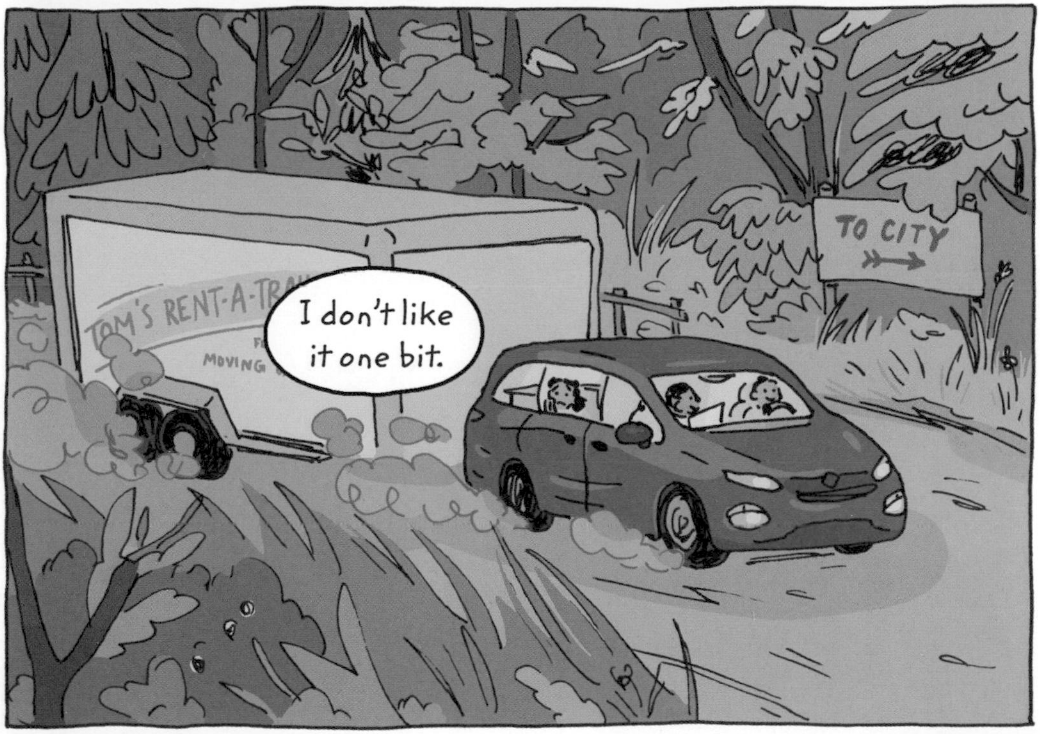
TO CITY
I don't like it one bit.

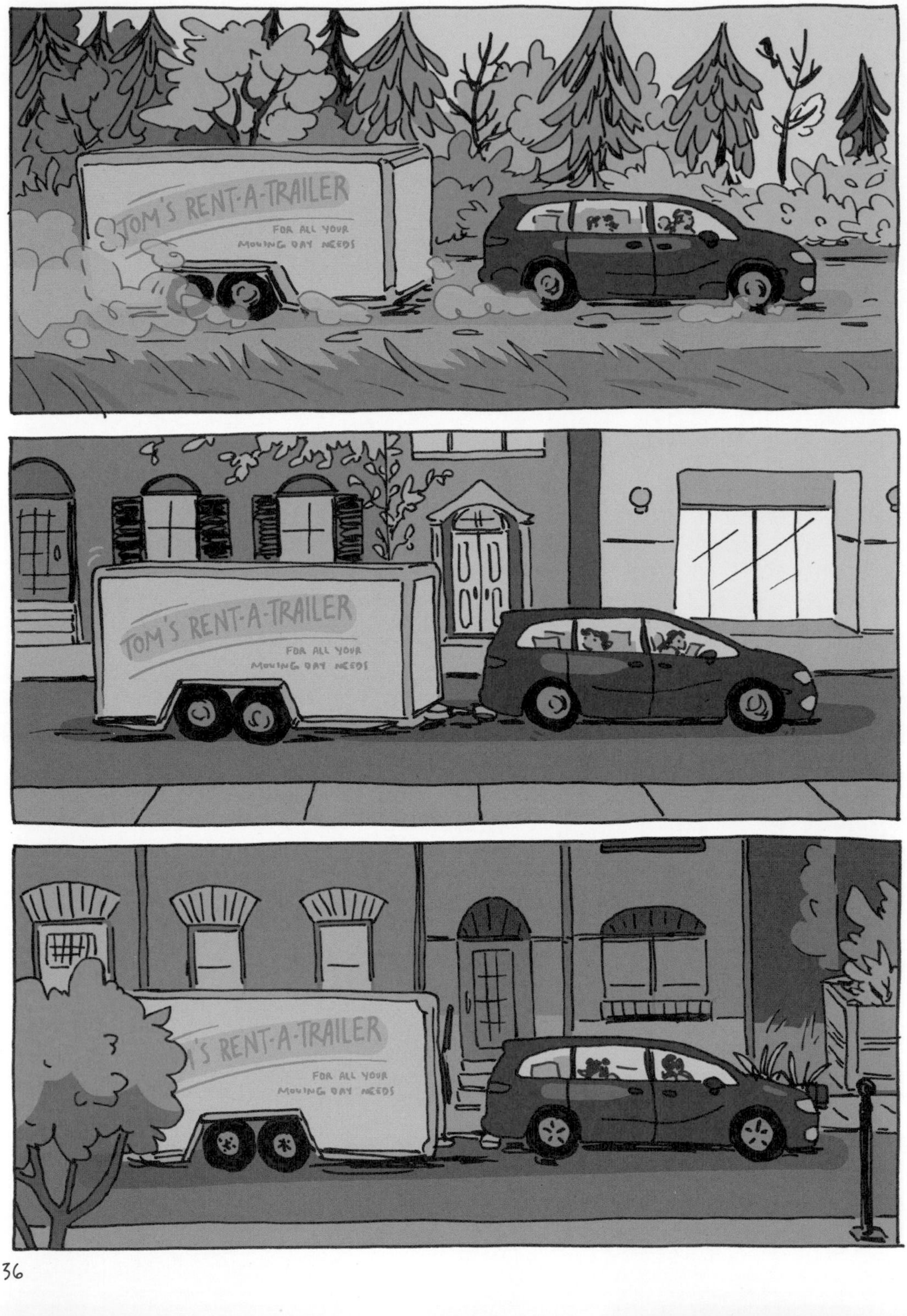
TOM'S RENT-A-TRAILER
FOR ALL YOUR MOVING DAY NEEDS
TOM'S RENT-A-TRAILER
FOR ALL YOUR MOVING DAY NEEDS
'S RENT-A-TRAILER
FOR ALL YOUR MOVING DAY NEEDS

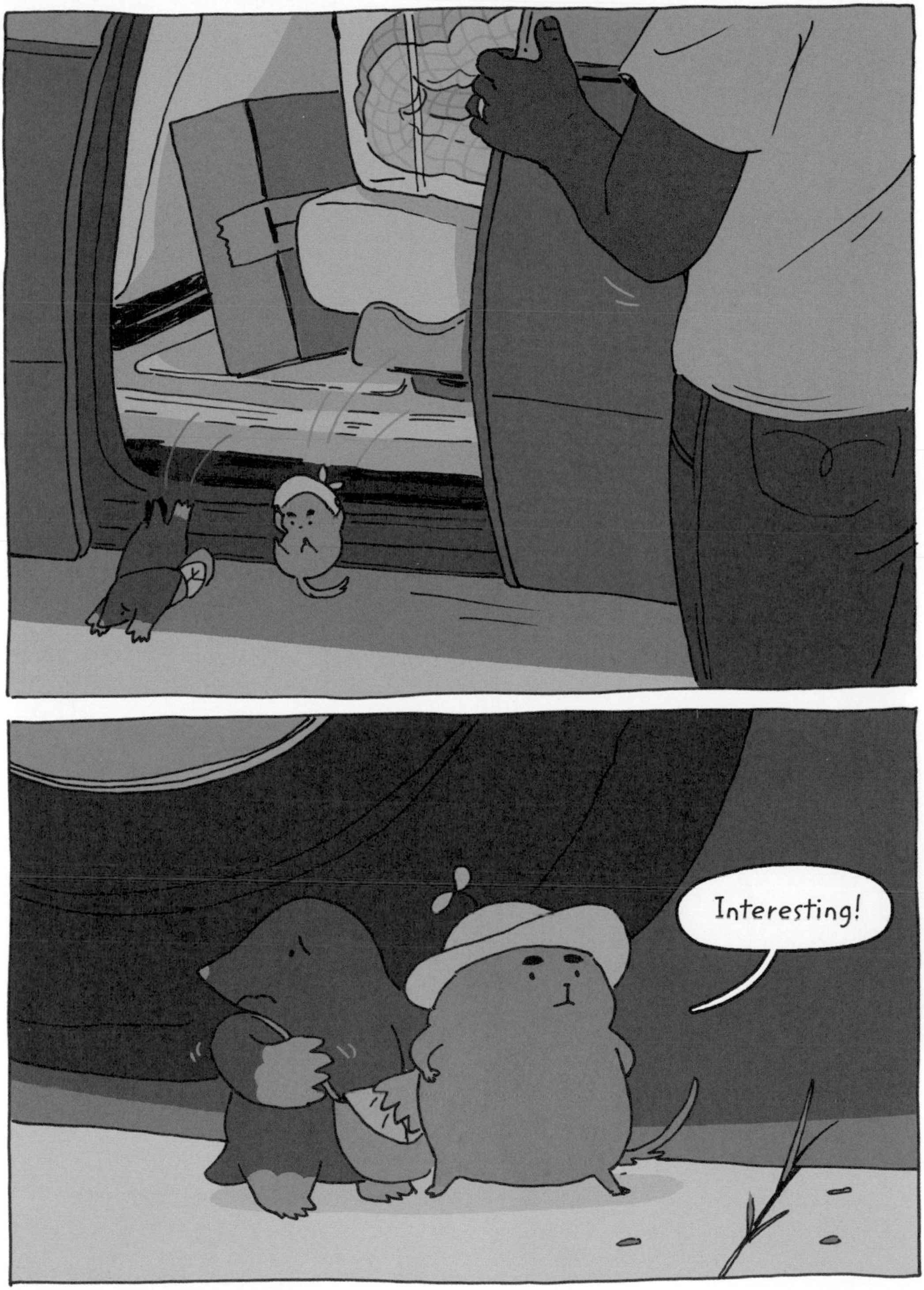
Interesting!

This place is different from the forest.
Vole, we're so far from our homes! What do we do?
What do we DO?
Hmm. If our homes are far away . . .
We must make new homes!

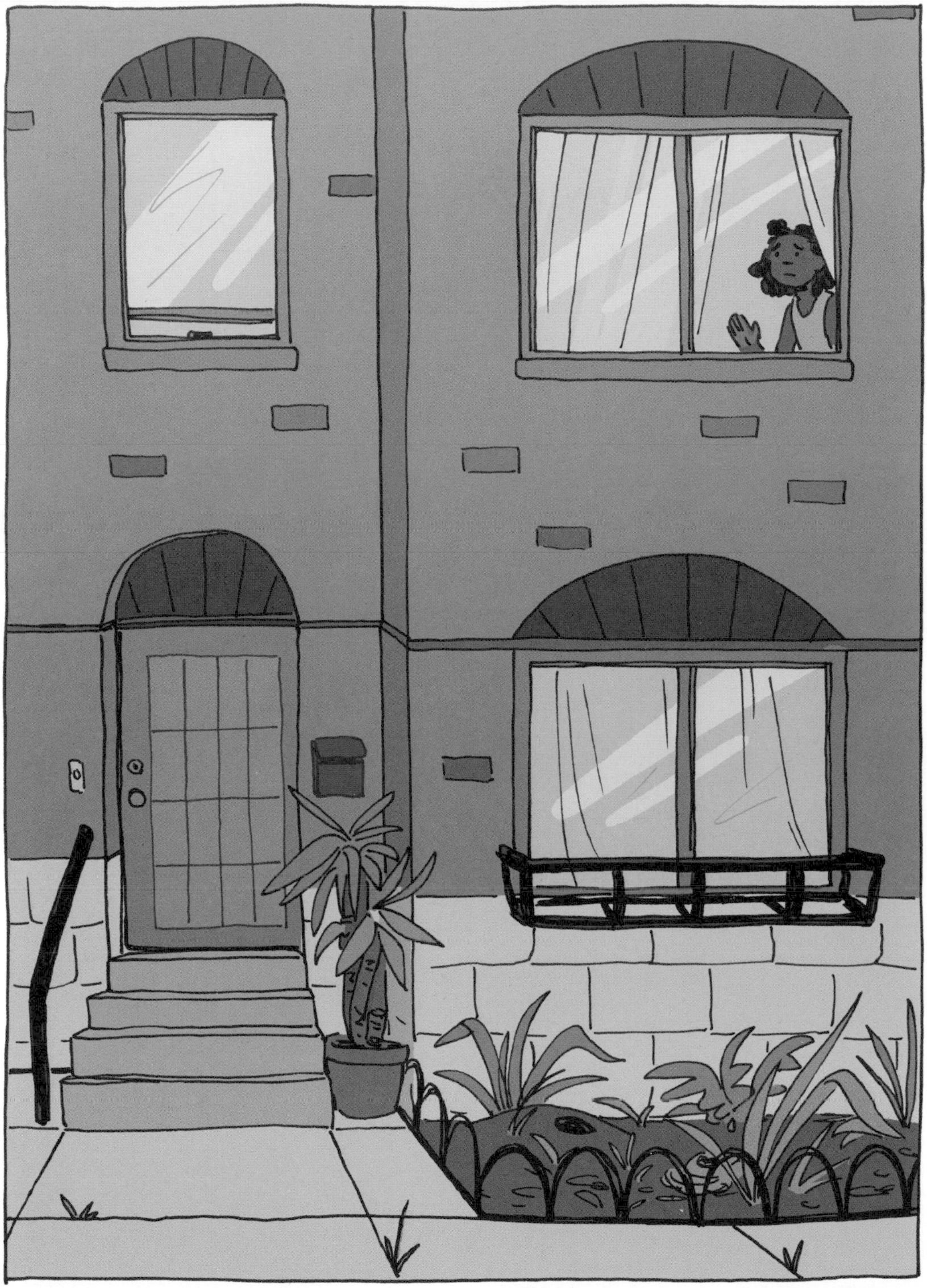

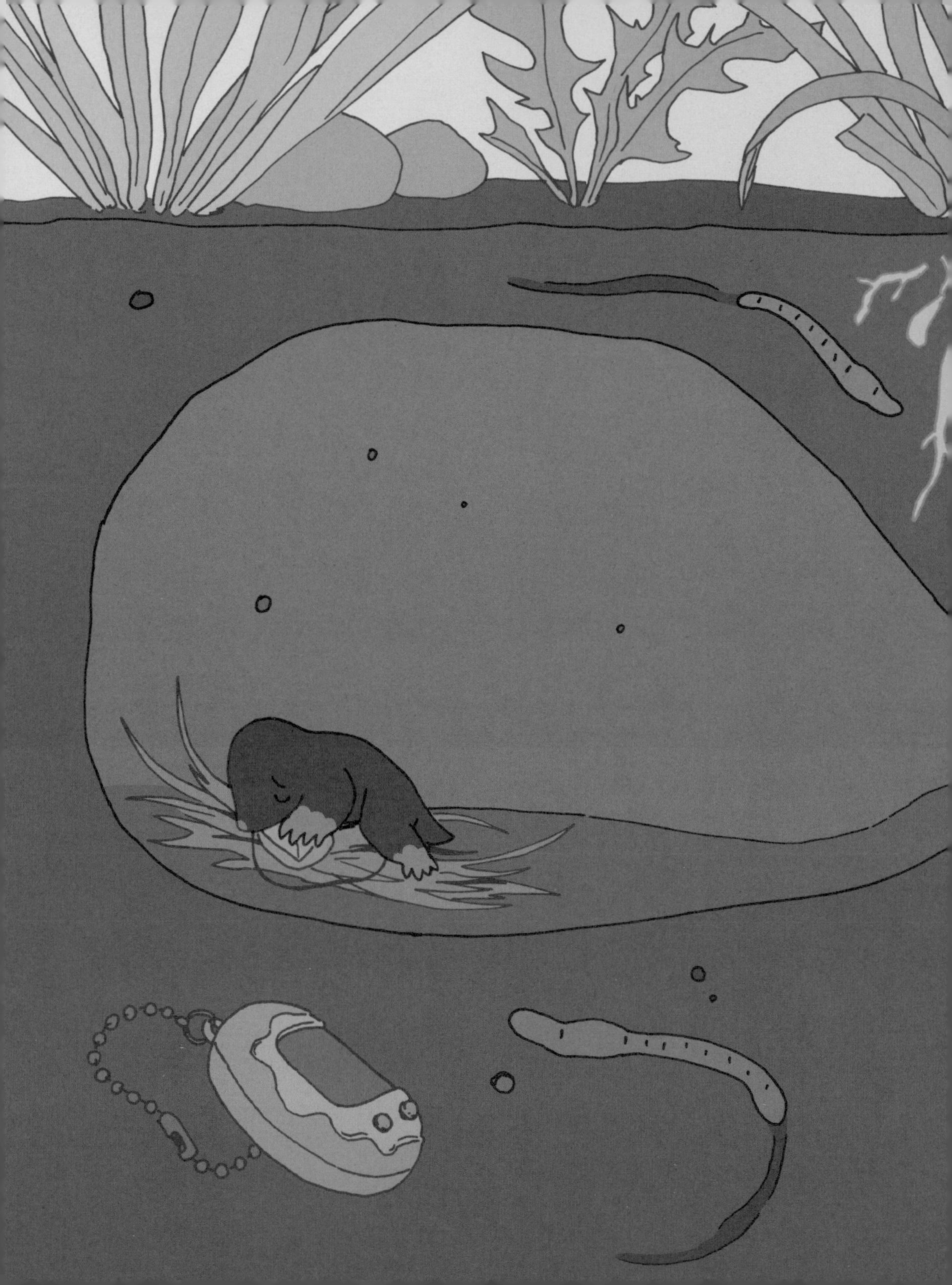

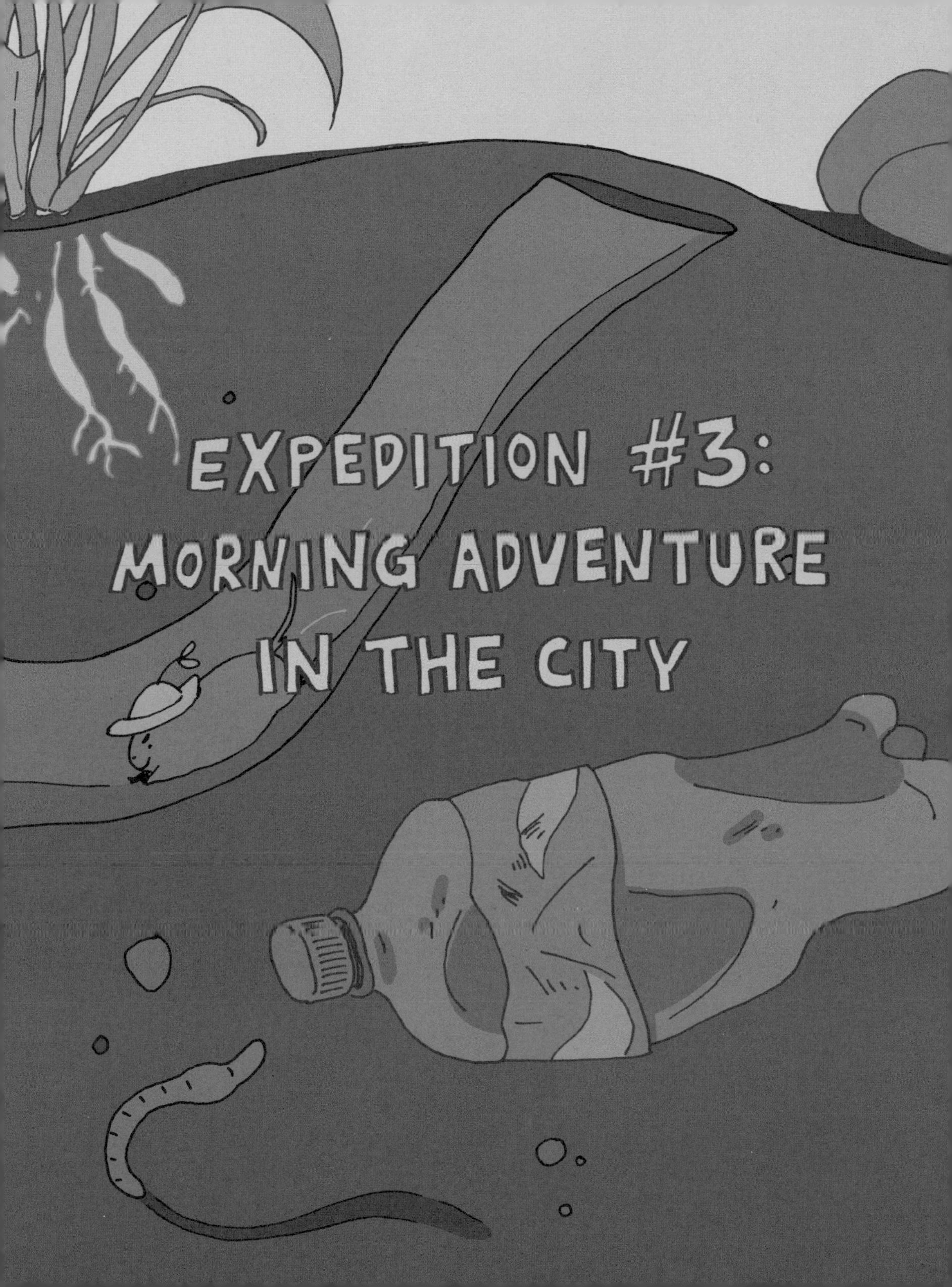
EXPEDITION #3:
MORNING ADVENTURE
IN THE CITY

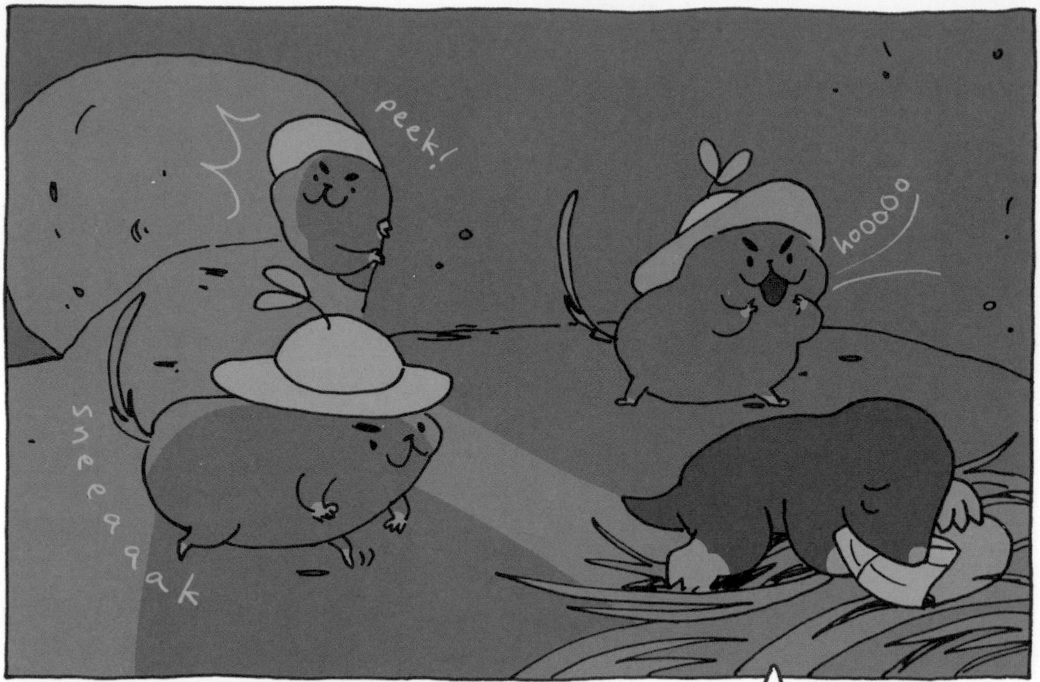
peek!
hooooo
sneeaaak
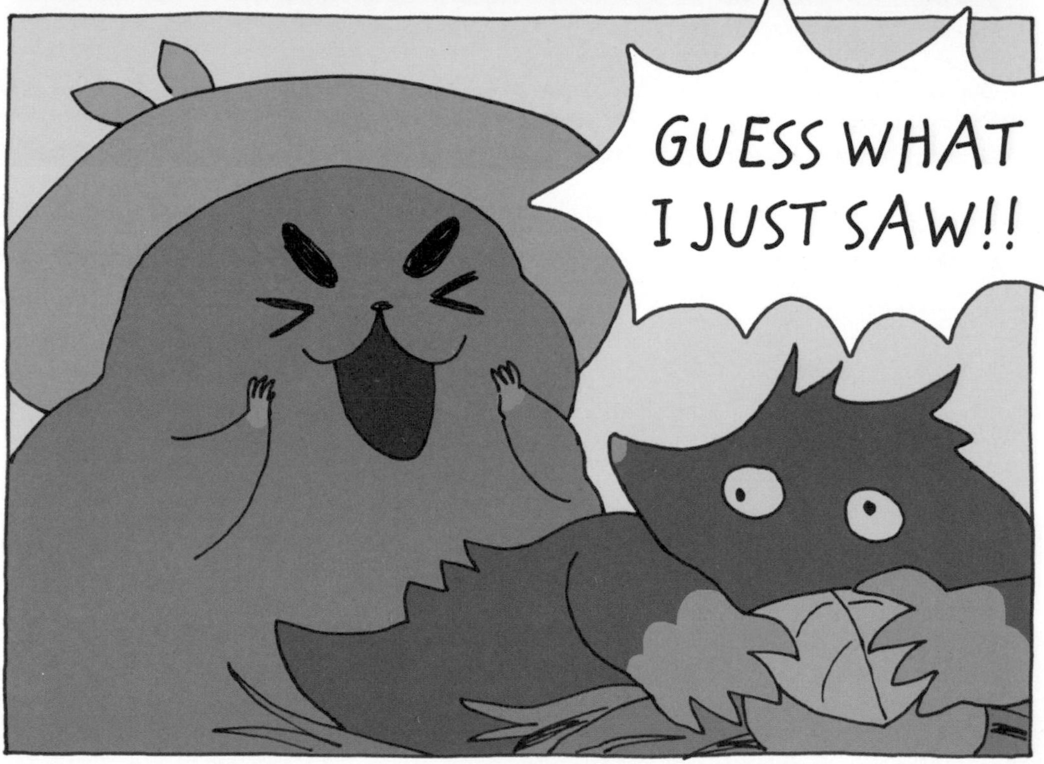
GUESS WHAT I JUST SAW!!

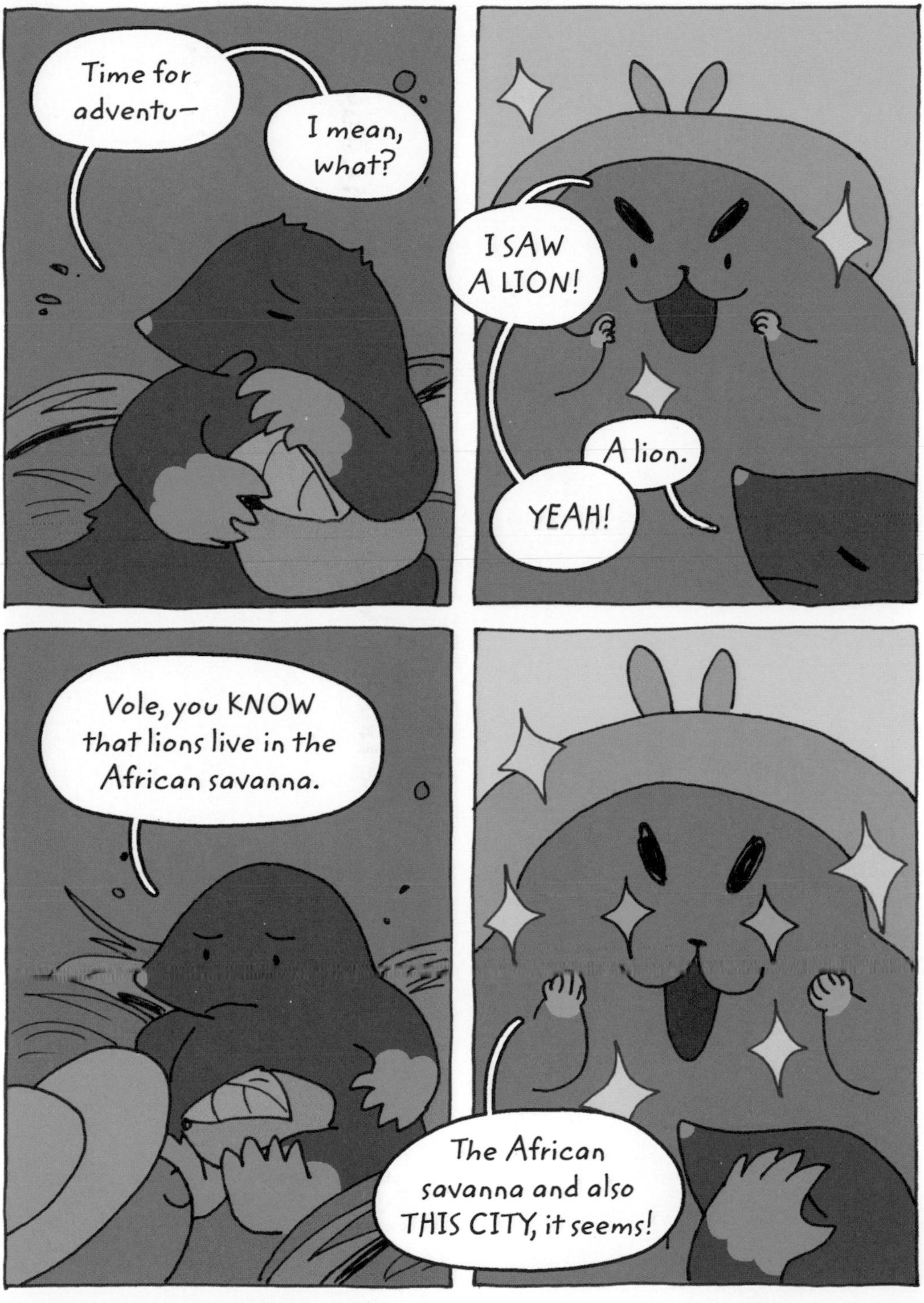
Time for adventu—
I mean, what?
I SAW A LION!
A lion.
YEAH!
Vole, you KNOW that lions live in the African savanna.
The African savanna and also THIS CITY, it seems!

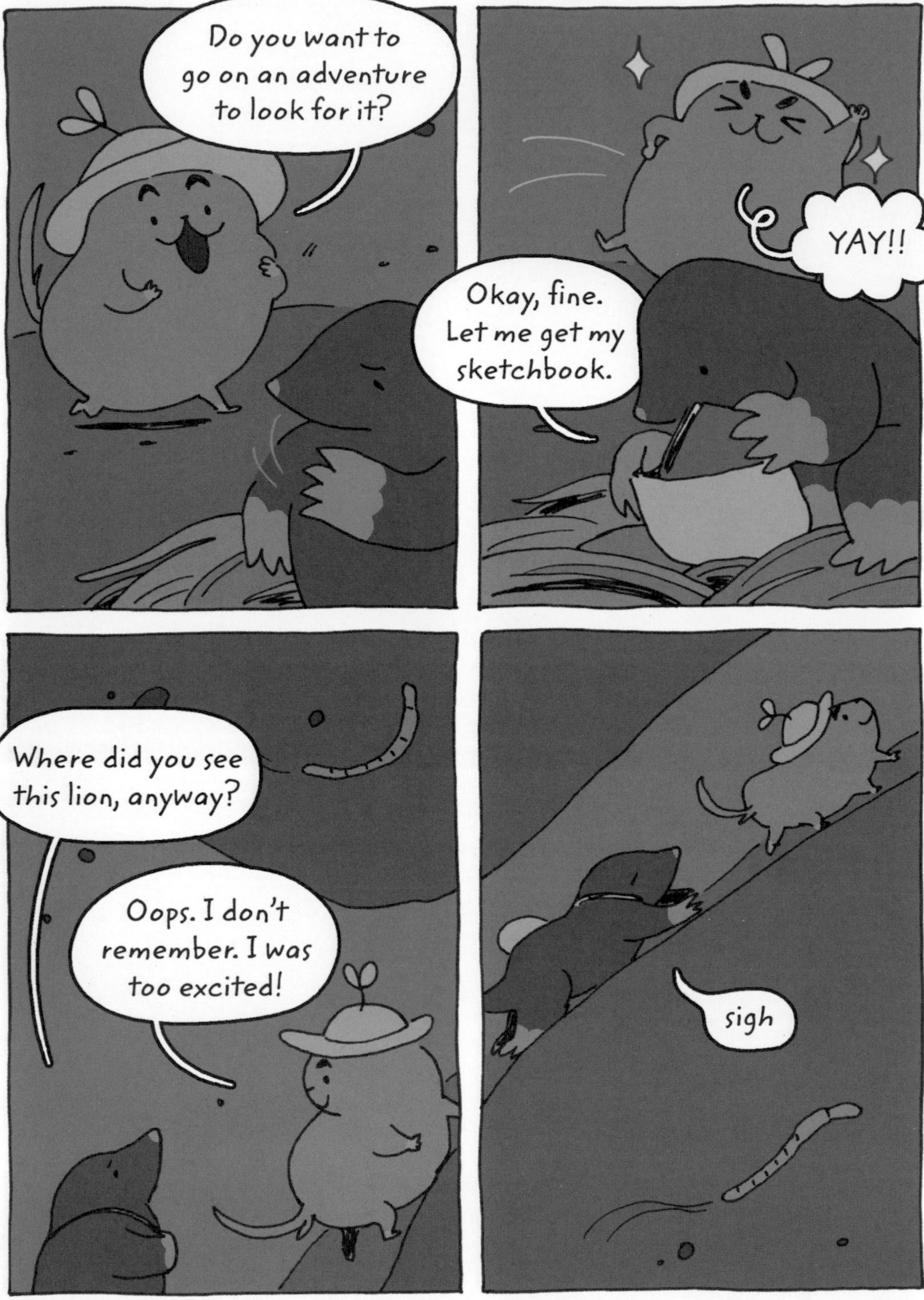
Do you want to go on an adventure to look for it?
YAY!!
Okay, fine. Let me get my sketchbook.
Where did you see this lion, anyway?
Oops. I don't remember. I was too excited!
sigh

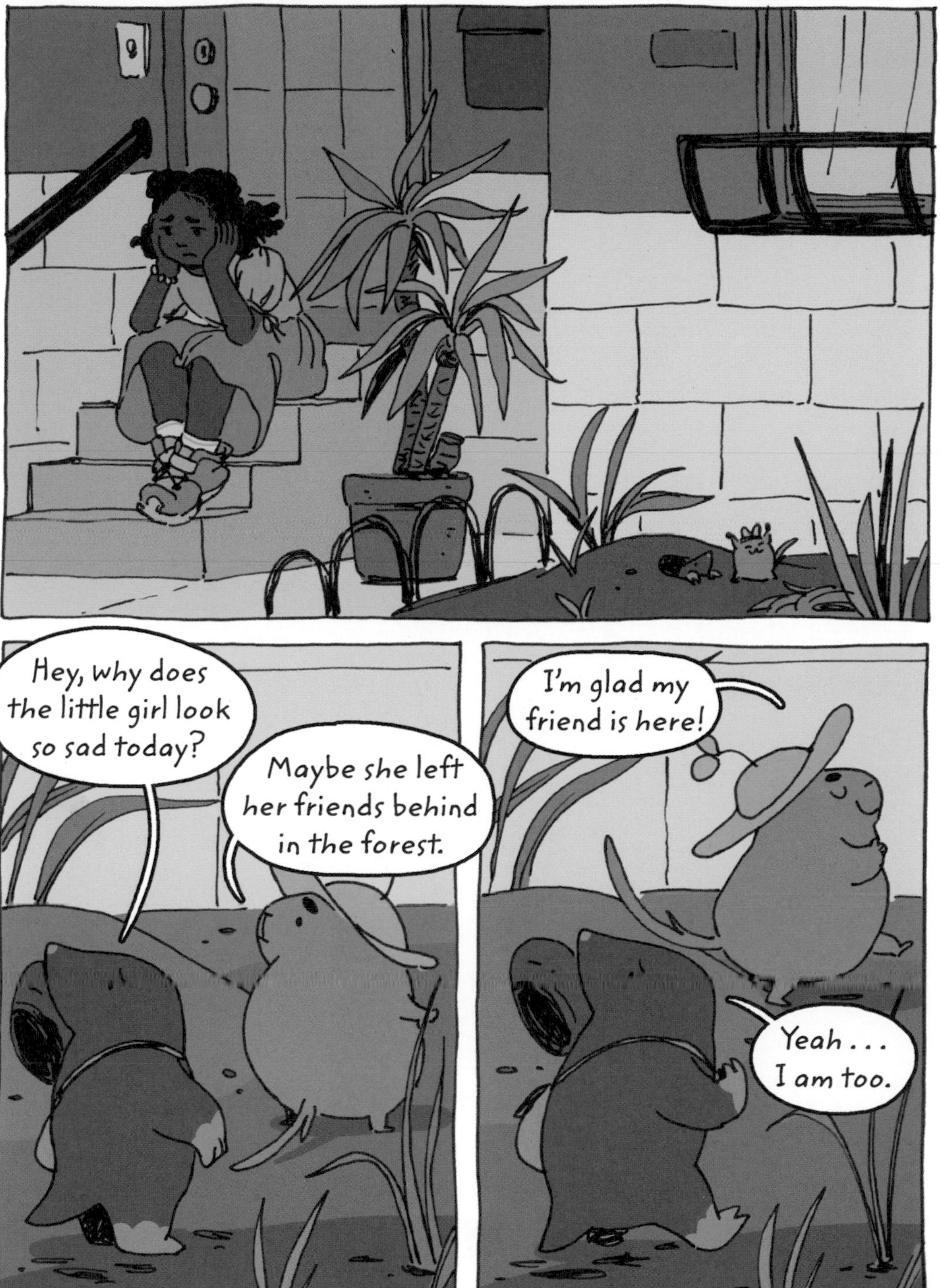
Hey, why does the little girl look so sad today?
Maybe she left her friends behind in the forest.
I'm glad my friend is here!
Yeah . . . I am too.

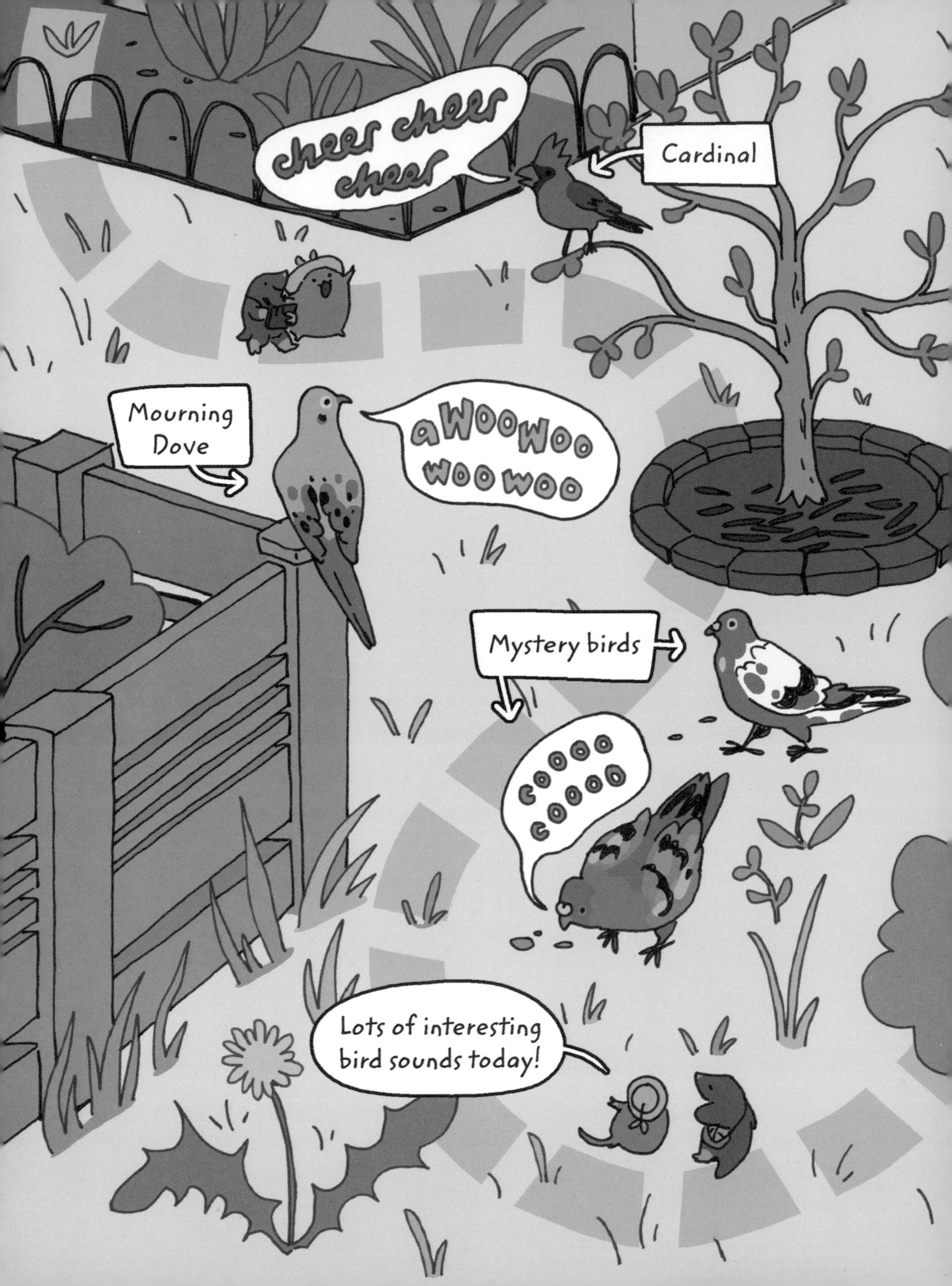
cheer cheer cheer
Cardinal
Mourning Dove
aWOOWOO WOO WOO
Mystery birds
COOOO COOOO
Lots of interesting bird sounds today!

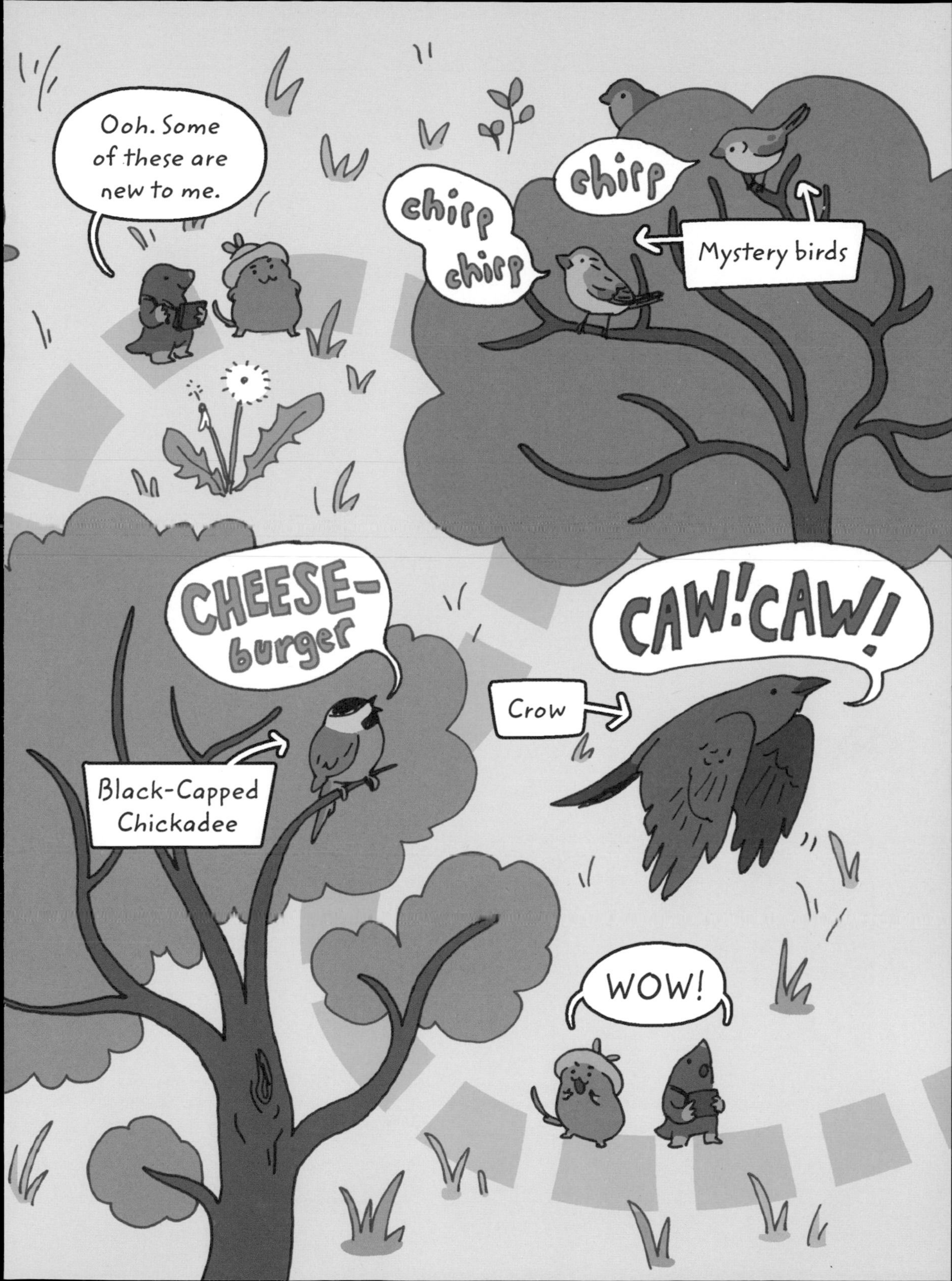
Ooh. Some of these are new to me.
chirp chirp
chirp
chirp
Mystery birds
CHEESE-burger
Black-Capped Chickadee
CAW! CAW!
Crow
WOW!

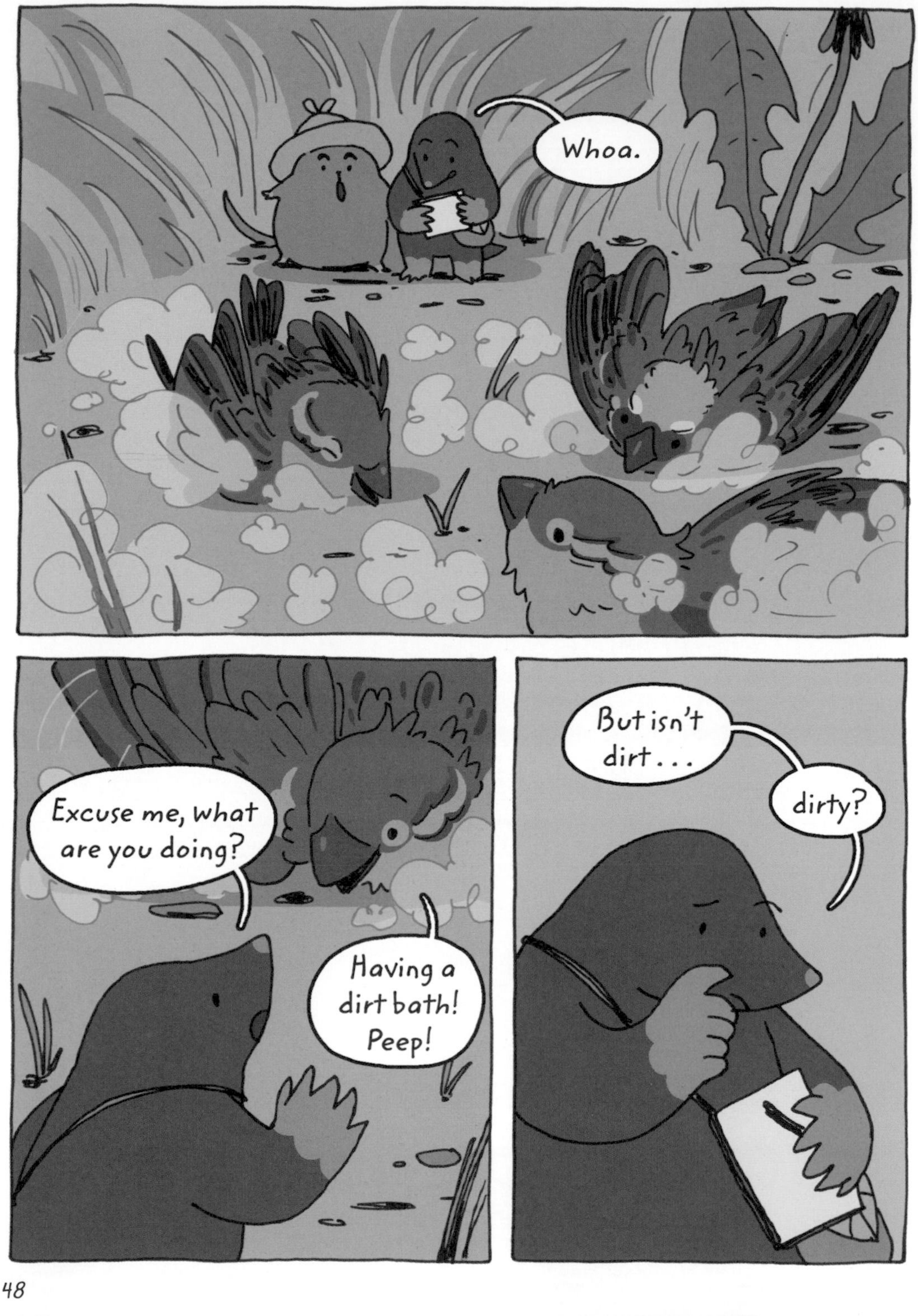
Whoa.
Excuse me, what are you doing?
Having a dirt bath! Peep!
But isn't dirt . . .
dirty?

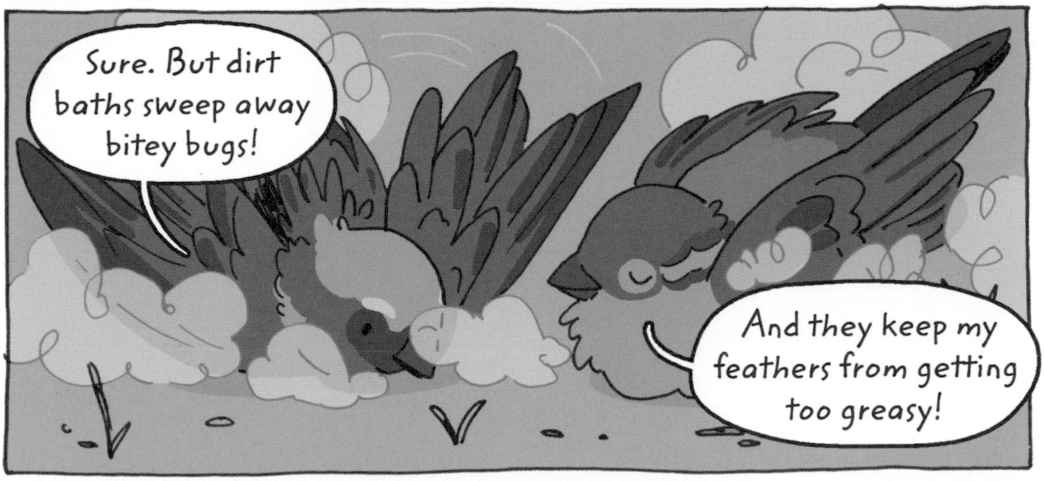
Sure. But dirt baths sweep away bitey bugs!
And they keep my feathers from getting too greasy!

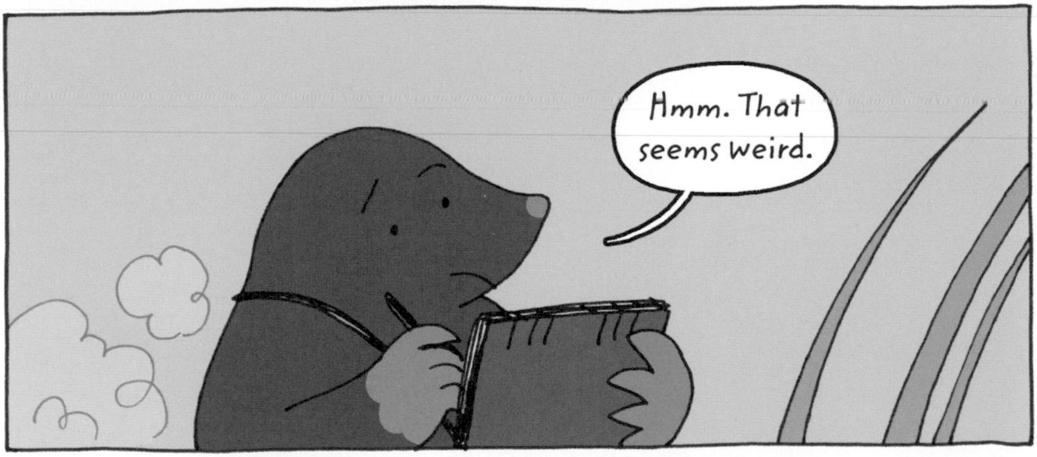
Hmm. That seems weird.

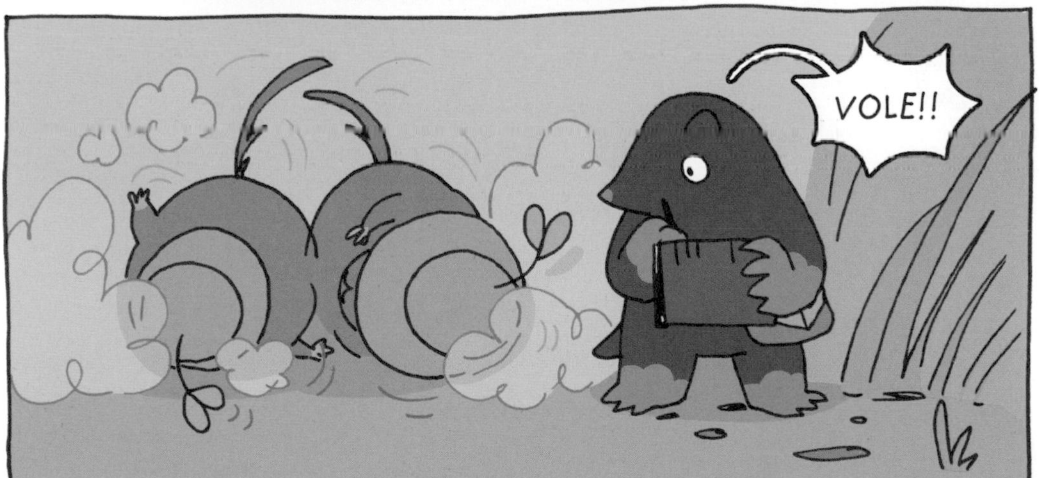
VOLE!!

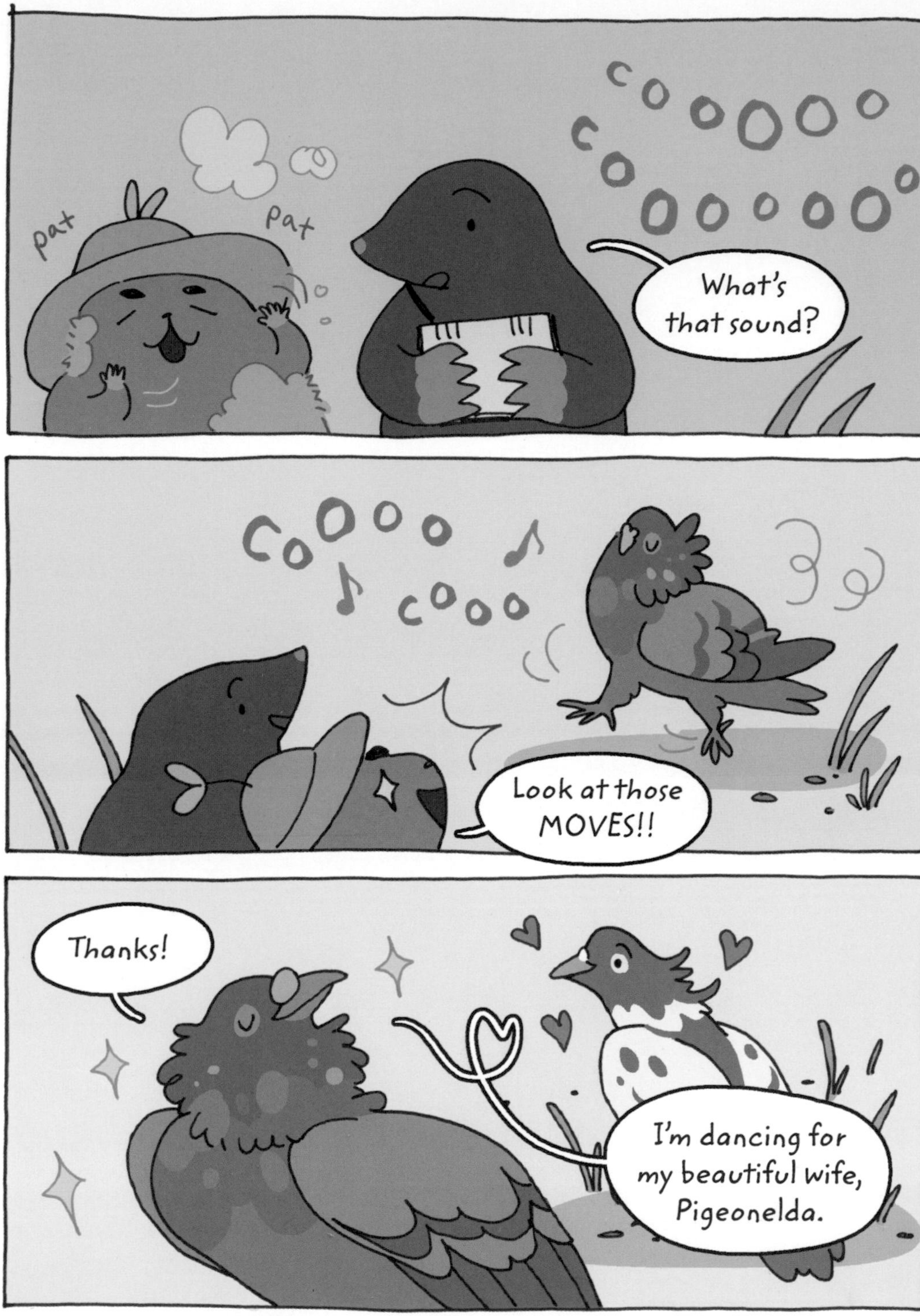
pat
pat
COOOOOO
COOOOOOOO
What's that sound?
COOOO
COOOO
Look at those MOVES!!
Thanks!
I'm dancing for my beautiful wife, Pigeonelda.

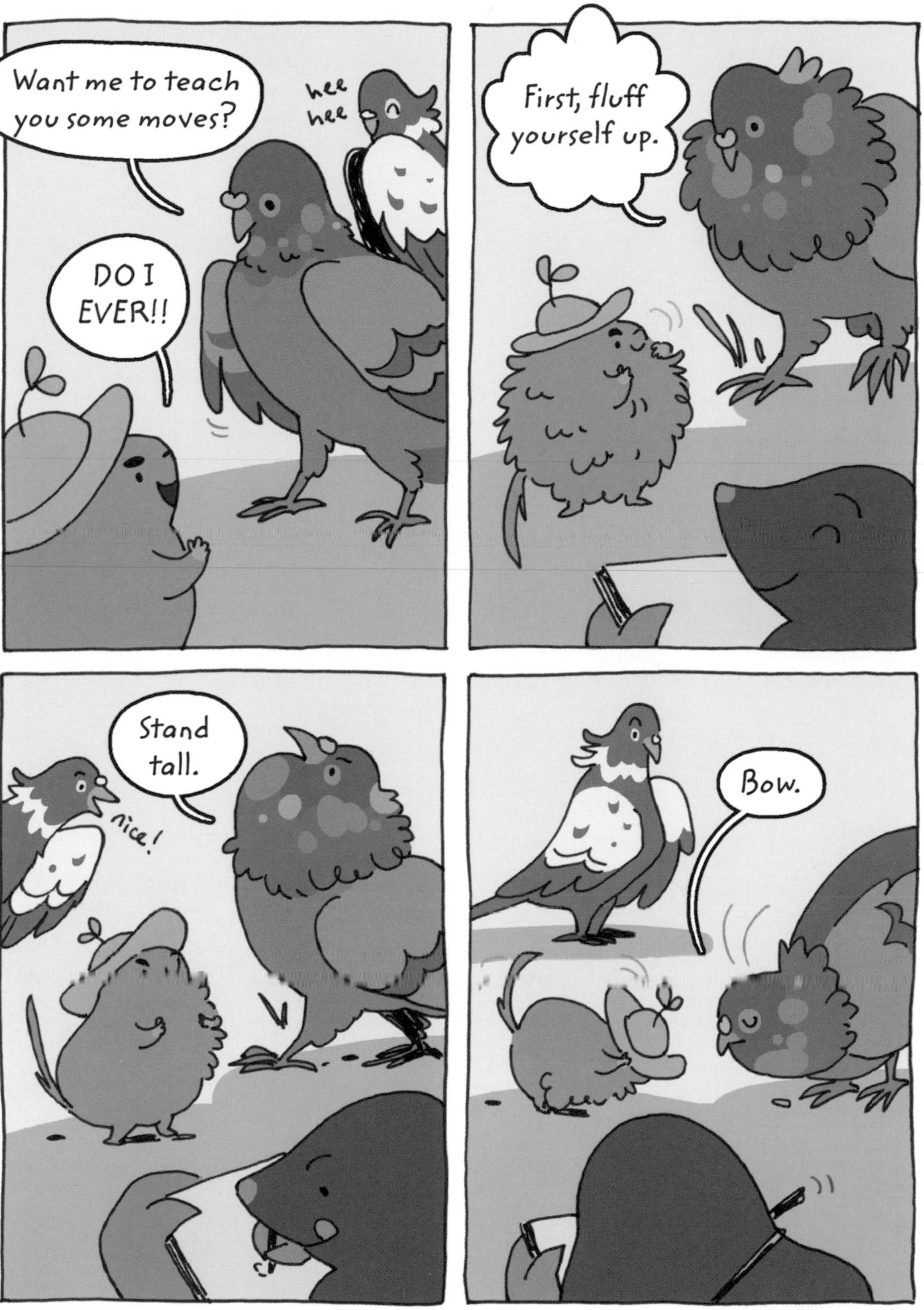
Want me to teach you some moves?
hee hee
DO I EVER!!
First, fluff yourself up.
Stand tall.
nice!
Bow.

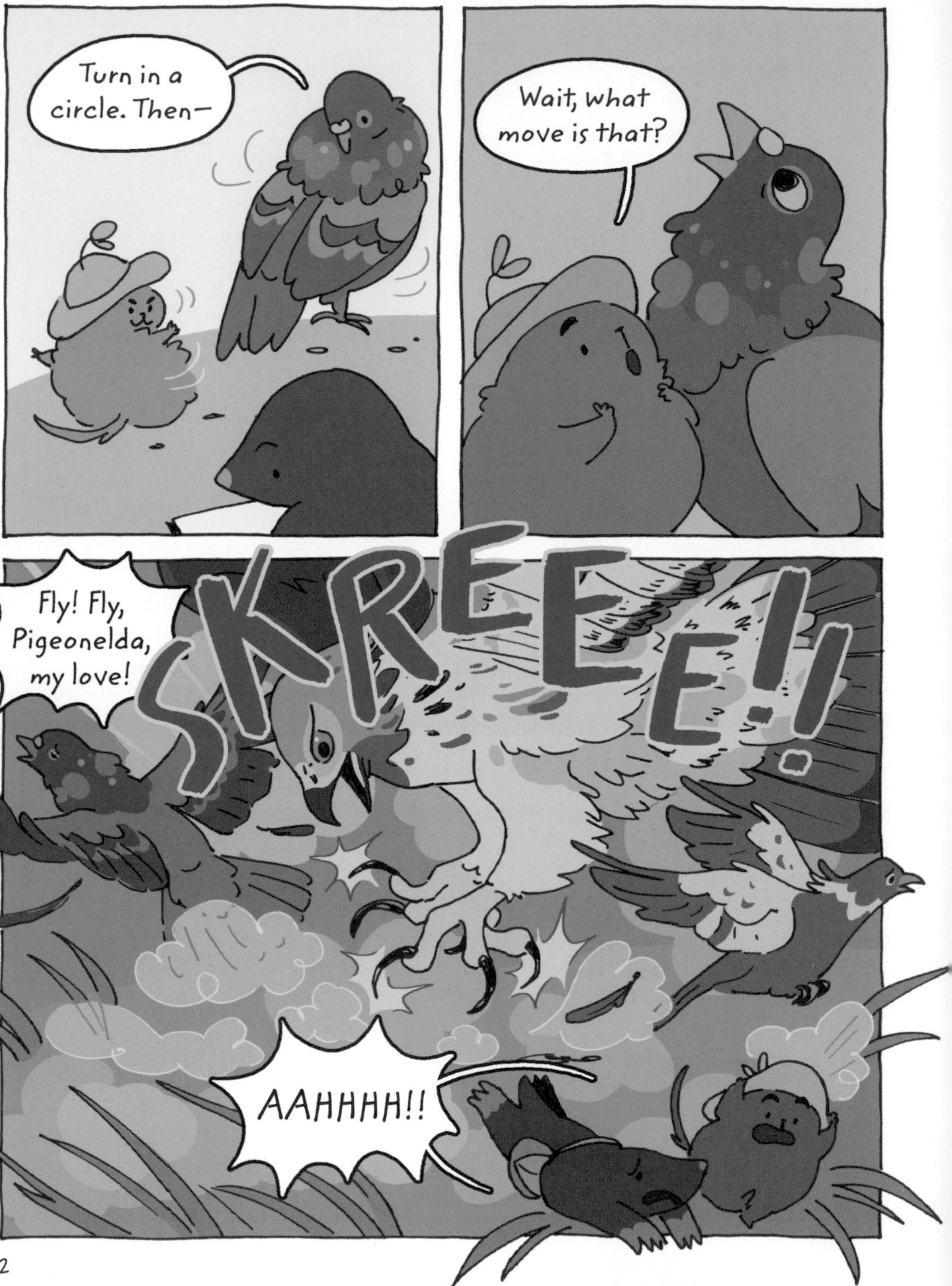
Turn in a circle. Then—
Wait, what move is that?
Fly! Fly, Pigeonelda, my love!
SKREEE!!
AAHHHH!!

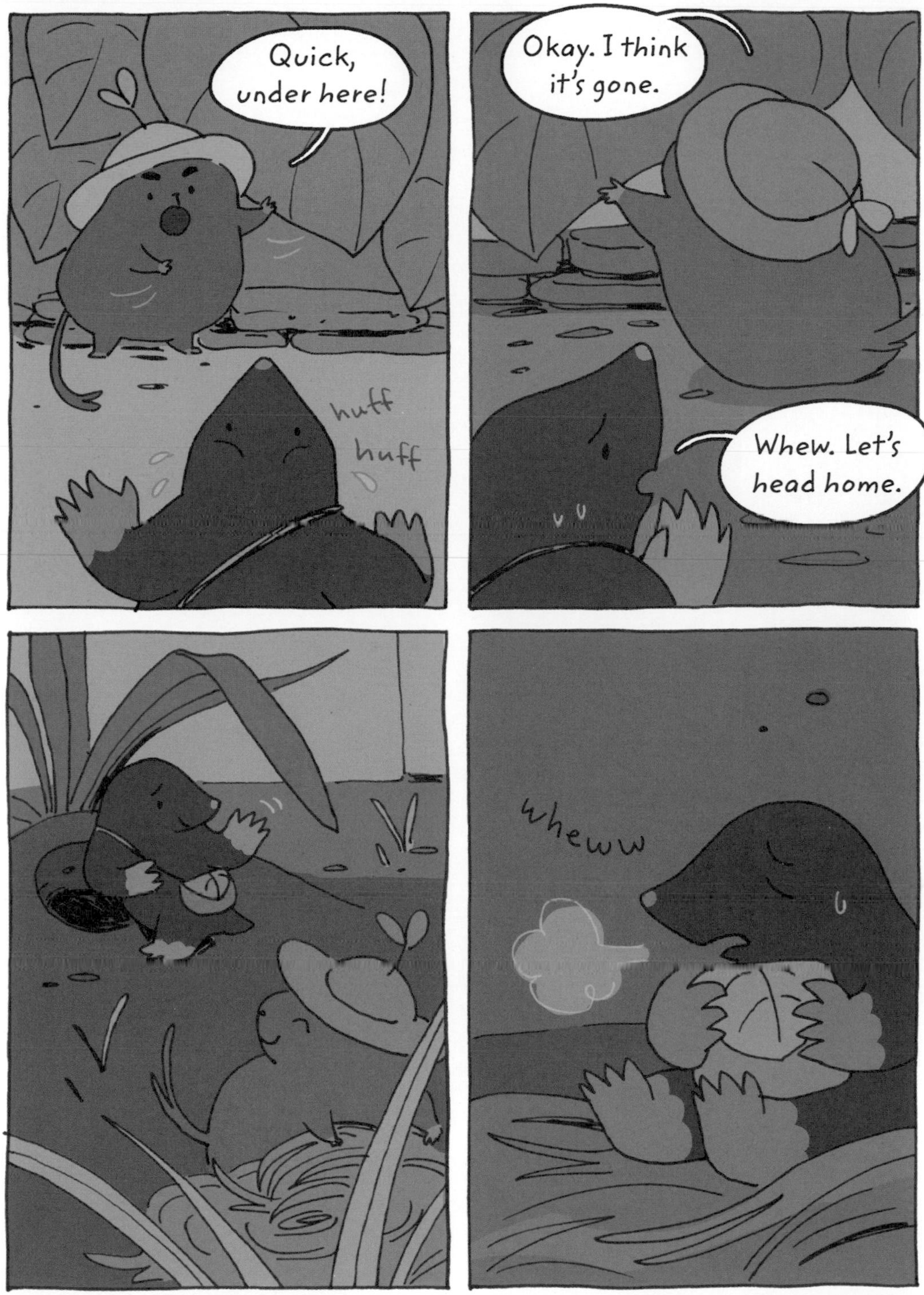

Quick, under here!
huff huff
Okay. I think it's gone.
Whew. Let's head home.
wheww

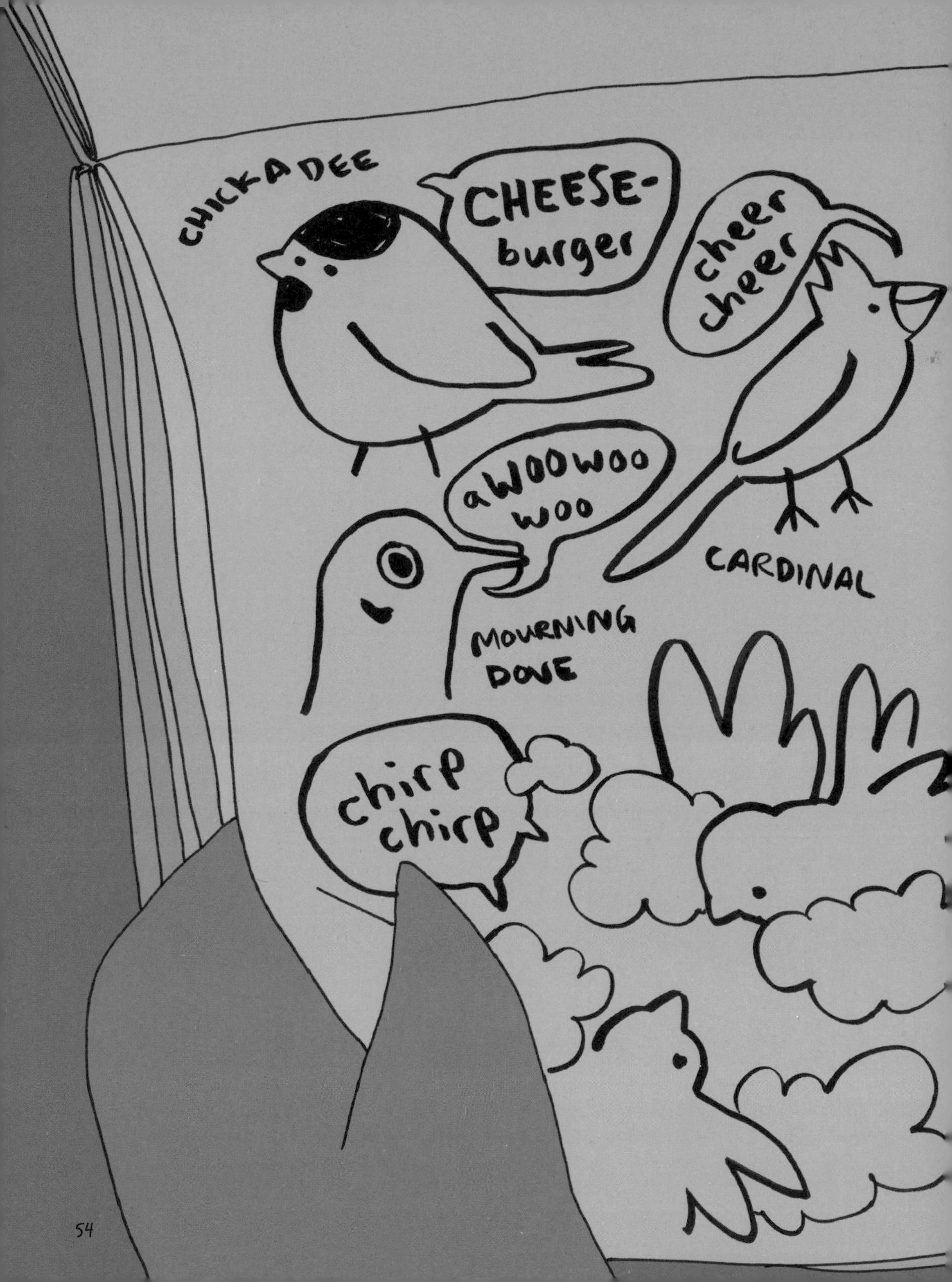
CHICKADEE
CHEESE-burger
cheer cheer
aWOOWOO woo
CARDINAL
MOURNING DOVE
chirp chirp

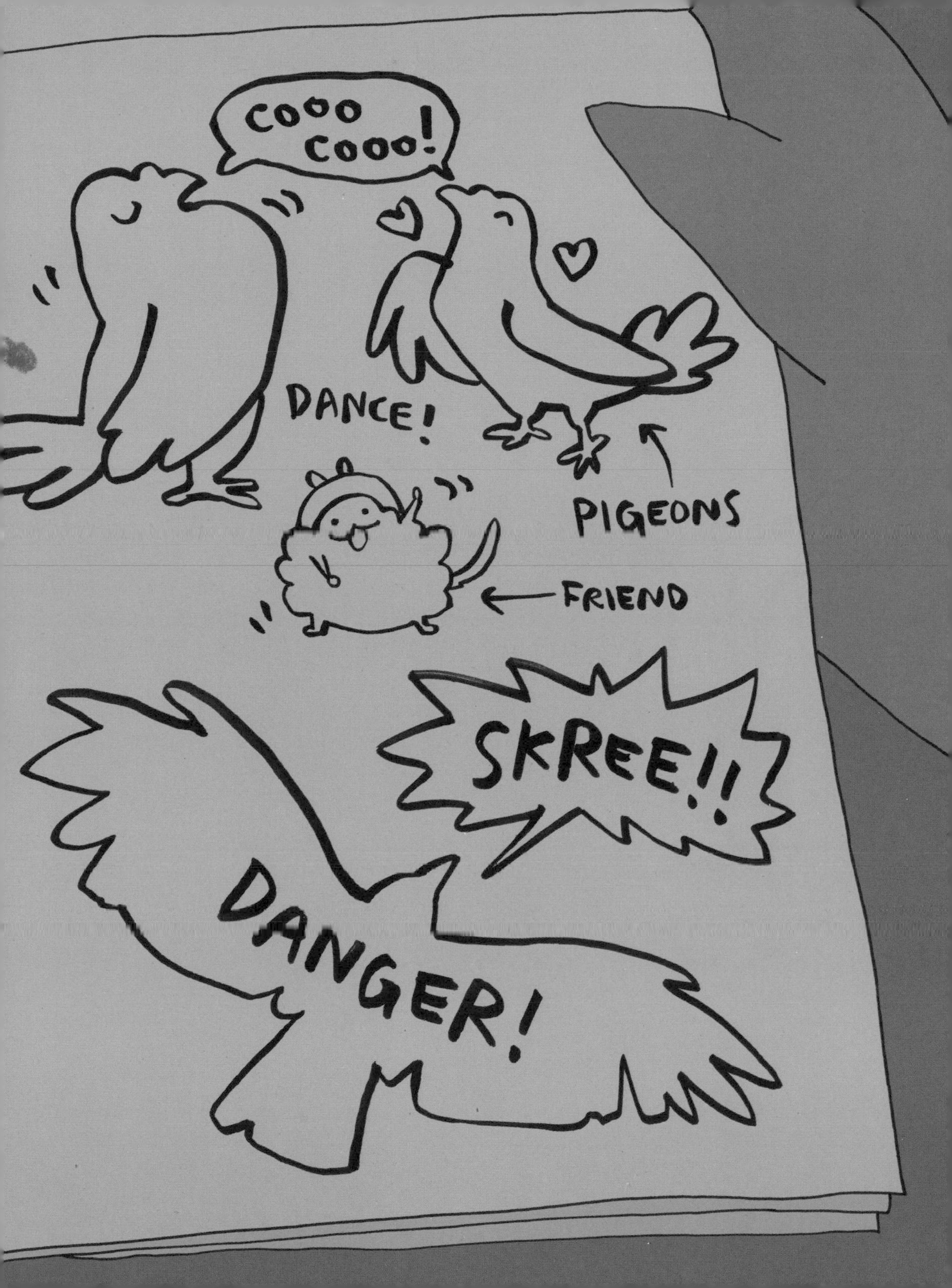
COOO COOO!
DANCE!
PIGEONS
FRIEND
SKREE!!
DANGER!

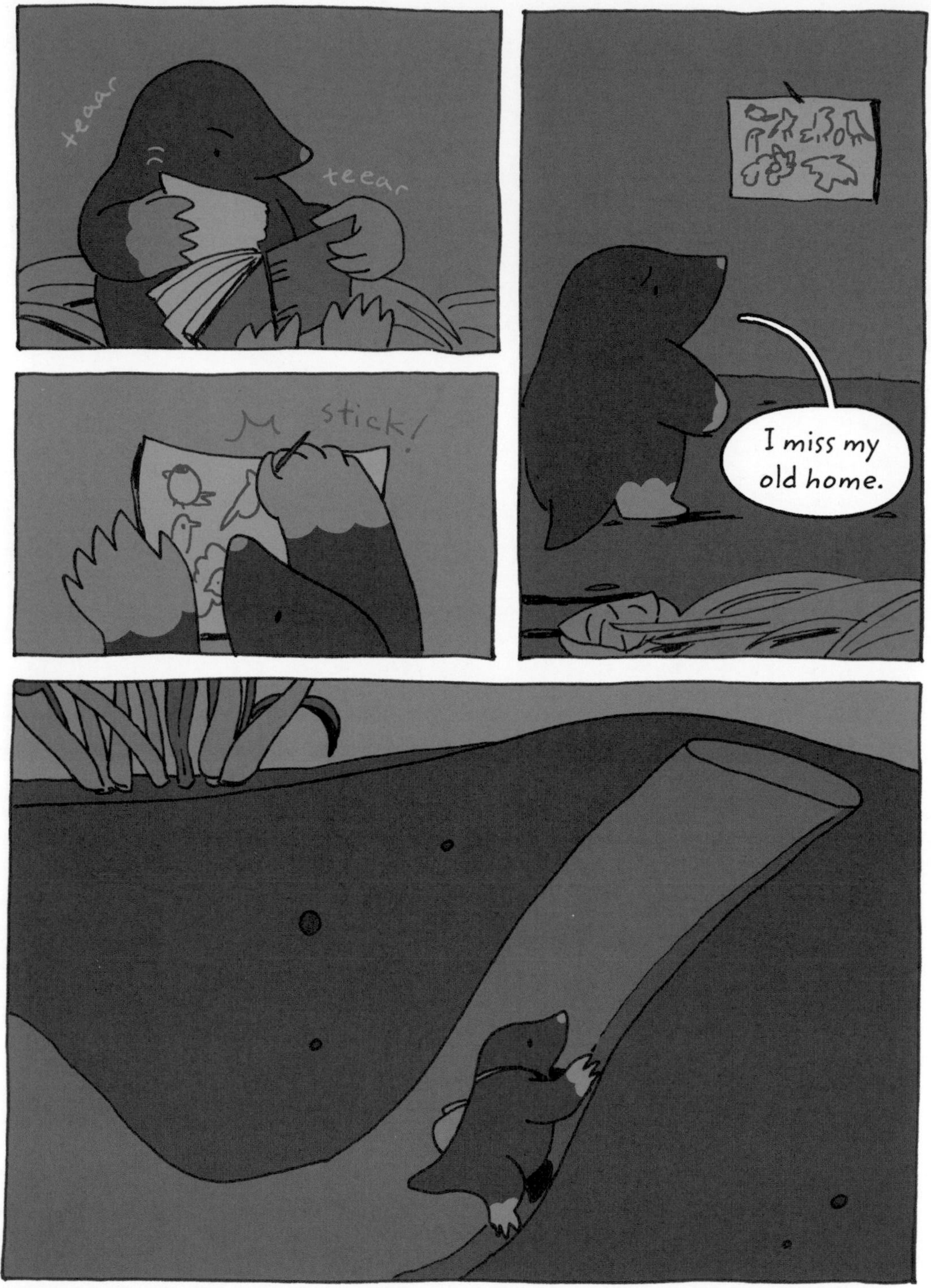
teaar
teear
stick!
I miss my old home.

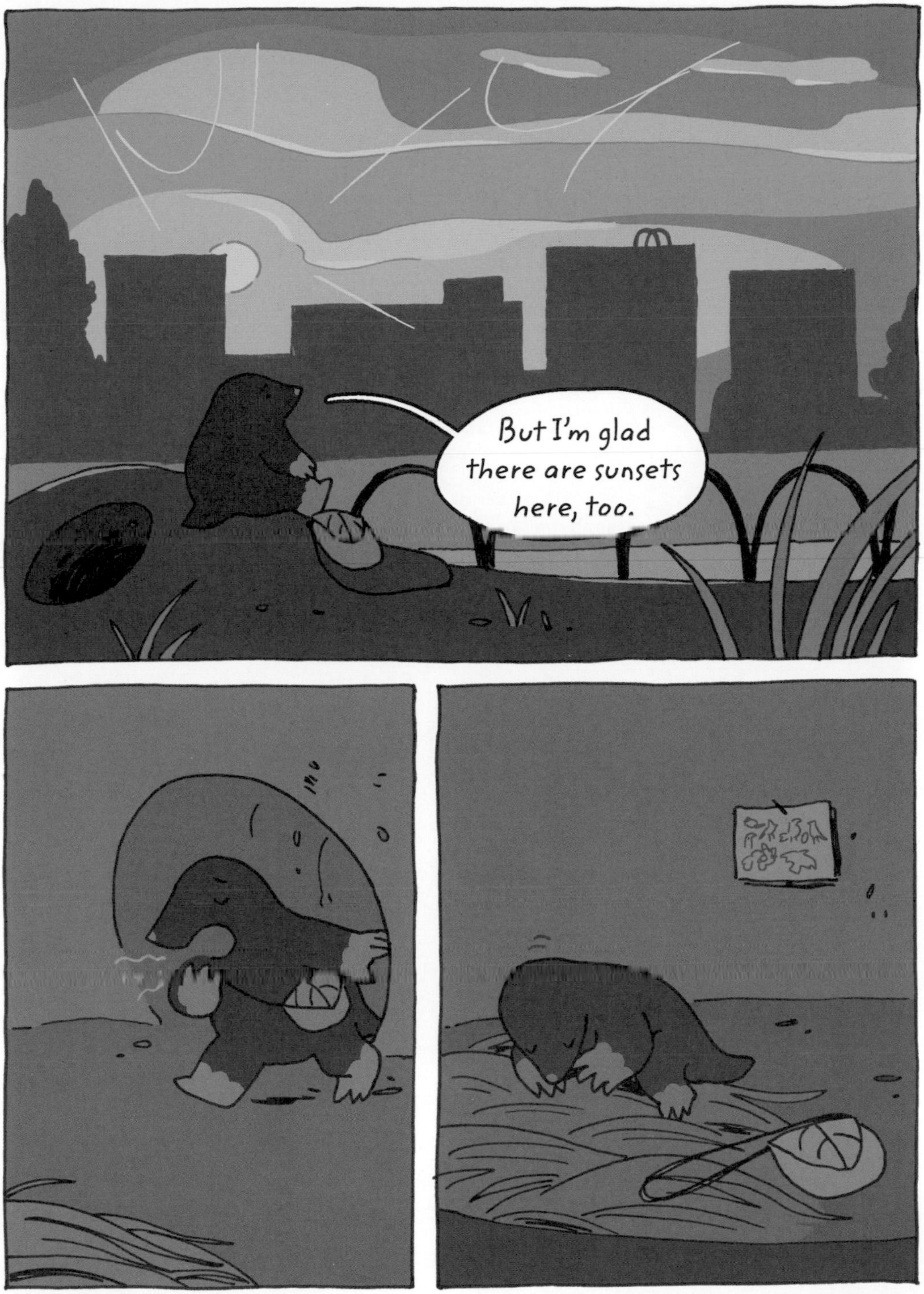
But I'm glad there are sunsets here, too.

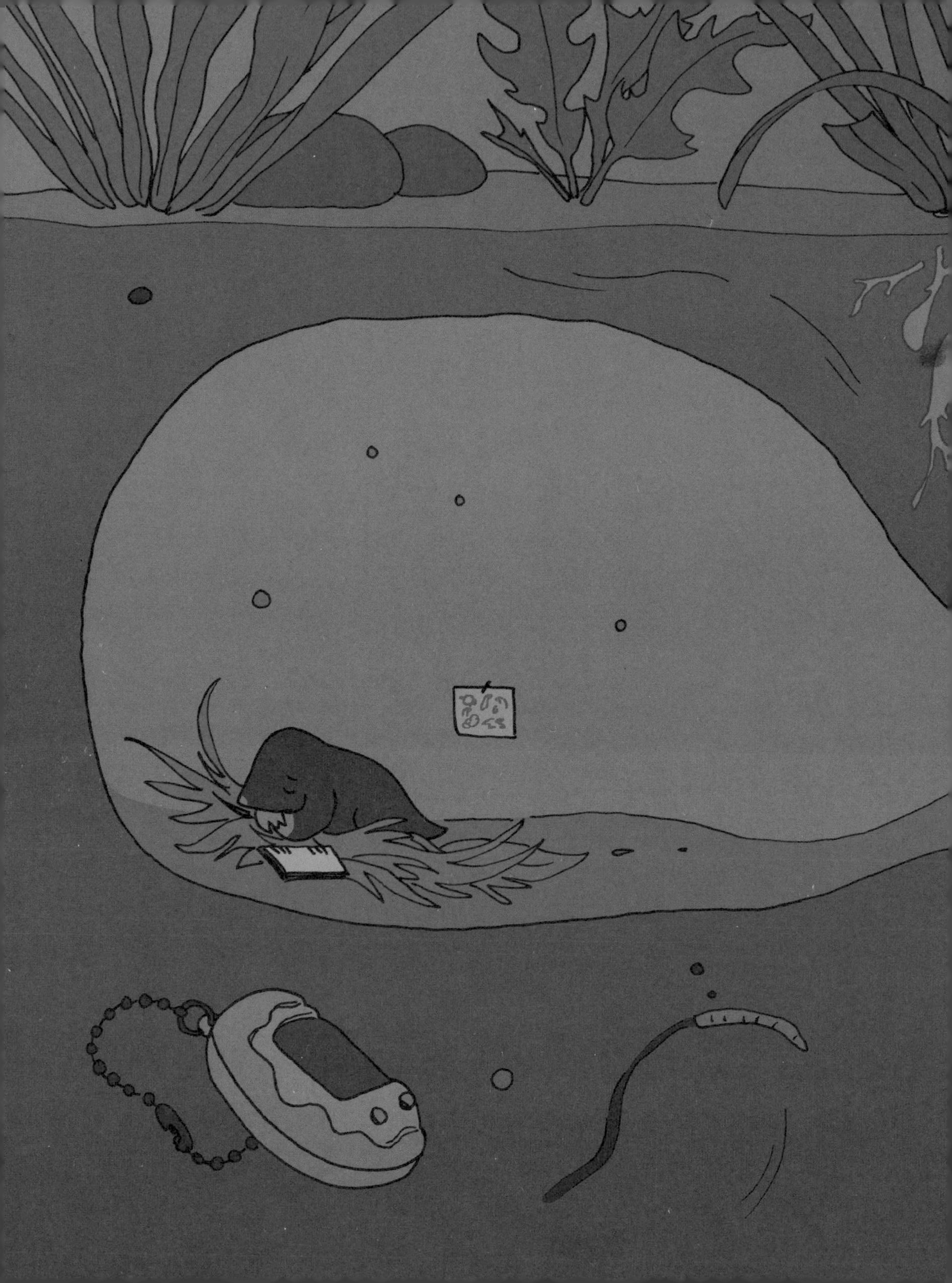

EXPEDITION #4: NIGHT ADVENTURE IN THE CITY

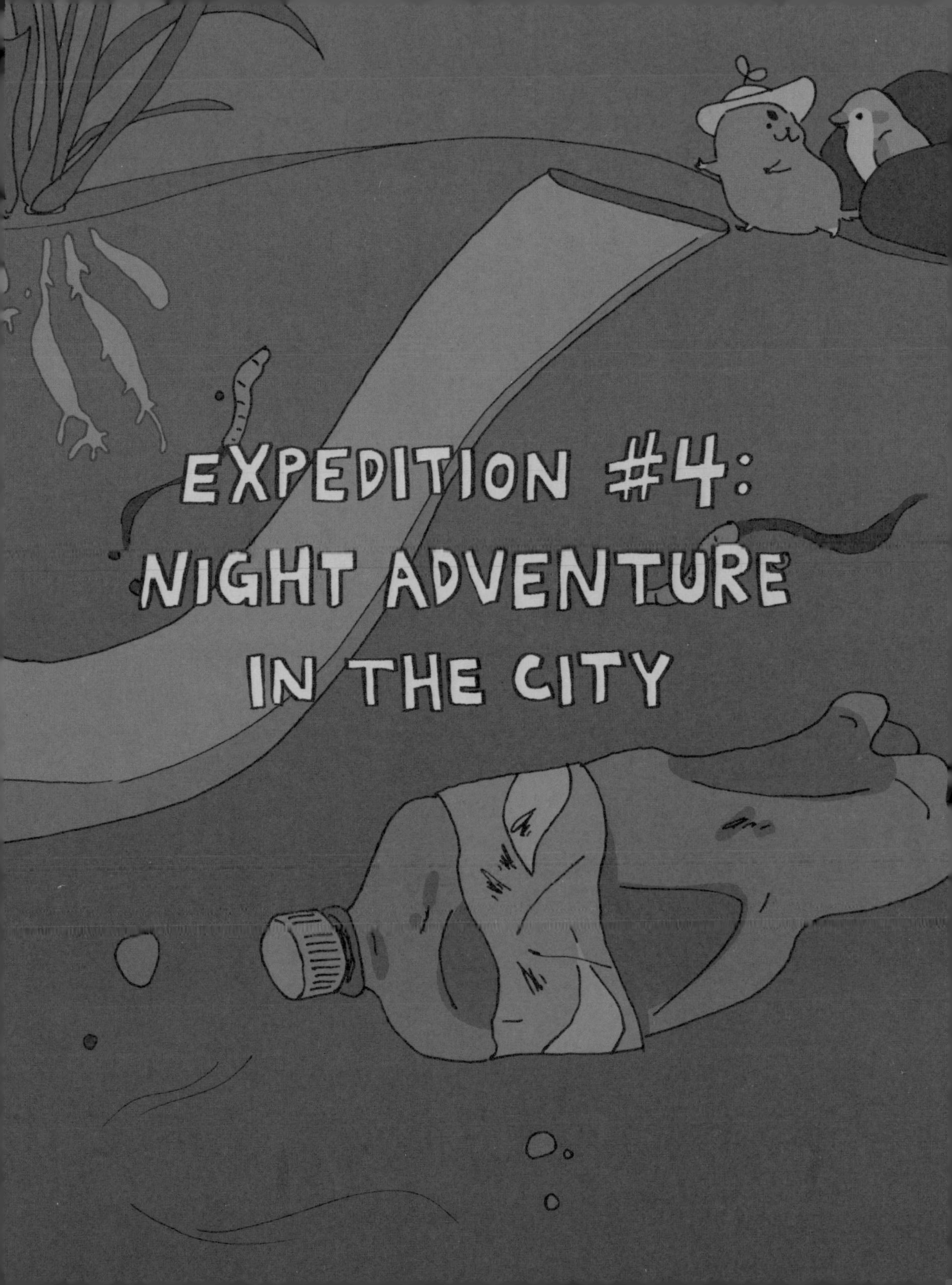

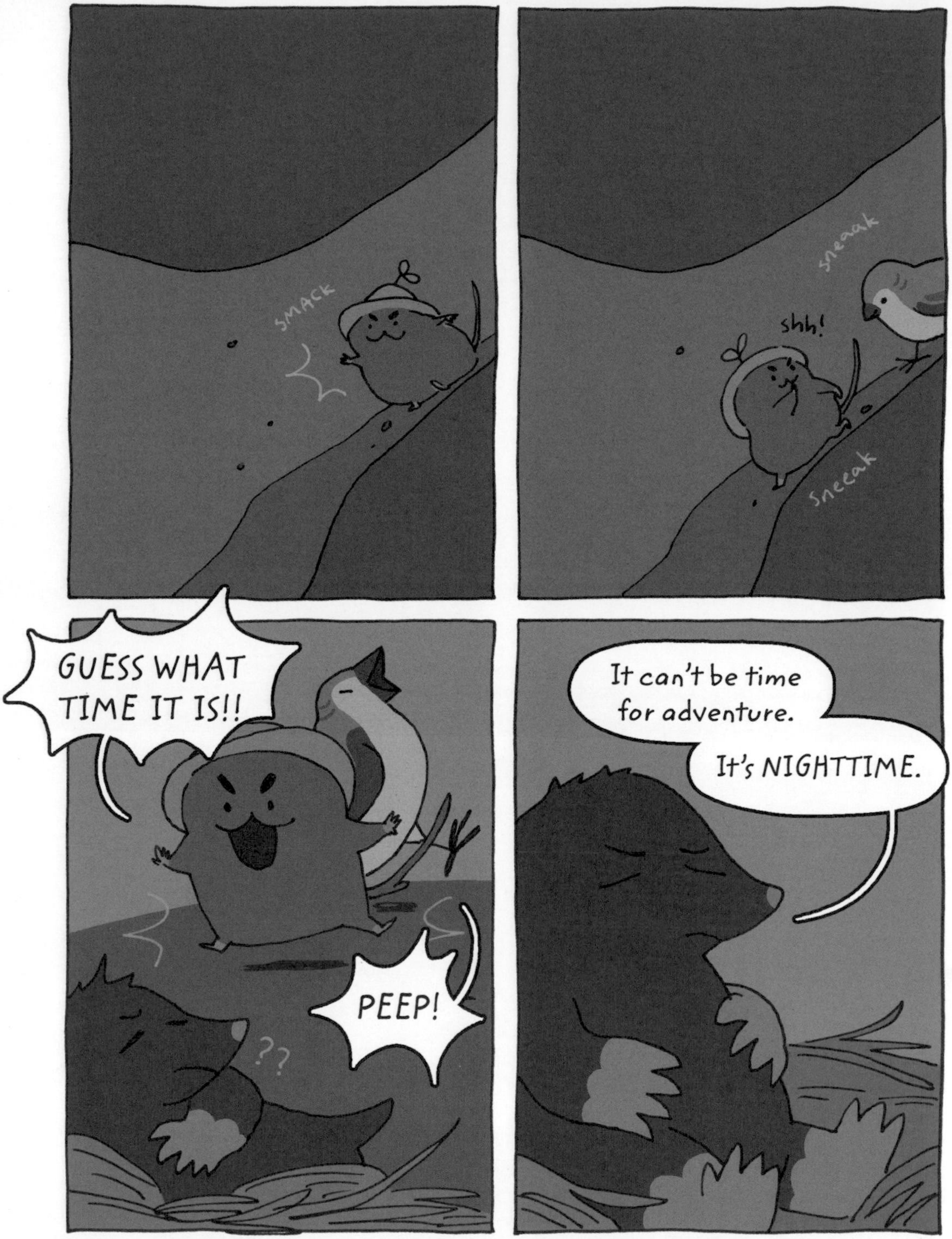
SMACK
sneaak
shh!
sneeak
GUESS WHAT TIME IT IS!!
PEEP!
??
It can't be time for adventure.
It's NIGHTTIME.

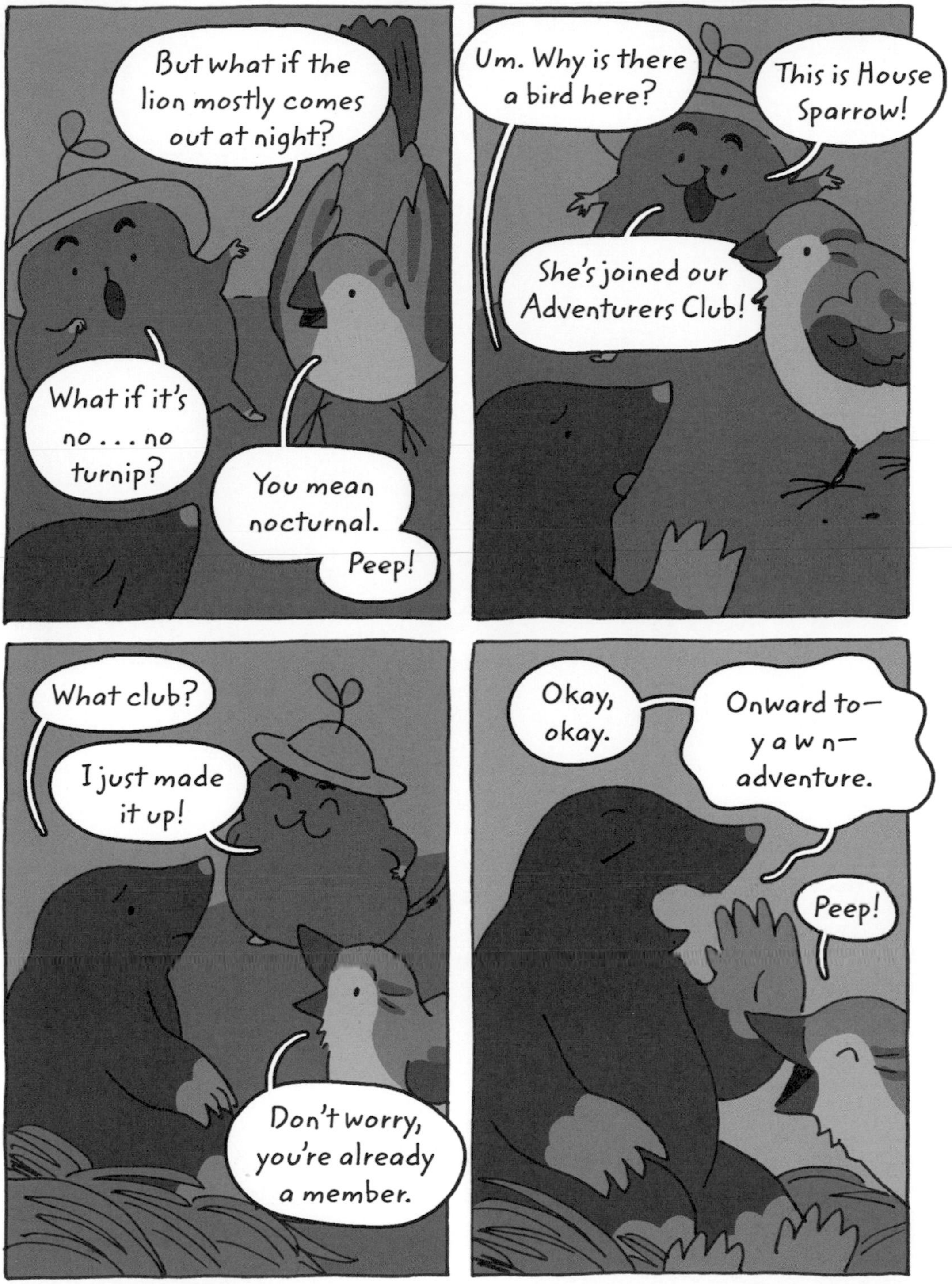

But what if the lion mostly comes out at night?
What if it's no . . . no turnip?
You mean nocturnal.
Peep!
Um. Why is there a bird here?
This is House Sparrow!
She's joined our Adventurers Club!
What club?
I just made it up!
Don't worry, you're already a member.
Okay, okay.
Onward to— y a w n— adventure.
Peep!

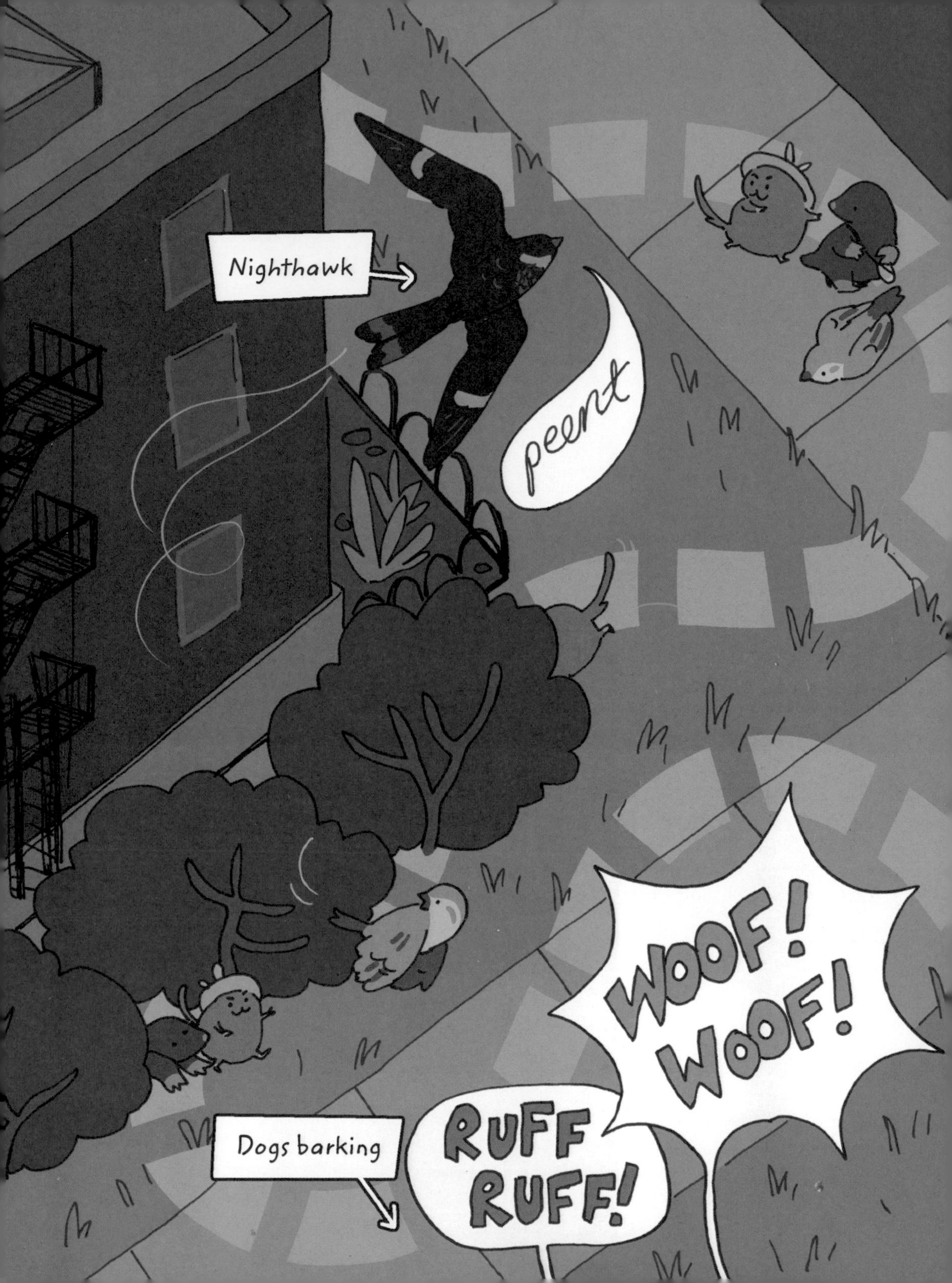
Nighthawk
peent
Dogs barking
WOOF! WOOF!
RUFF RUFF!

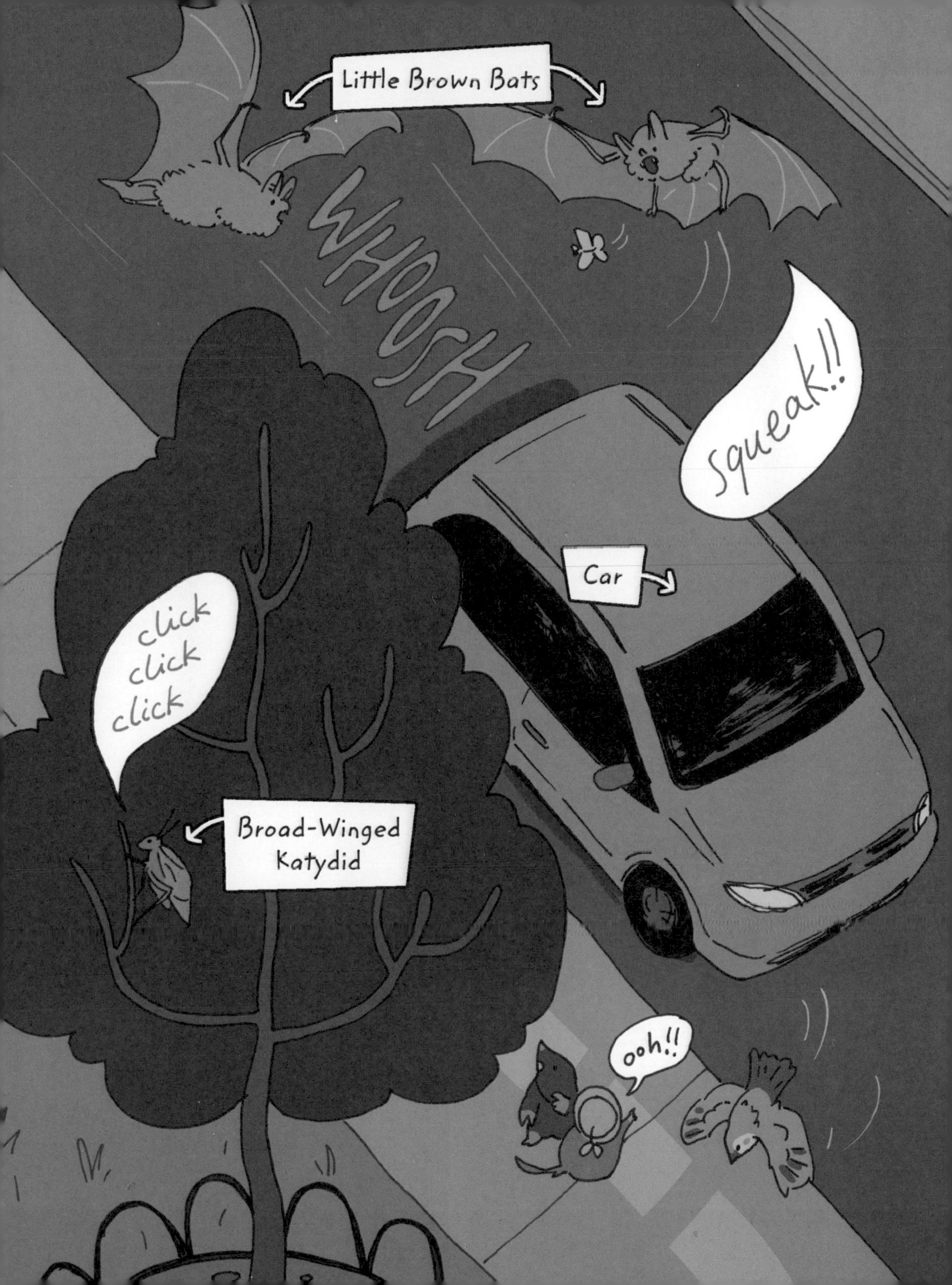
Little Brown Bats
WHOOSH
squeak!!
Car
click click click
Broad-Winged Katydid
ooh!!

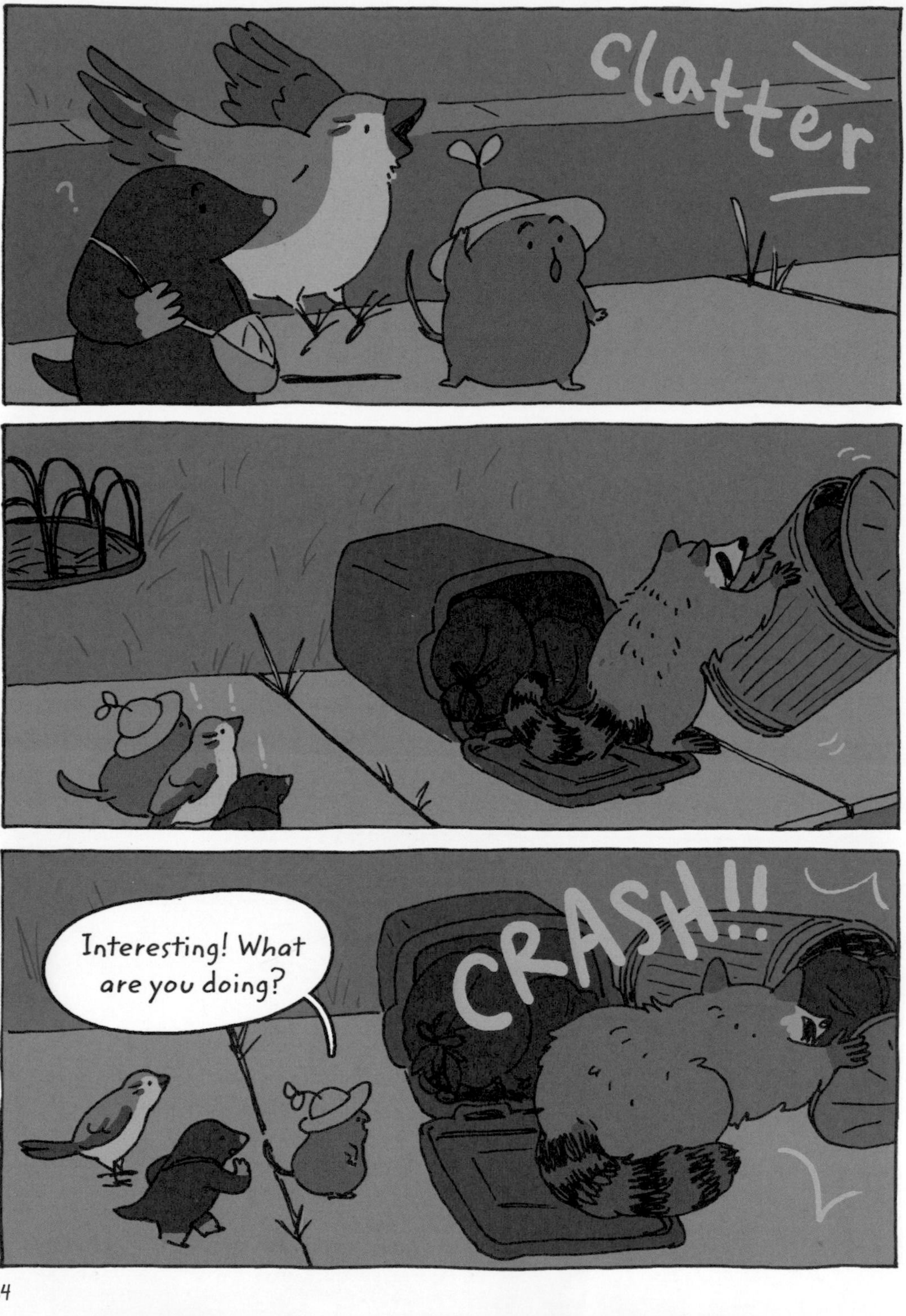
clatter
CRASH!!
Interesting! What are you doing?

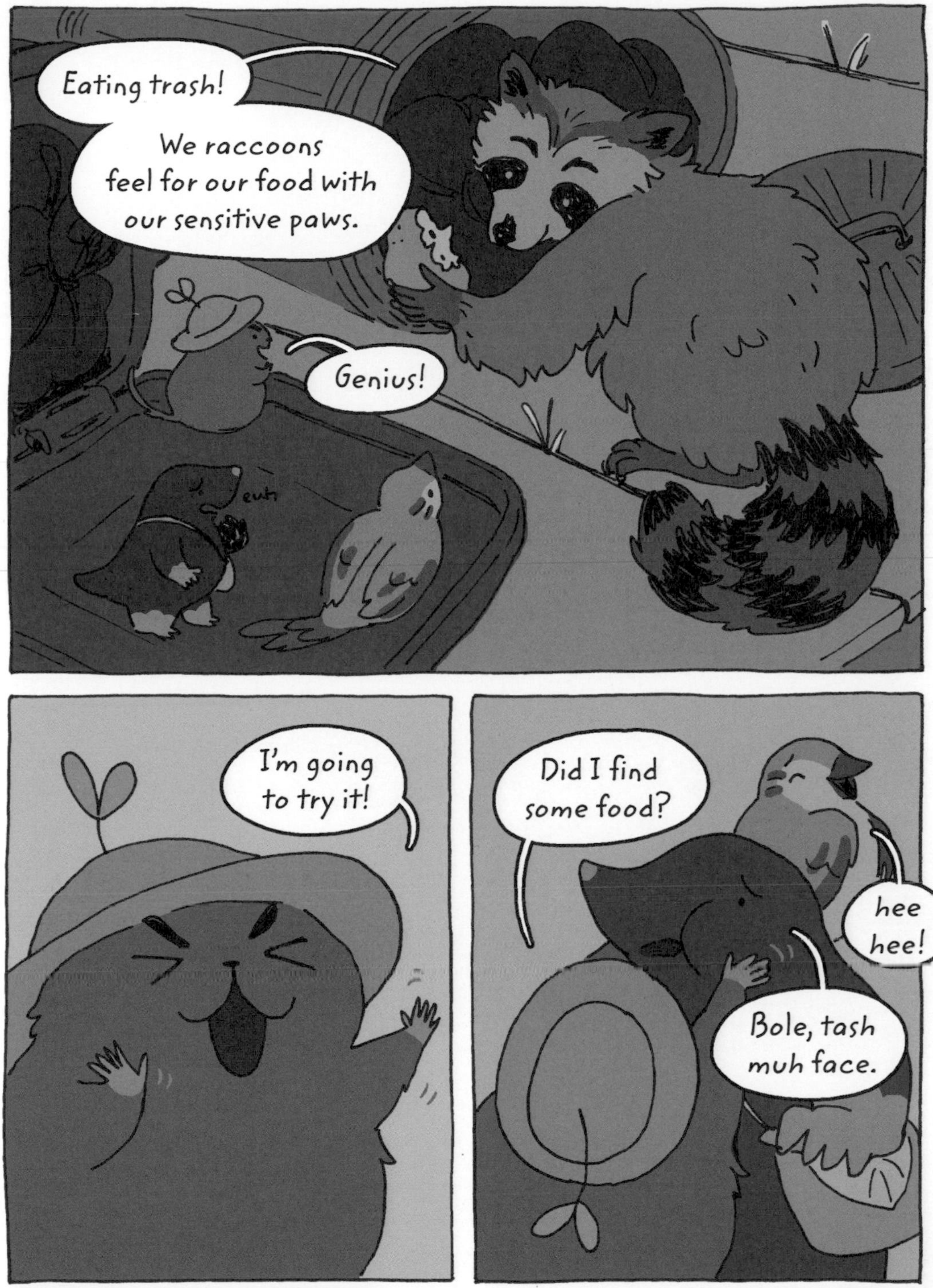
Eating trash!
We raccoons feel for our food with our sensitive paws.
Genius!
I'm going to try it!
Did I find some food?
hee hee!
Bole, tash muh face.

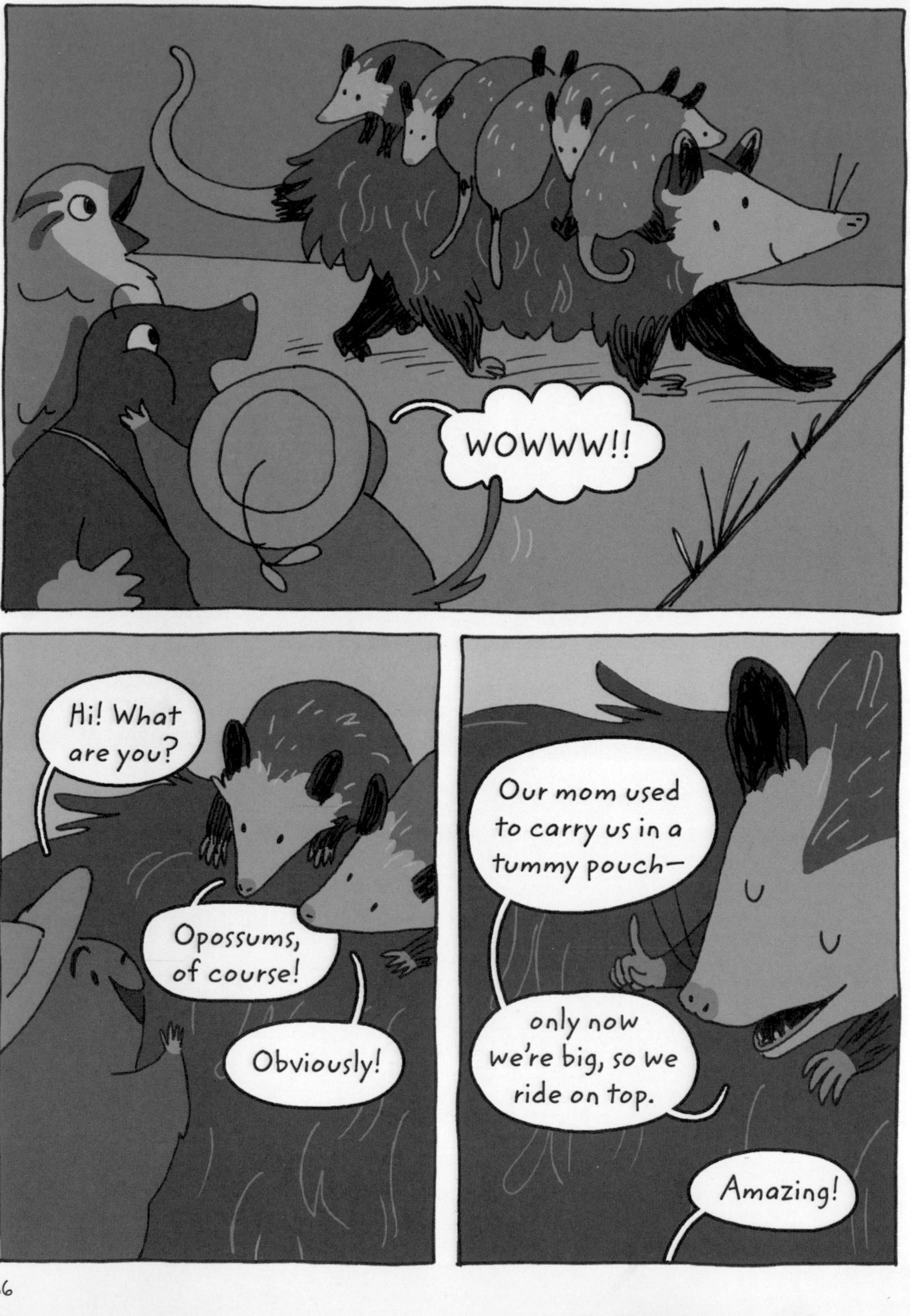
WOWWW!!
Hi! What are you?
Opossums, of course!
Obviously!
Our mom used to carry us in a tummy pouch—
only now we're big, so we ride on top.
Amazing!

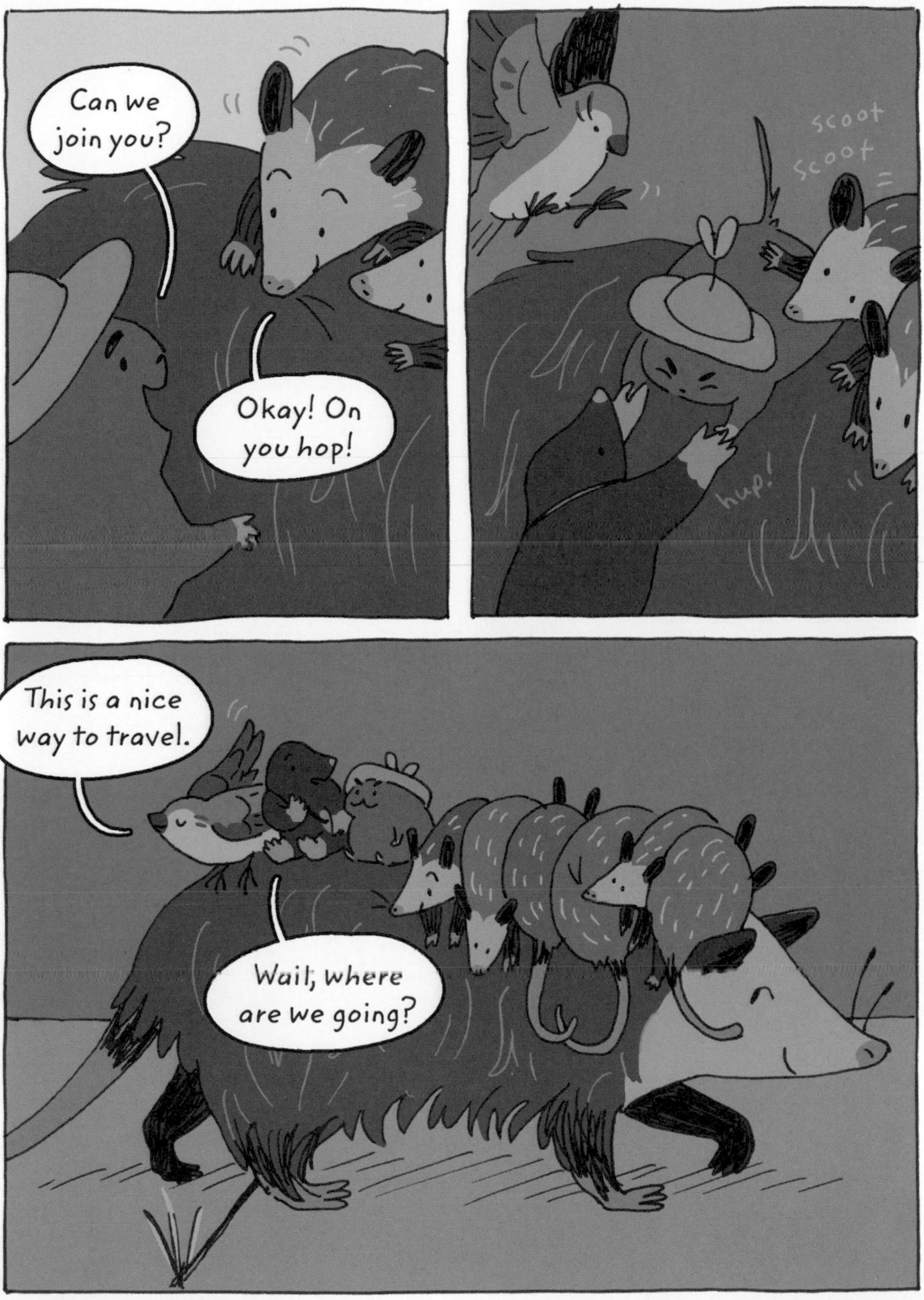
Can we join you?
Okay! On you hop!
scoot scoot
hup!
This is a nice way to travel.
Wait, where are we going?

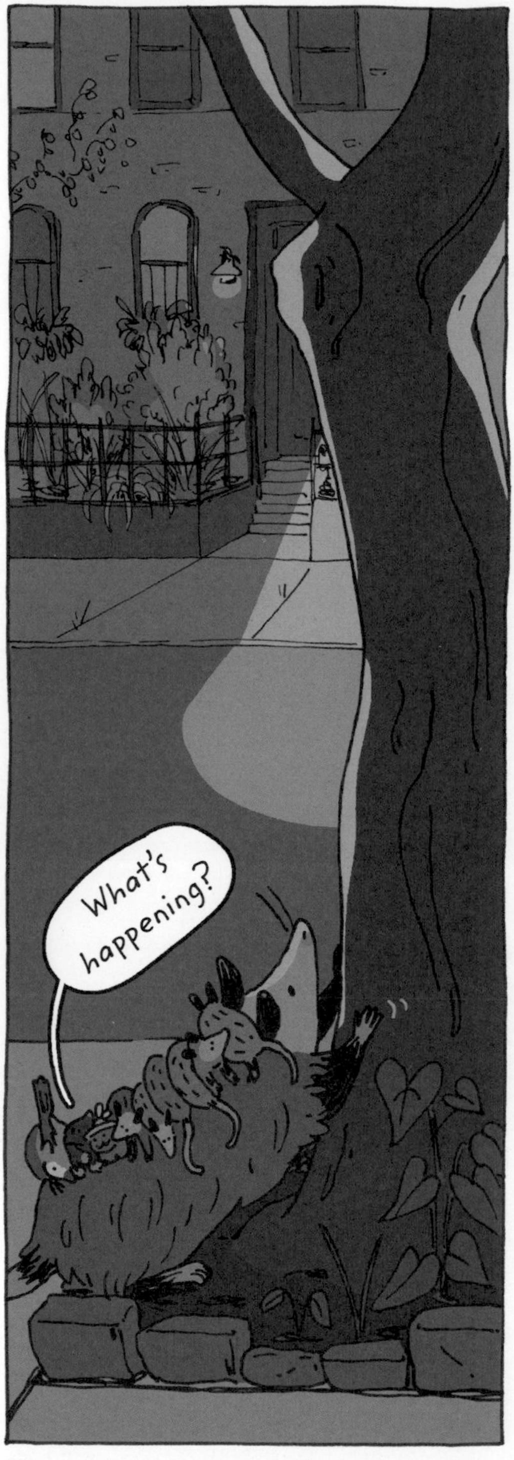
What's happening?

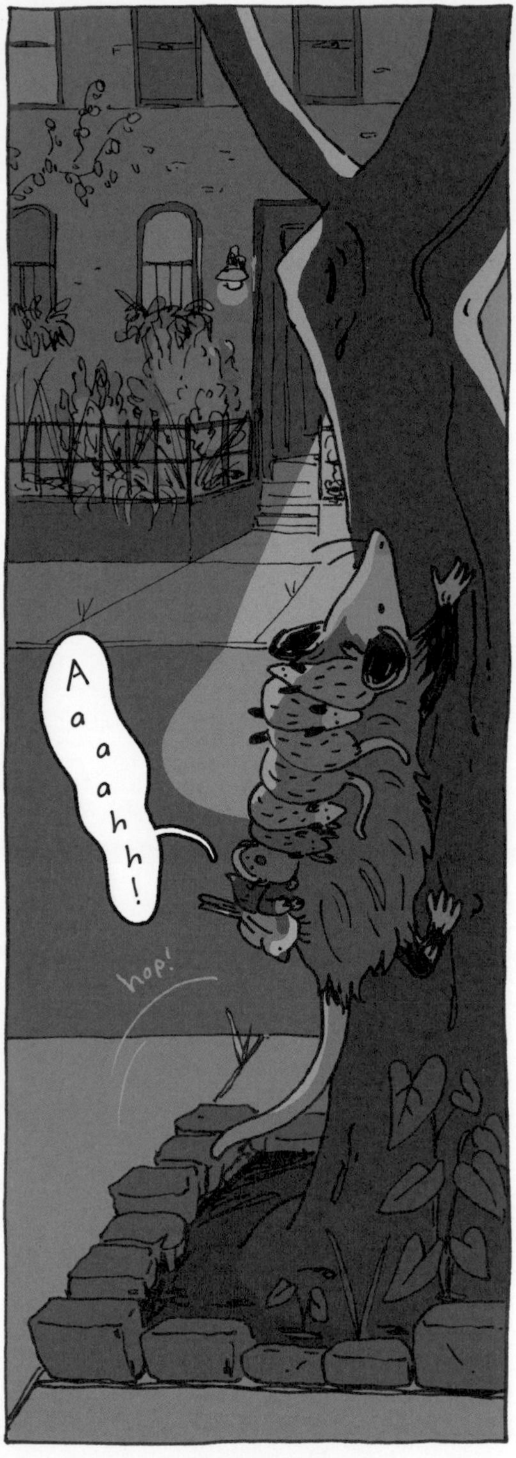
Aaaahh!
hop!

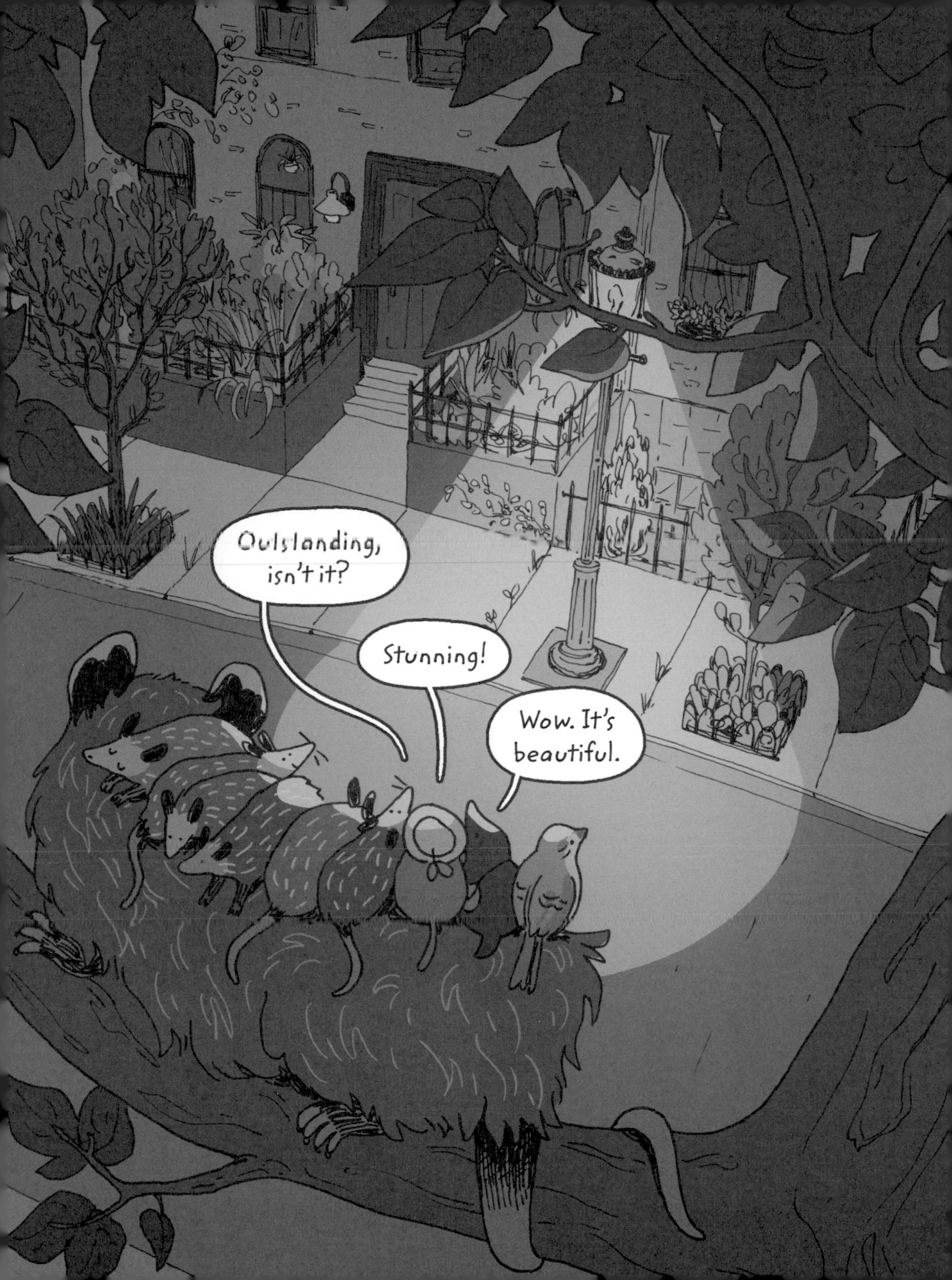
Outstanding, isn't it?
Stunning!
Wow. It's beautiful.

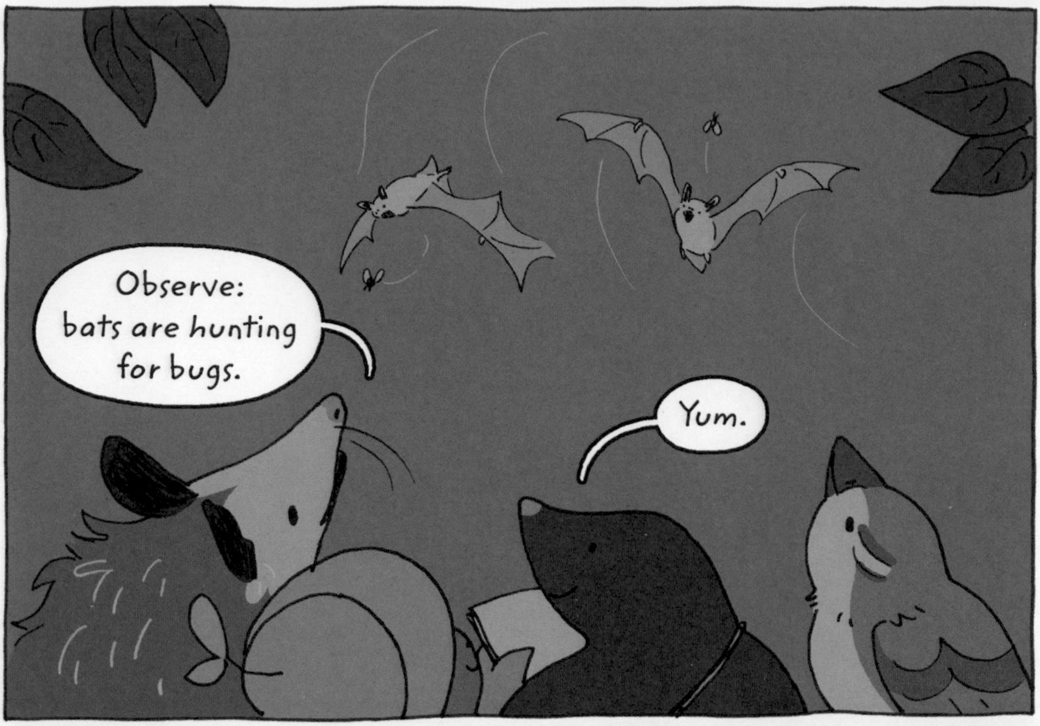
Observe: bats are hunting for bugs.
Yum.

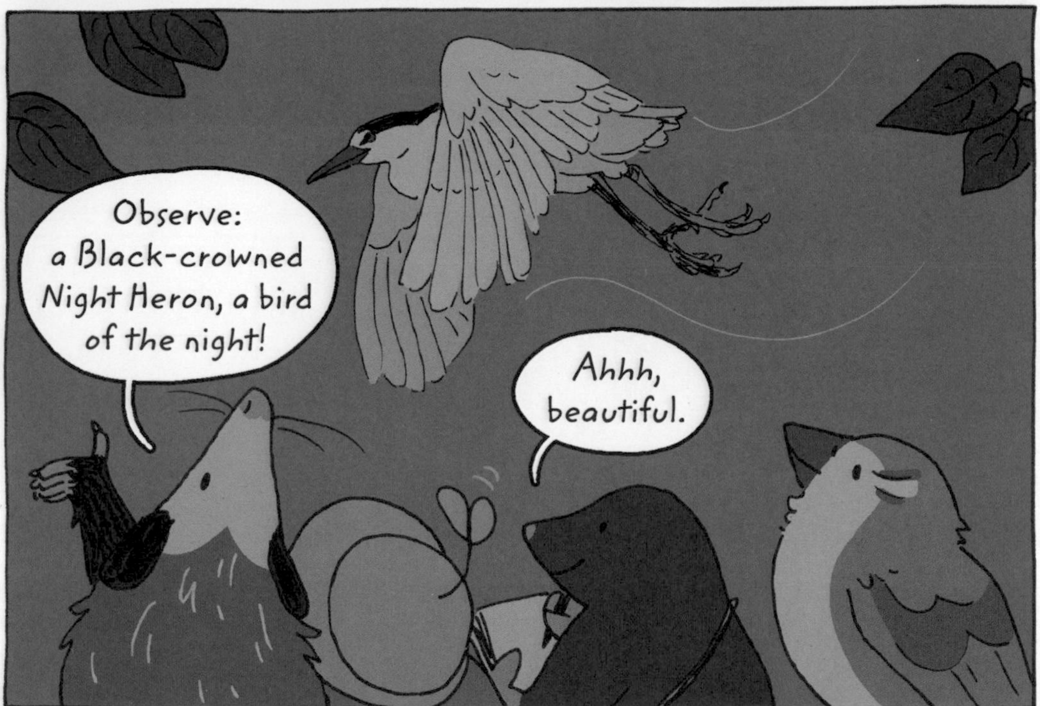
Observe: a Black-crowned Night Heron, a bird of the night!
Ahhh, beautiful.

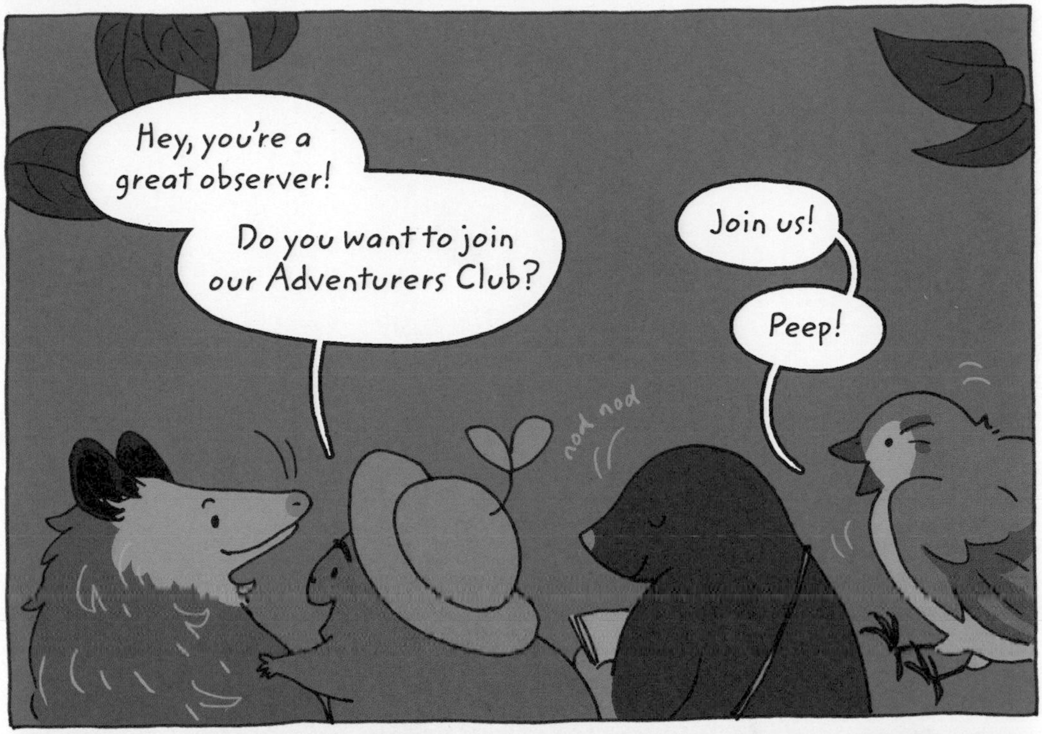
Hey, you're a great observer!
Do you want to join our Adventurers Club?
Join us!
Peep!
nod nod

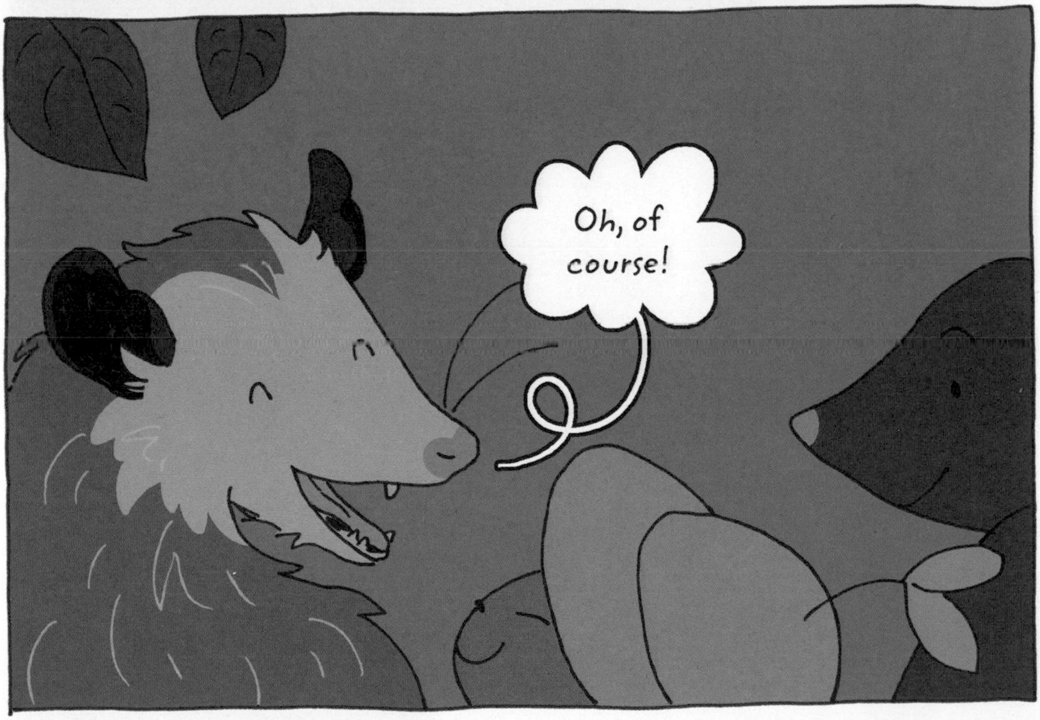
Oh, of course!

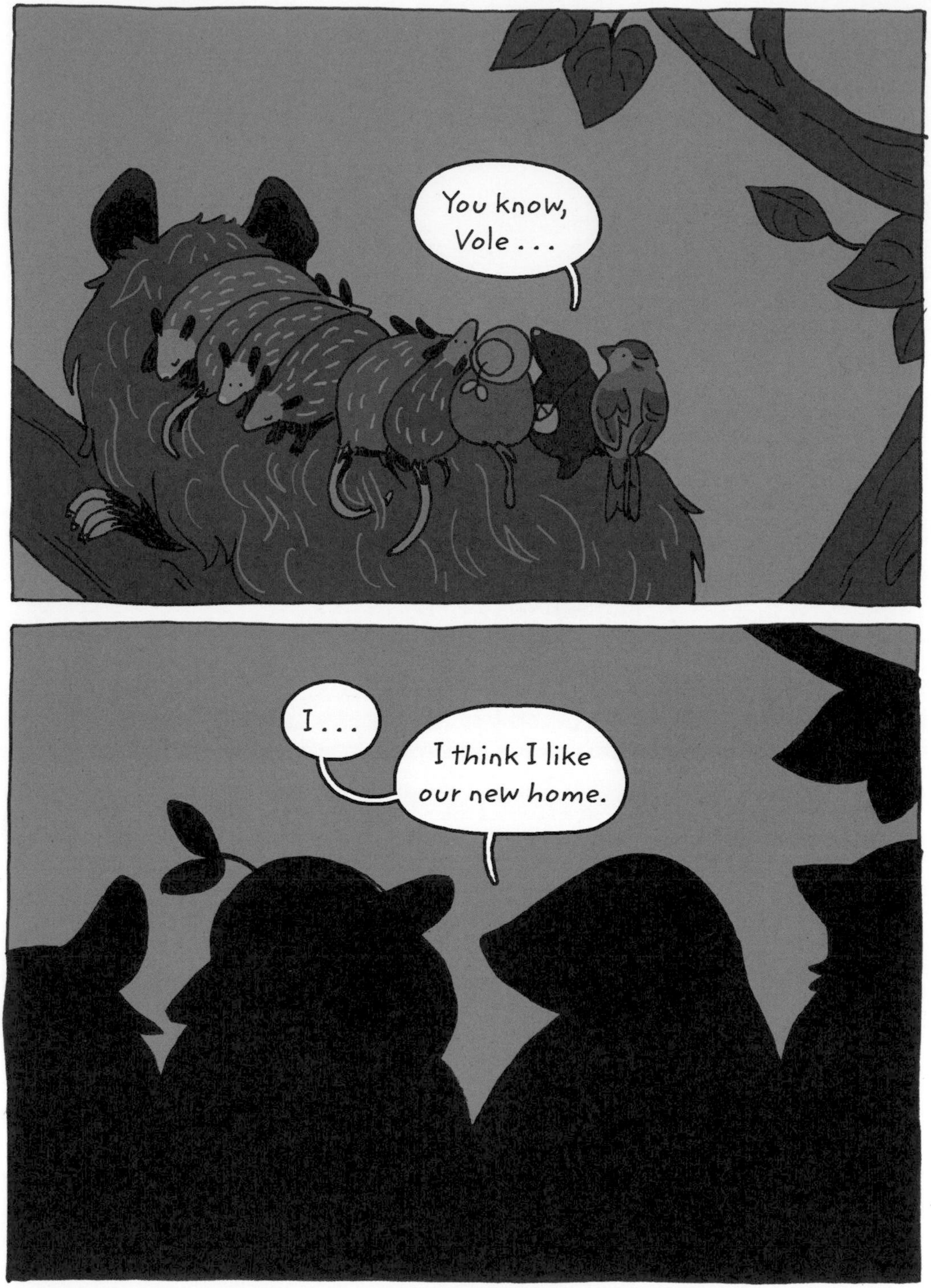
You know, Vole . . .
I . . .
I think I like our new home.

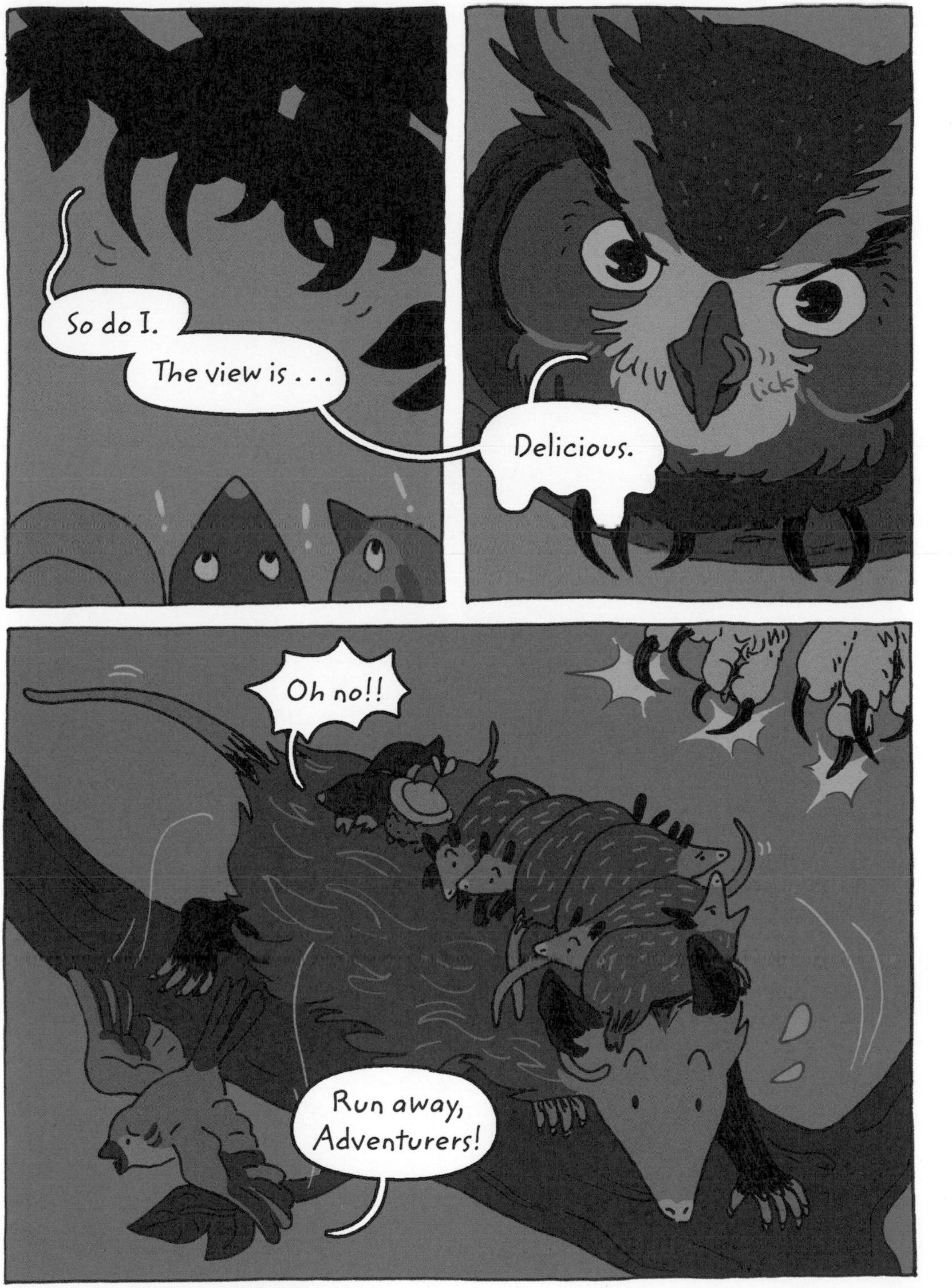
So do I.
The view is . . .
lick
Delicious.
Oh no!!
Run away, Adventurers!

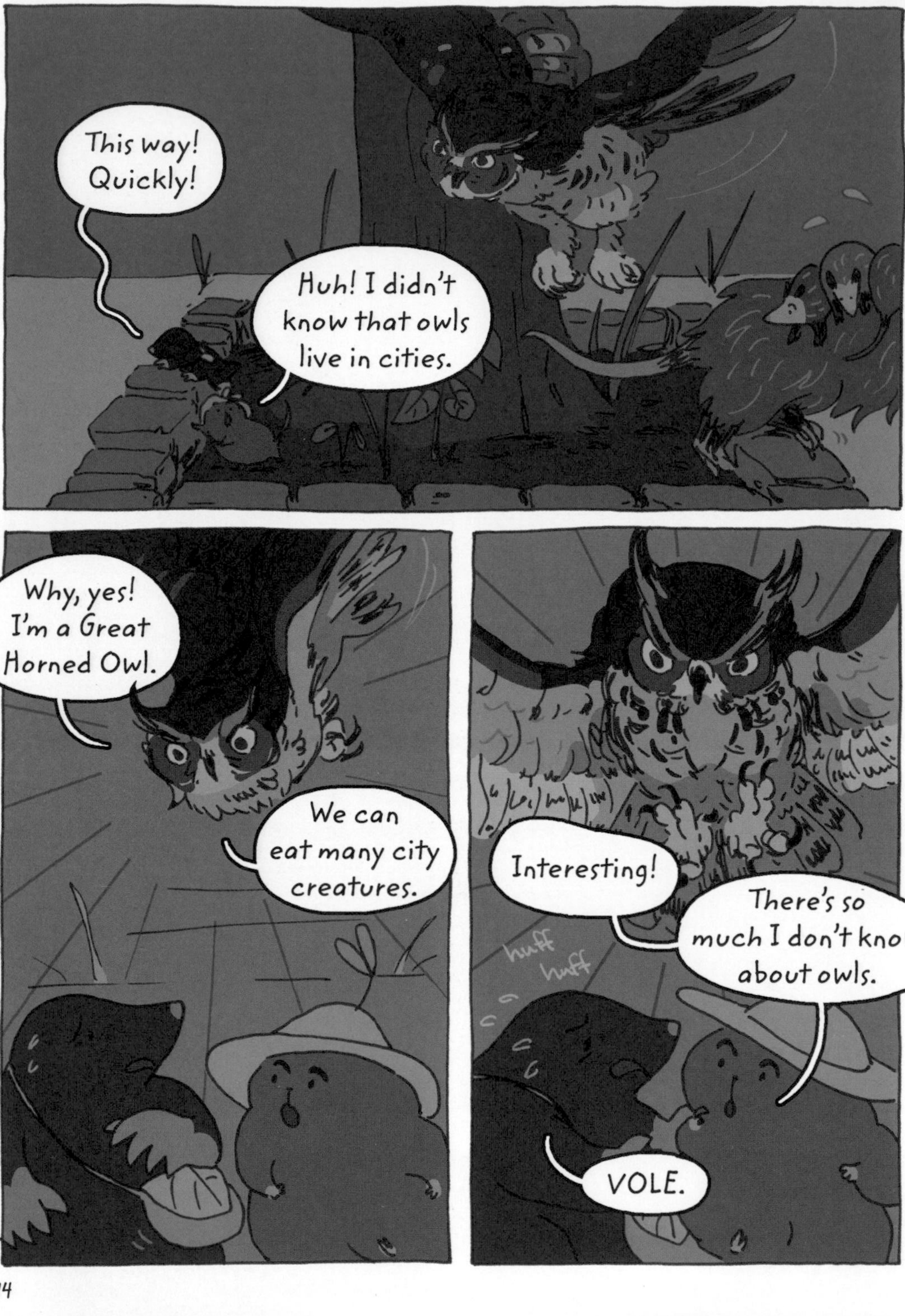
This way! Quickly!
Huh! I didn't know that owls live in cities.
Why, yes! I'm a Great Horned Owl.
We can eat many city creatures.
Interesting!
There's so much I don't know about owls.
huff huff
VOLE.

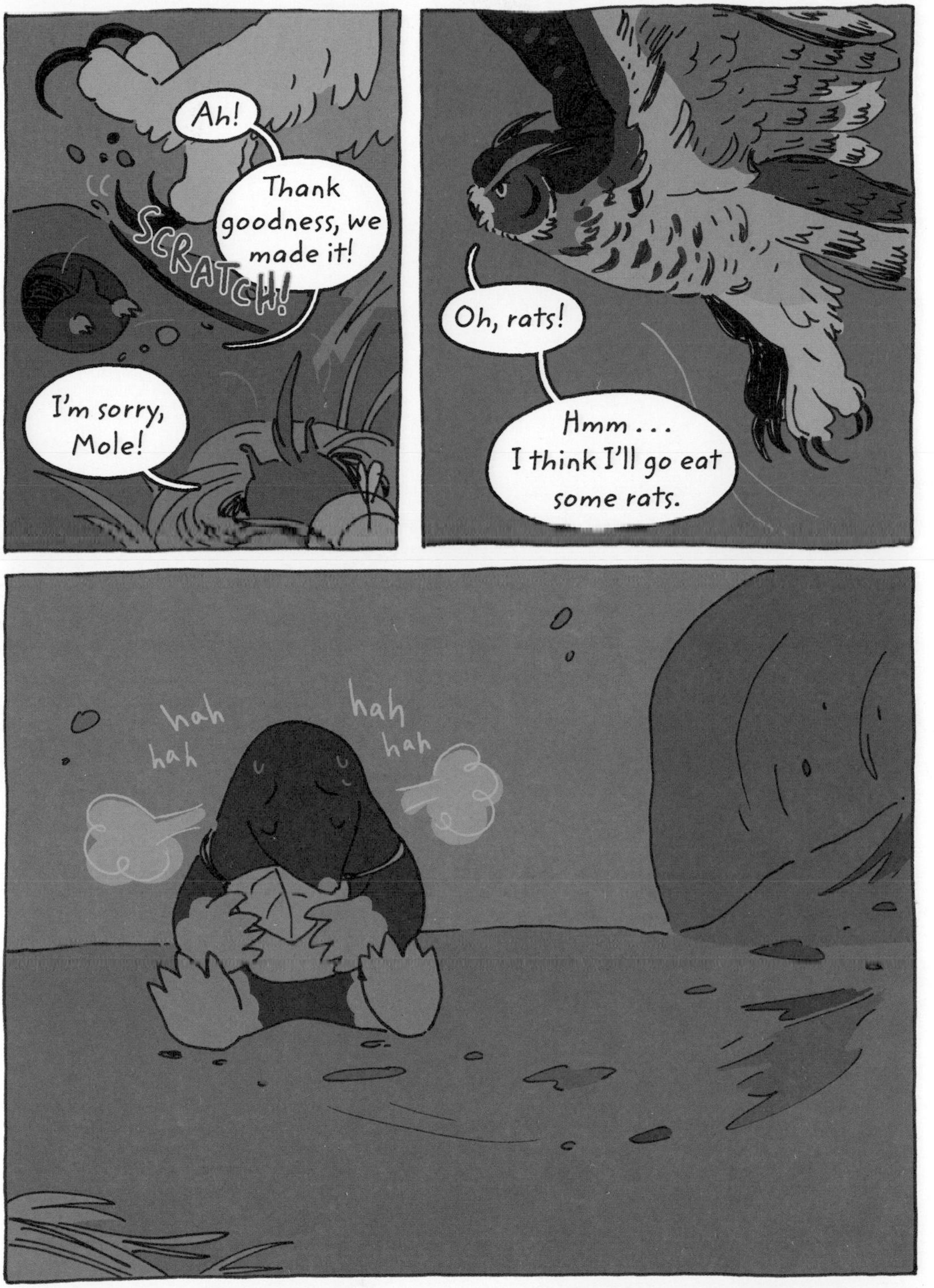
Ah!
Thank goodness, we made it!
SCRATCH!
I'm sorry, Mole!
Oh, rats!
Hmm . . . I think I'll go eat some rats.
hah hah
hah hah

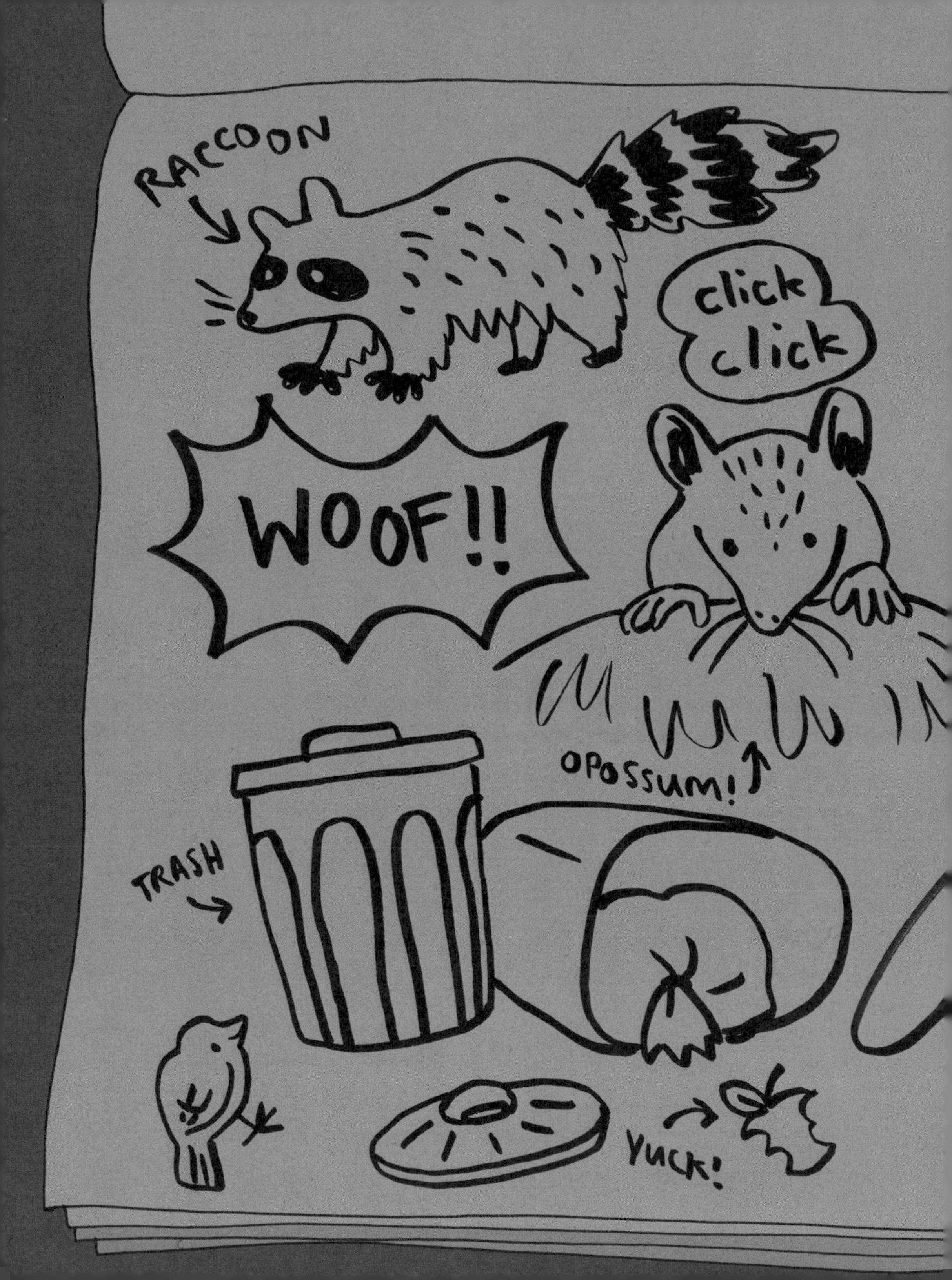
RACCOON
click click
WOOF!!
OPOSSUM!
TRASH
YUCK!

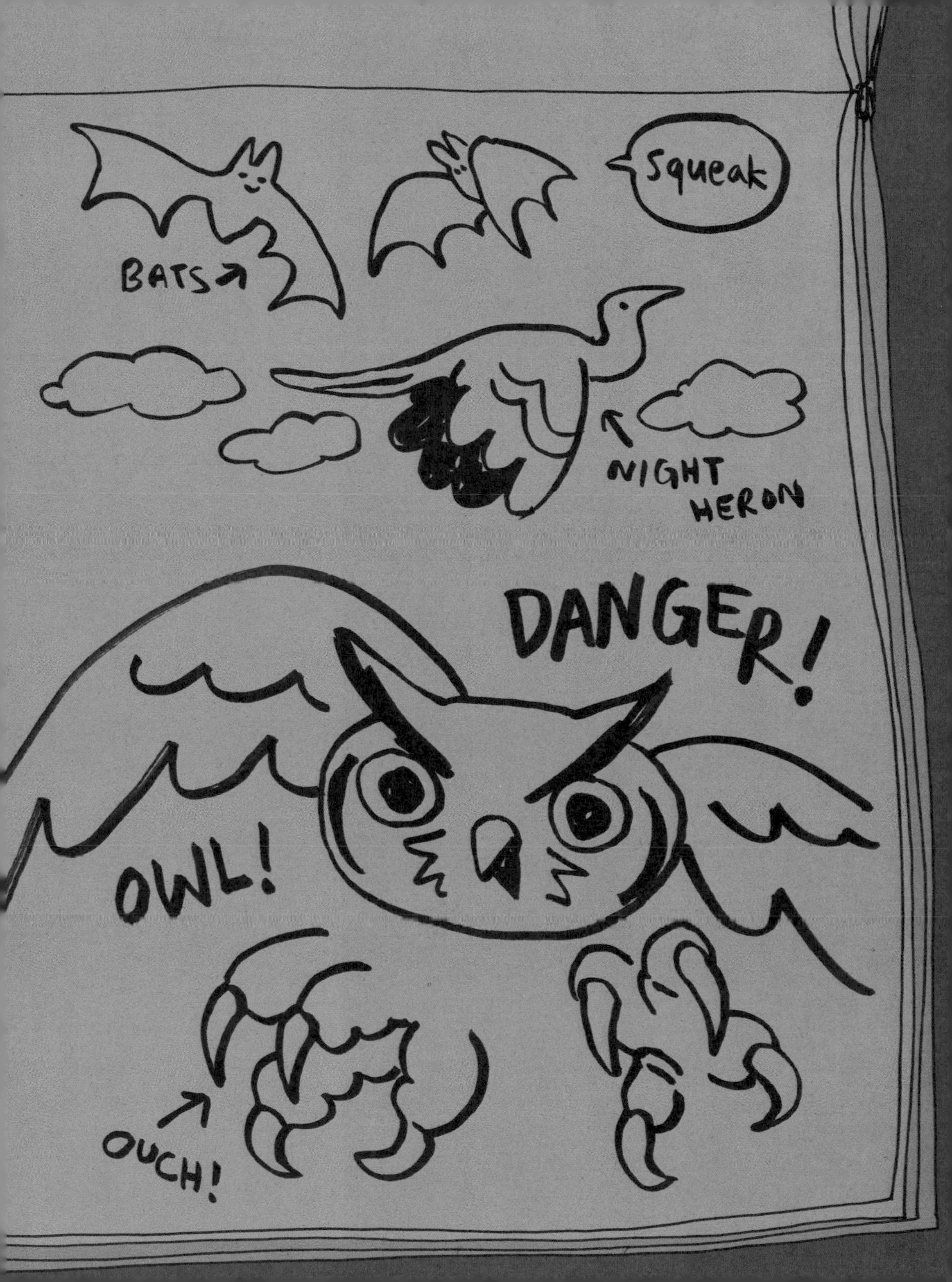
Squeak
BATS
NIGHT HERON
DANGER!
OWL!
OUCH!

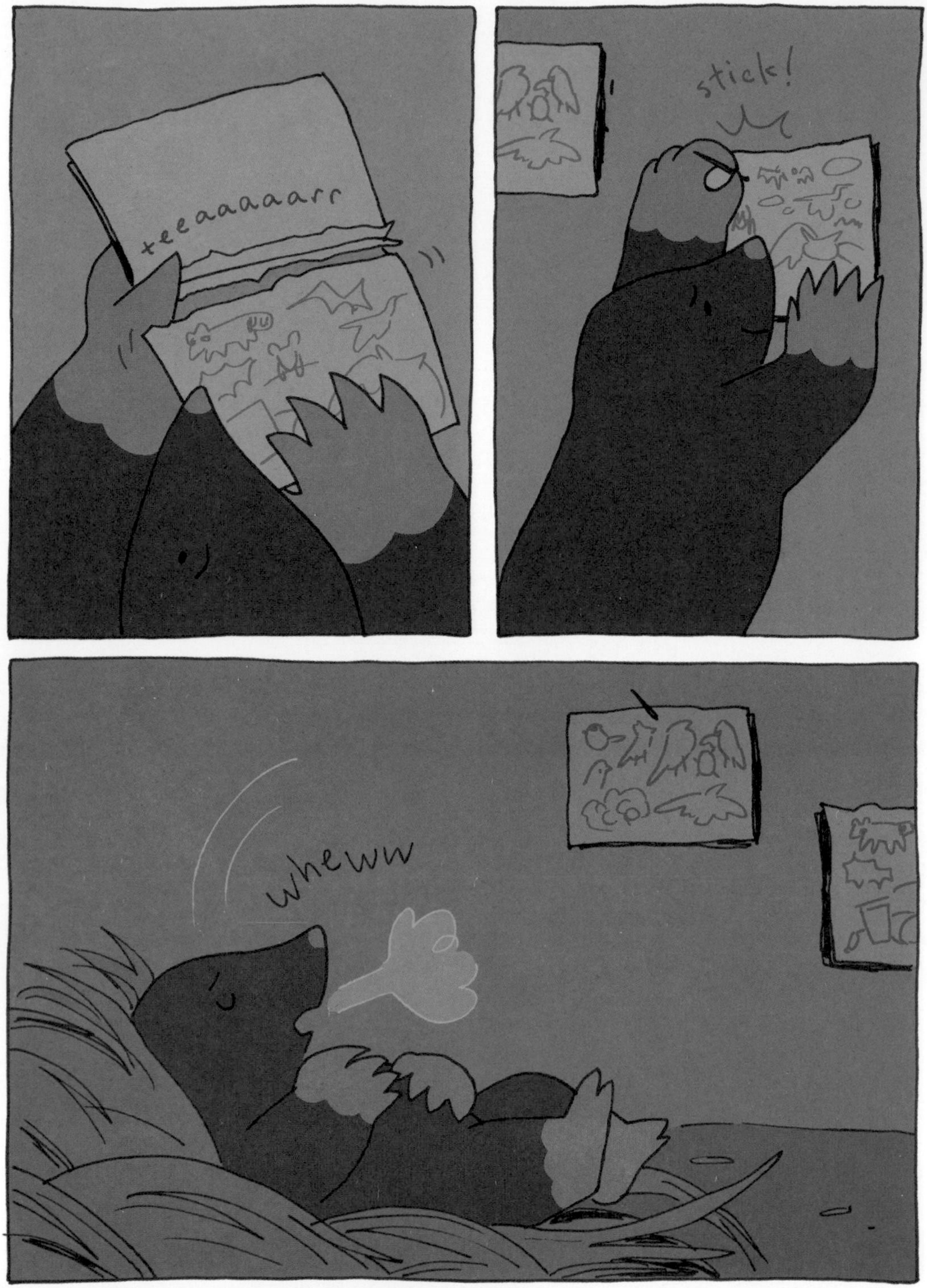
teeaaaaaarr
stick!
whewww

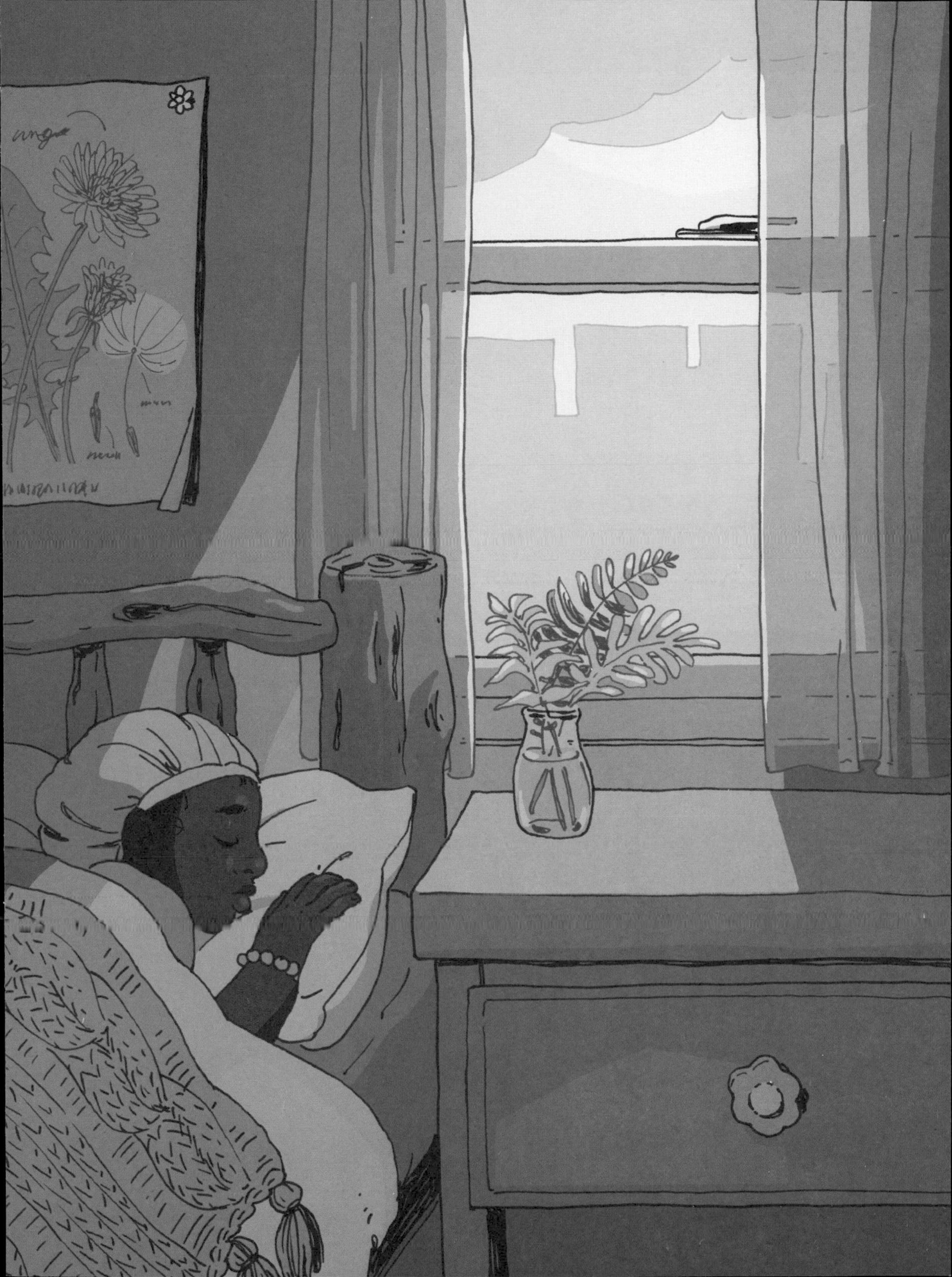

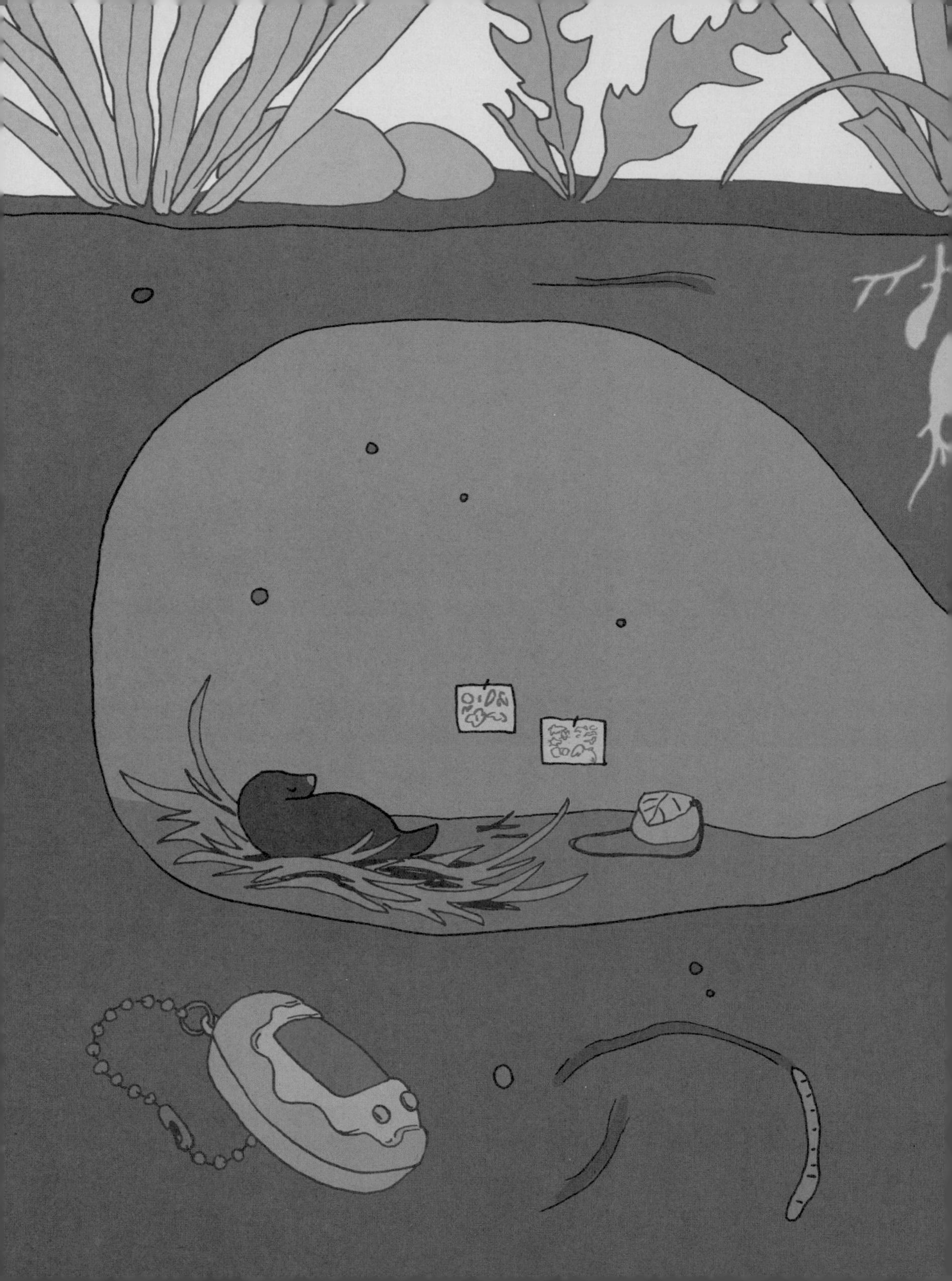

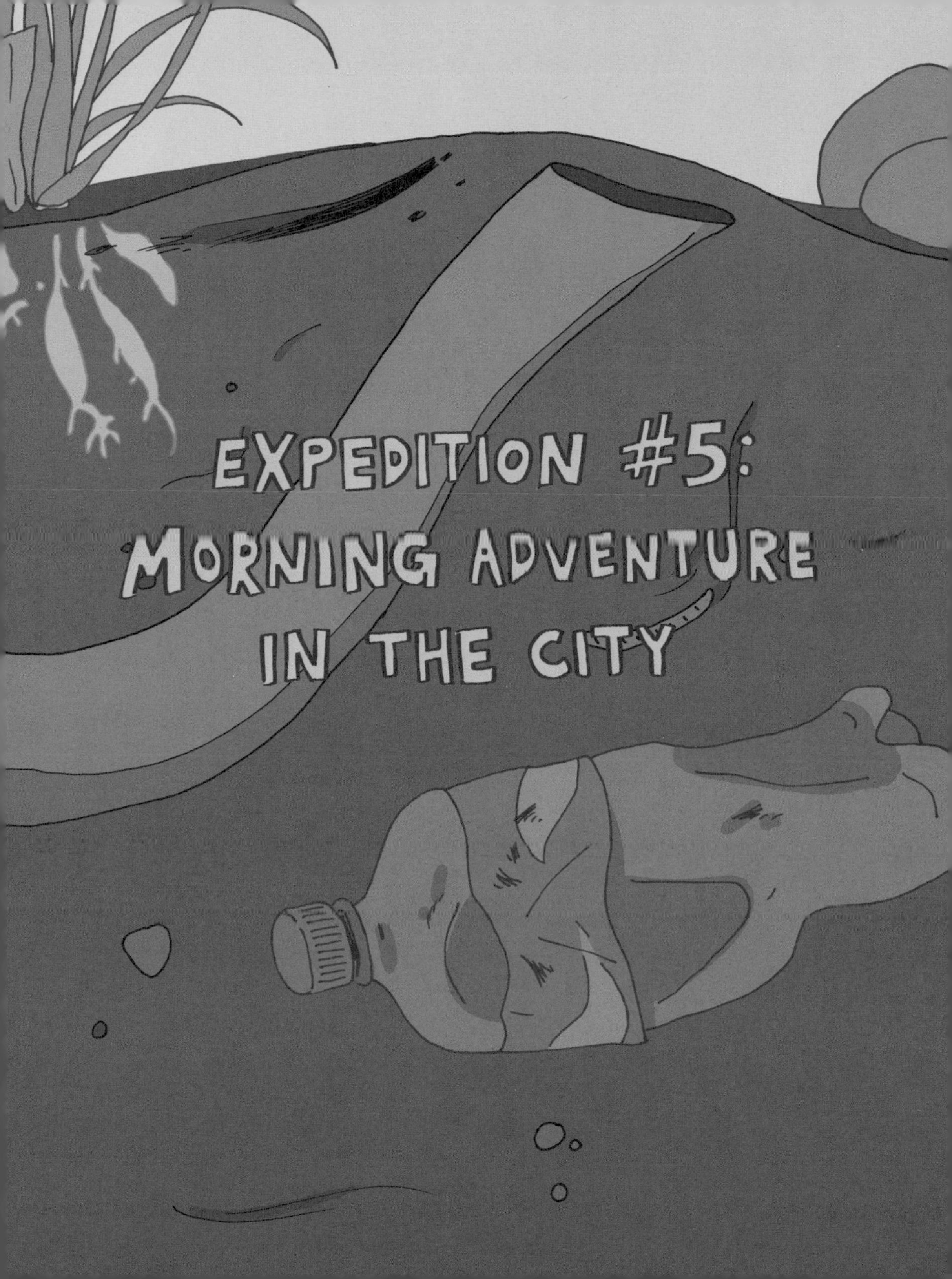
EXPEDITION #5:
MORNING ADVENTURE
IN THE CITY

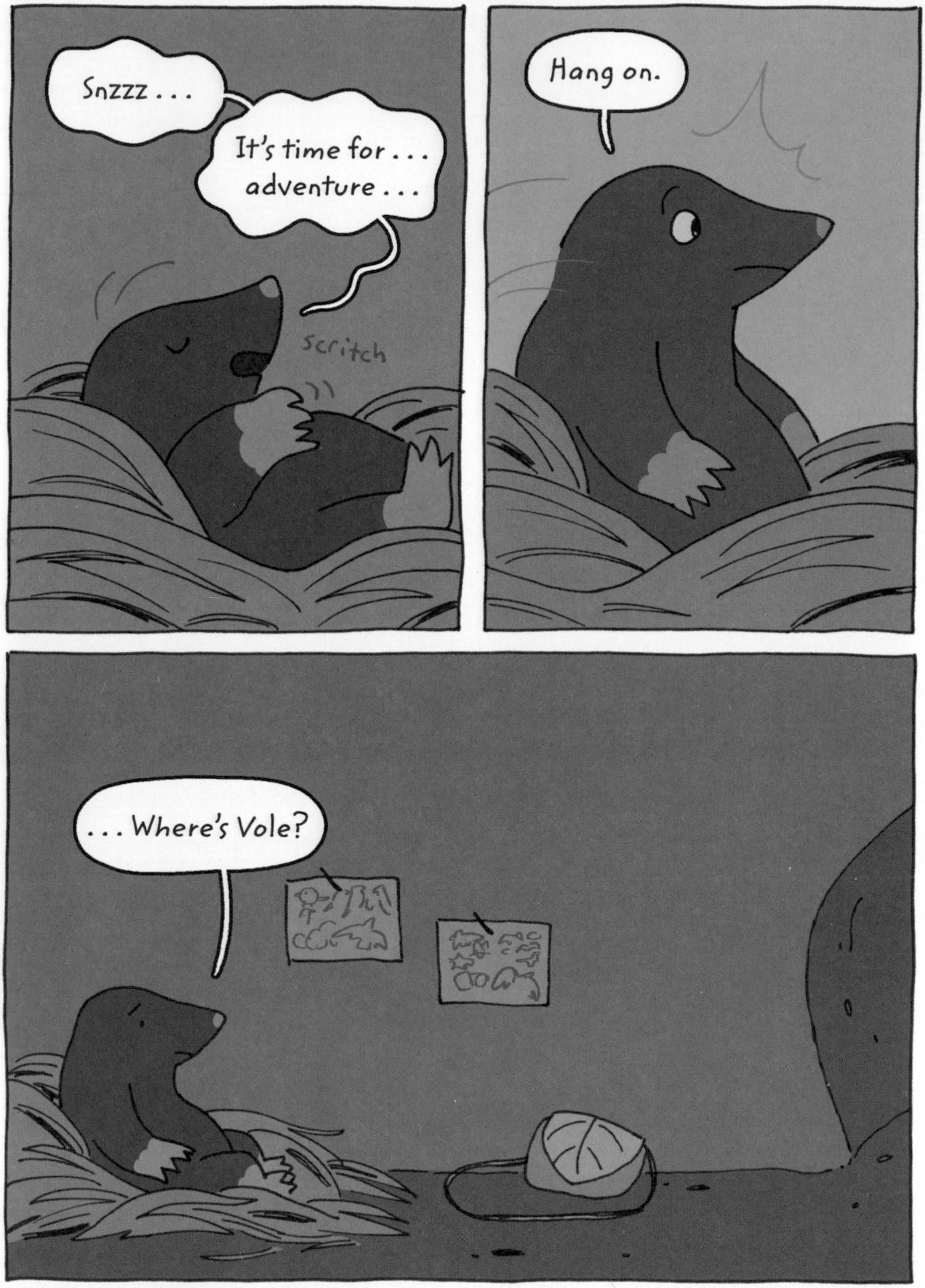
Snzzz . . .
It's time for . . . adventure . . .
scritch
Hang on.
. . . Where's Vole?

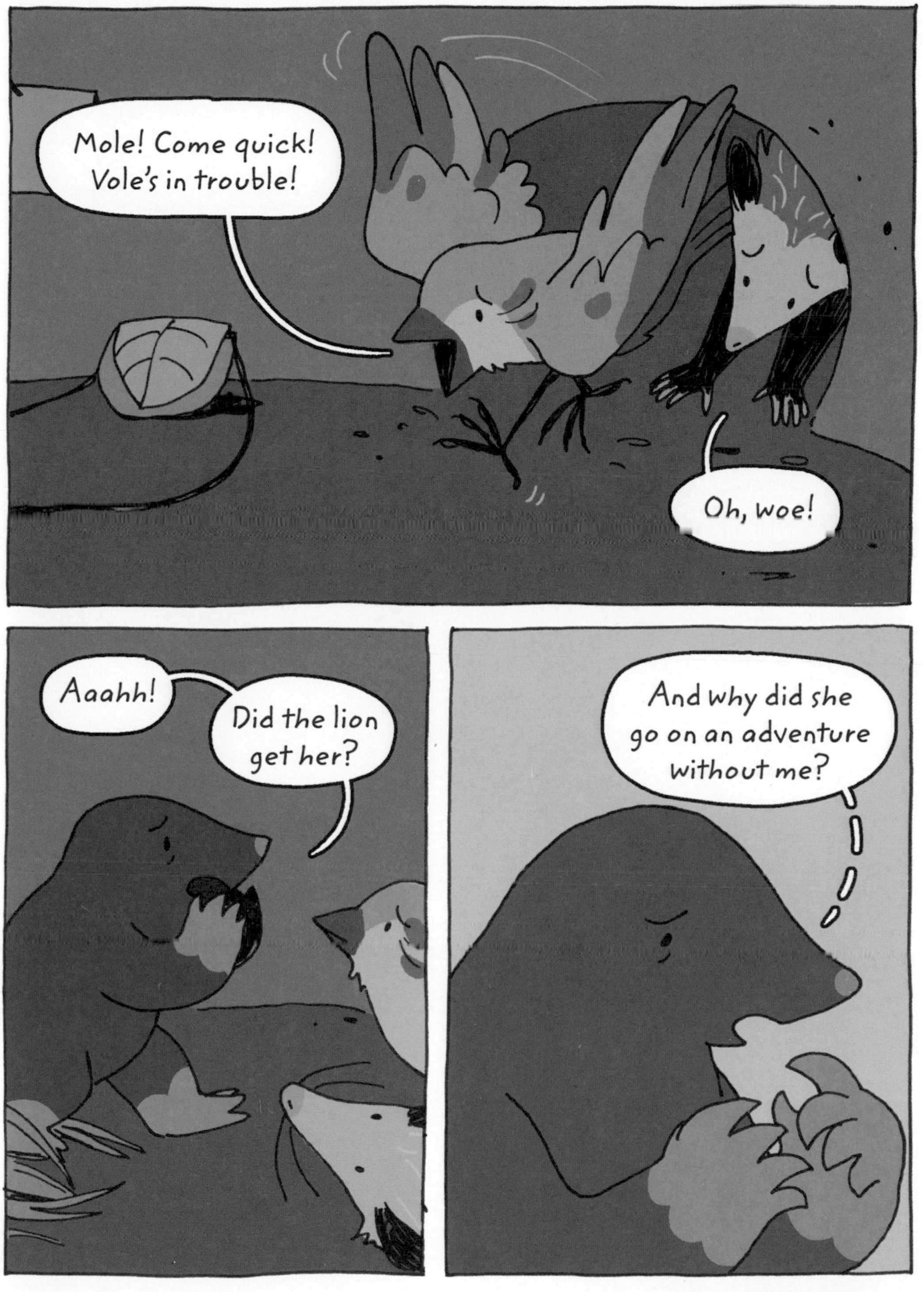
Mole! Come quick! Vole's in trouble!
Oh, woe!
Aaahh!
Did the lion get her?
And why did she go on an adventure without me?

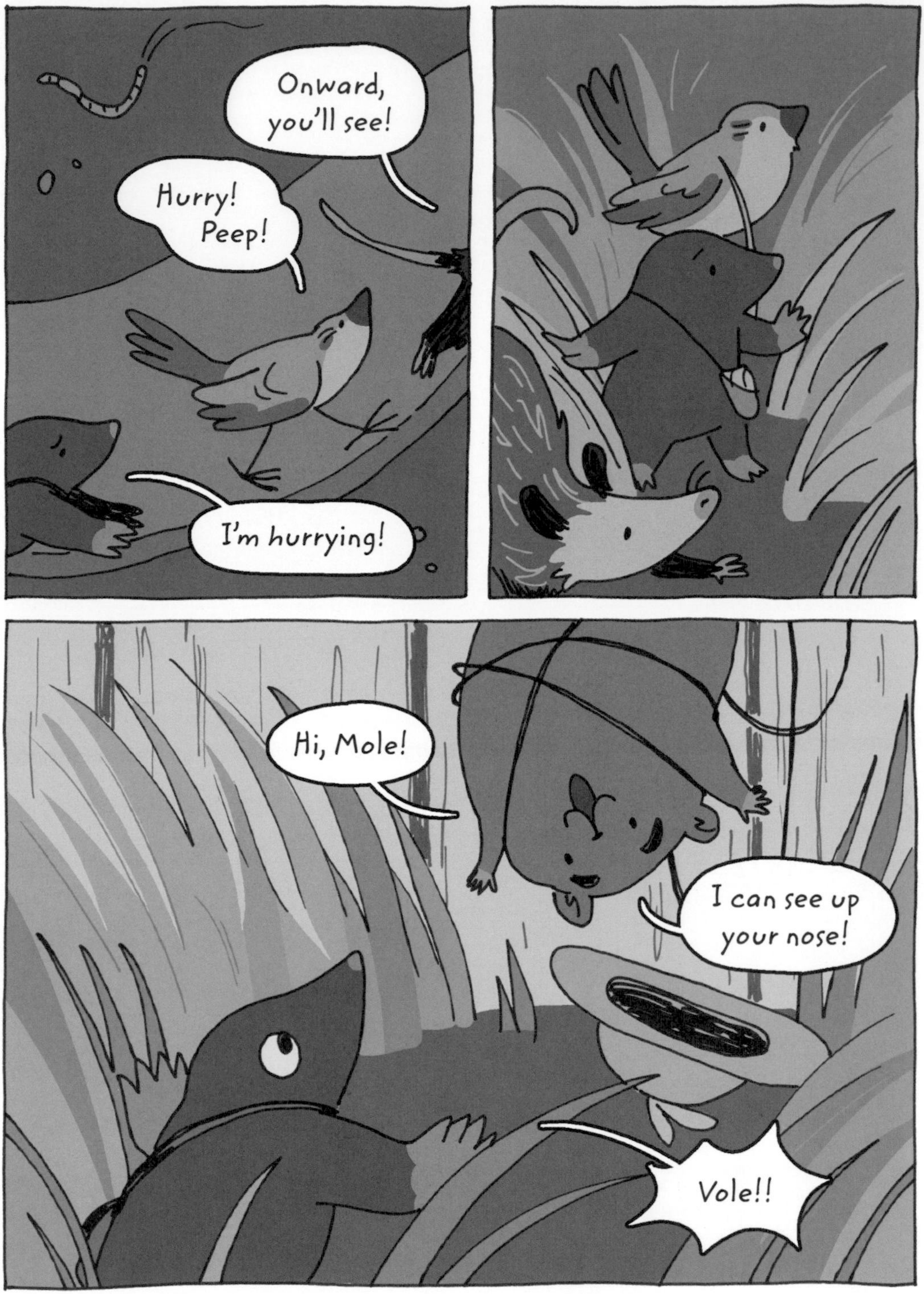
Onward, you'll see!
Hurry! Peep!
I'm hurrying!
Hi, Mole!
I can see up your nose!
Vole!!

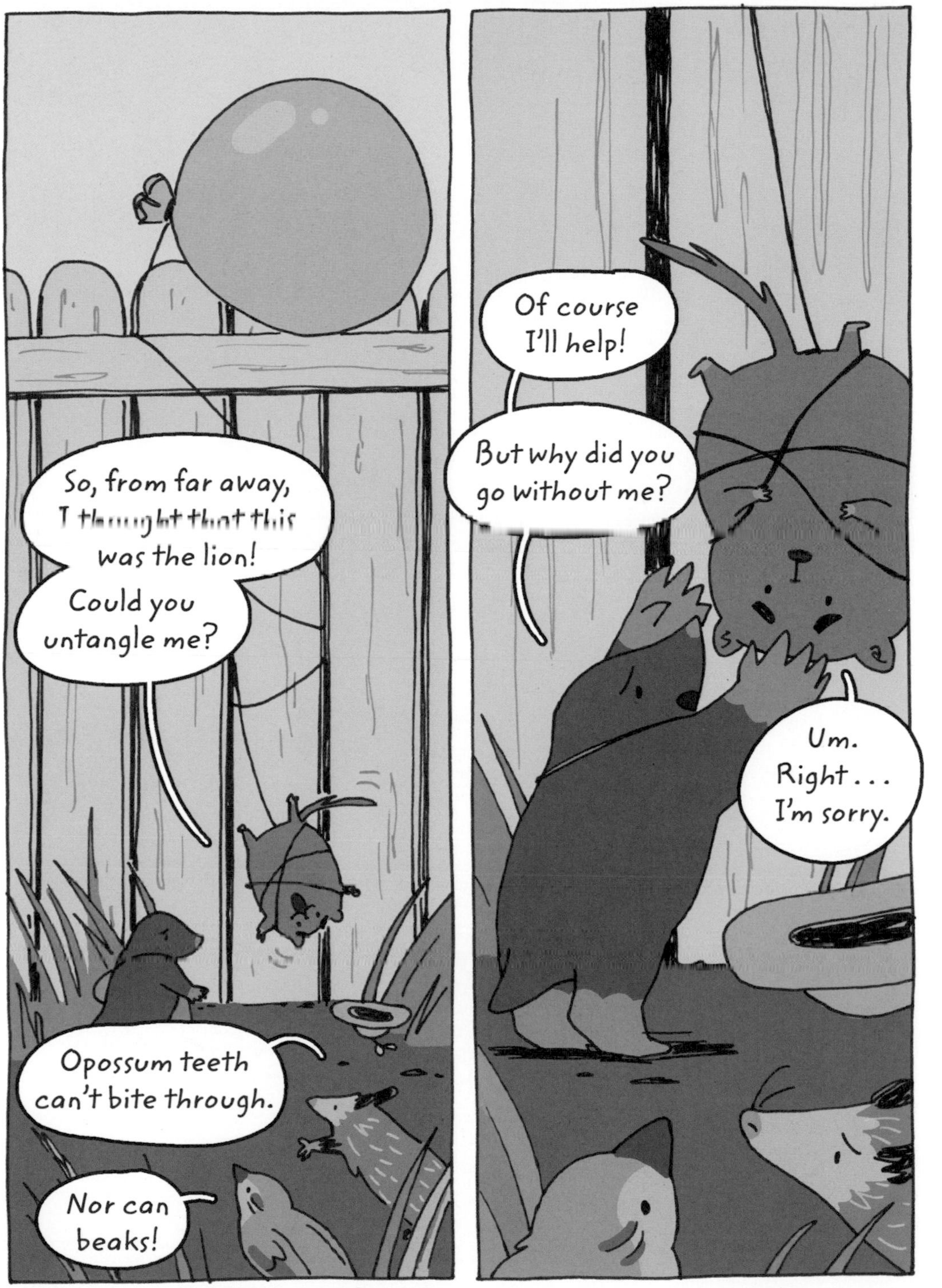
So, from far away, I thought that this was the lion!
Could you untangle me?
Opossum teeth can't bite through.
Nor can beaks!
Of course I'll help!
But why did you go without me?
Um. Right . . . I'm sorry.

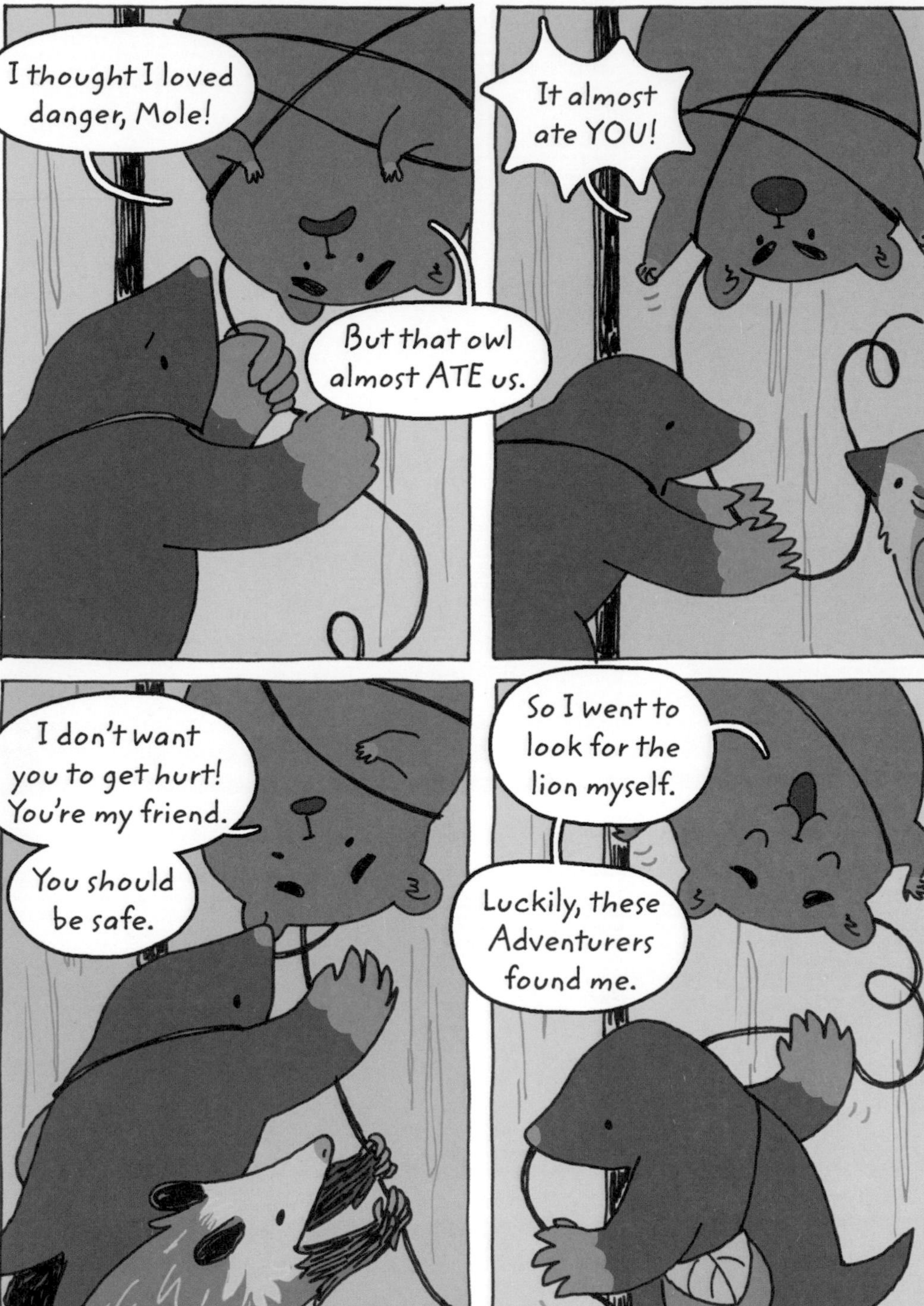
I thought I loved danger, Mole!
But that owl almost ATE us.
It almost ate YOU!
I don't want you to get hurt! You're my friend.
You should be safe.
So I went to look for the lion myself.
Luckily, these Adventurers found me.

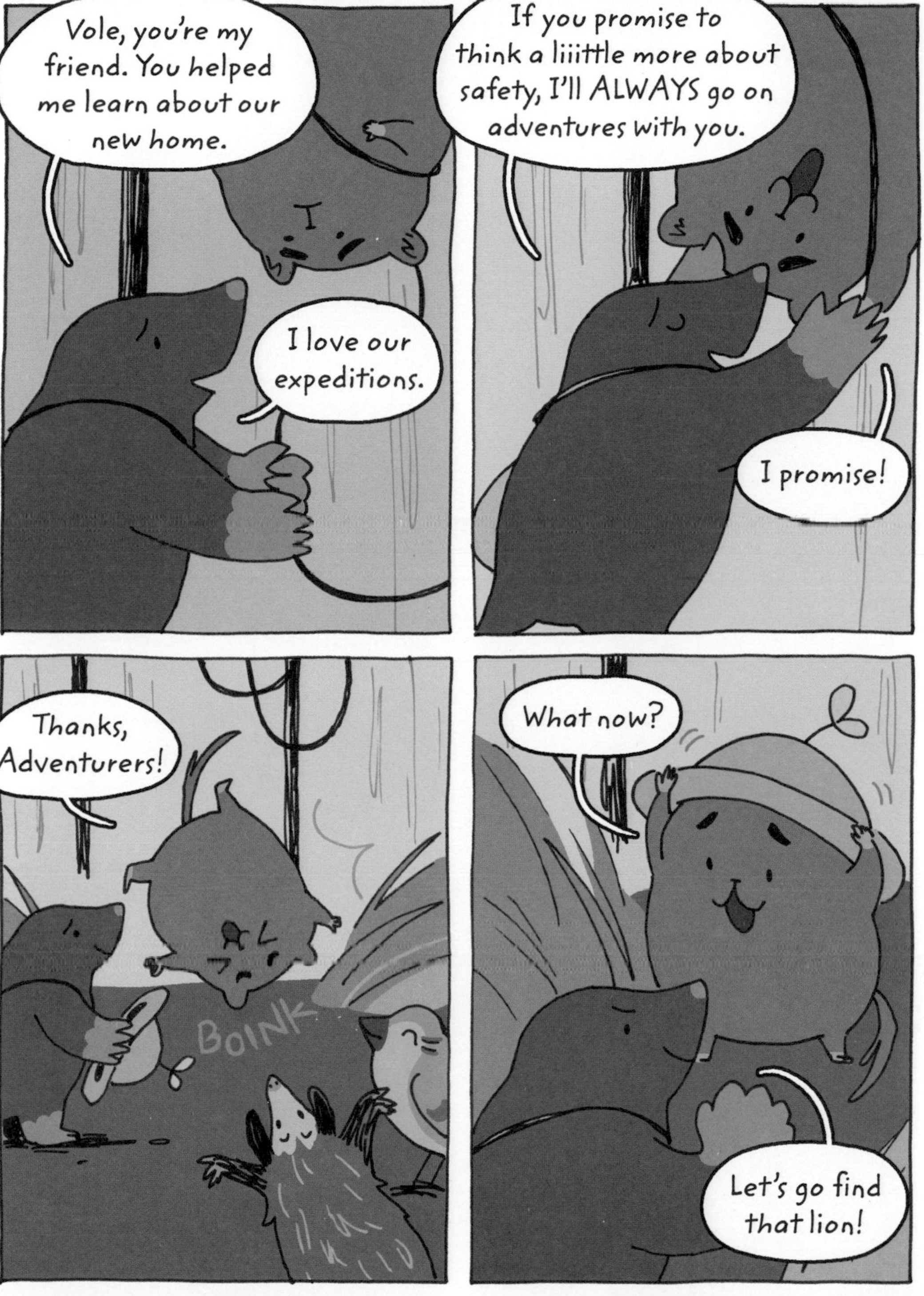
Vole, you're my friend. You helped me learn about our new home.
I love our expeditions.
If you promise to think a liiittle more about safety, I'll ALWAYS go on adventures with you.
I promise!
Thanks, Adventurers!
BOINK
What now?
Let's go find that lion!

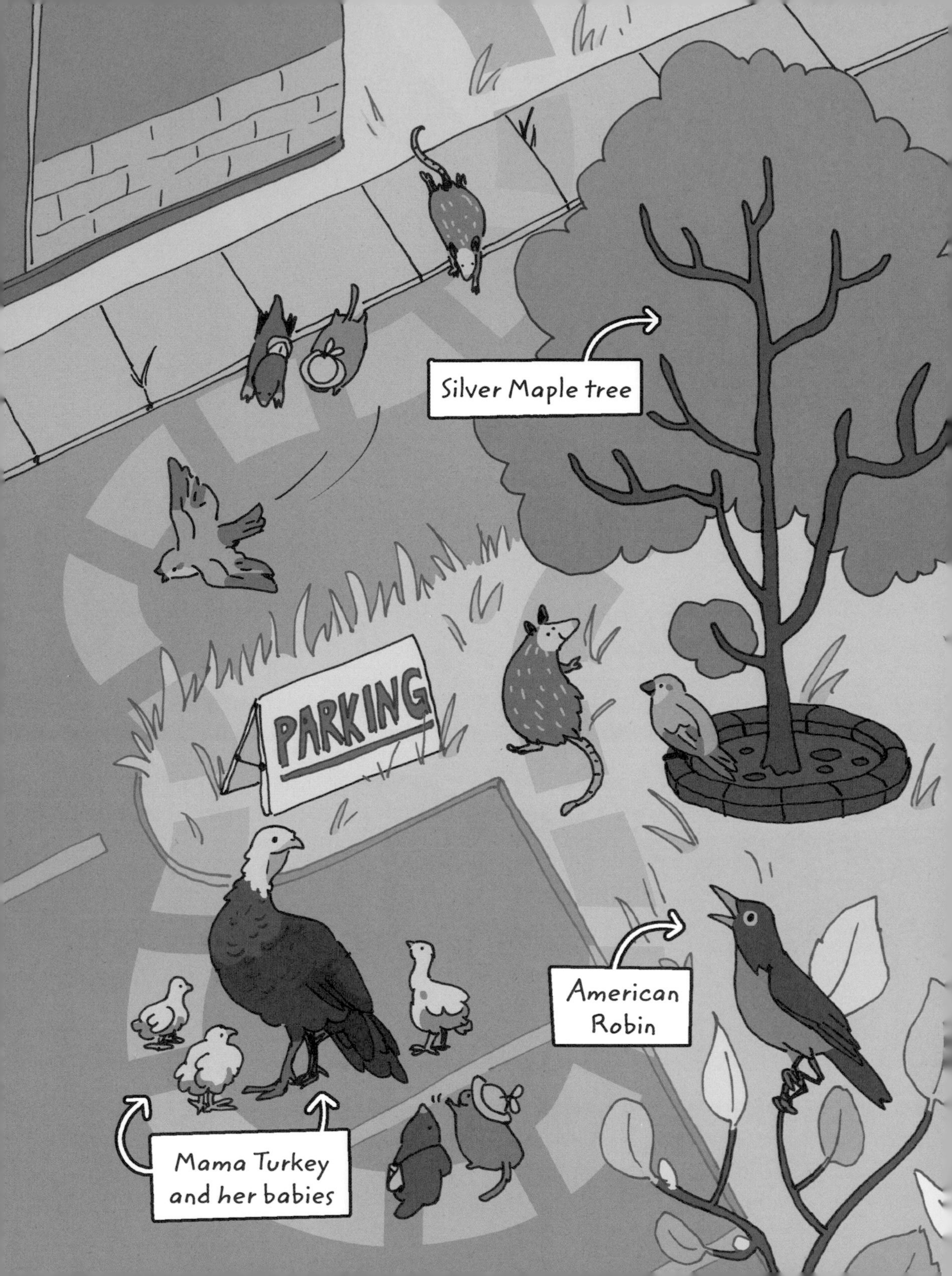
Silver Maple tree
PARKING
American
Robin
Mama Turkey
and her babies

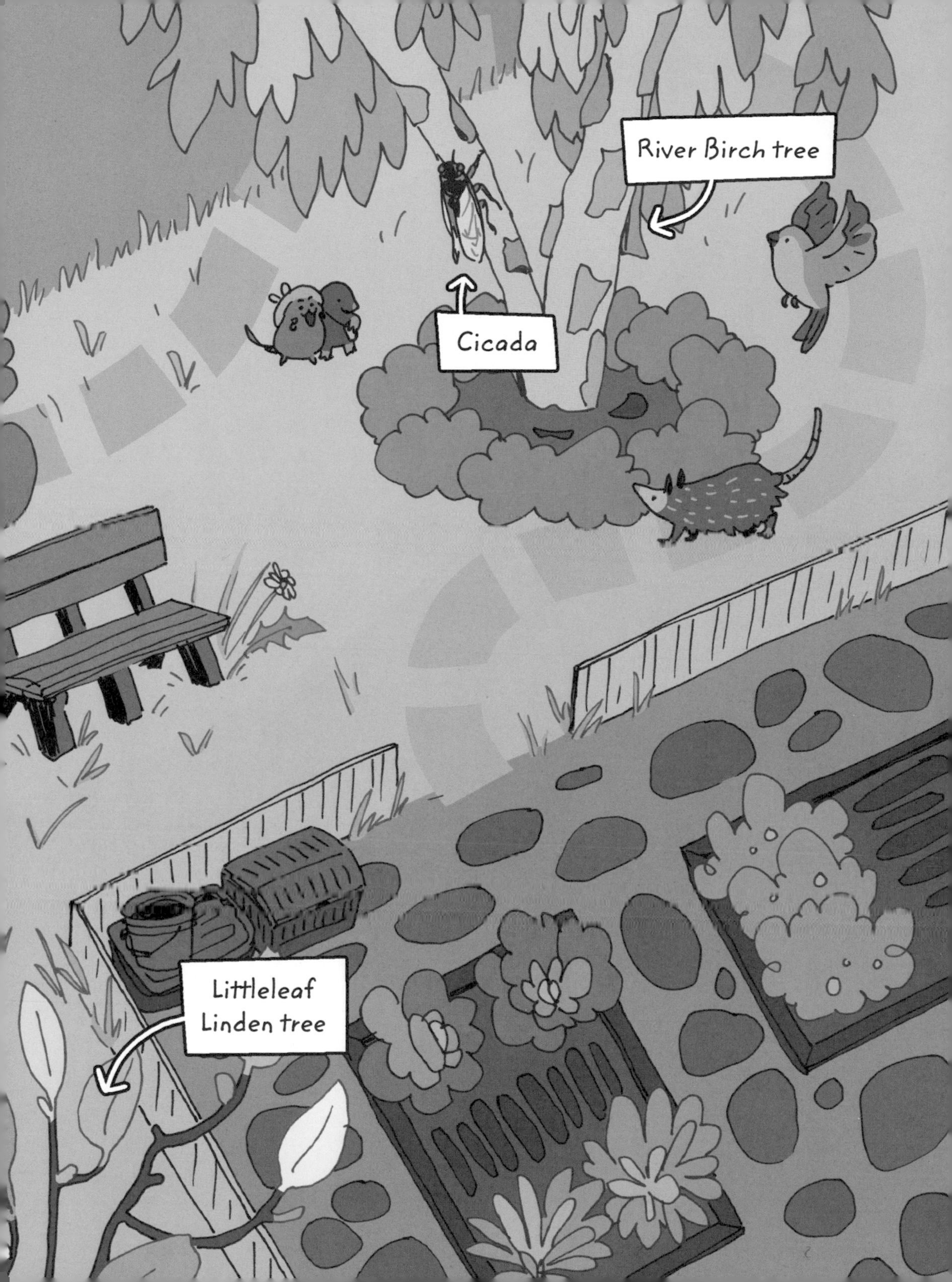
River Birch tree
Cicada
Littleleaf
Linden tree

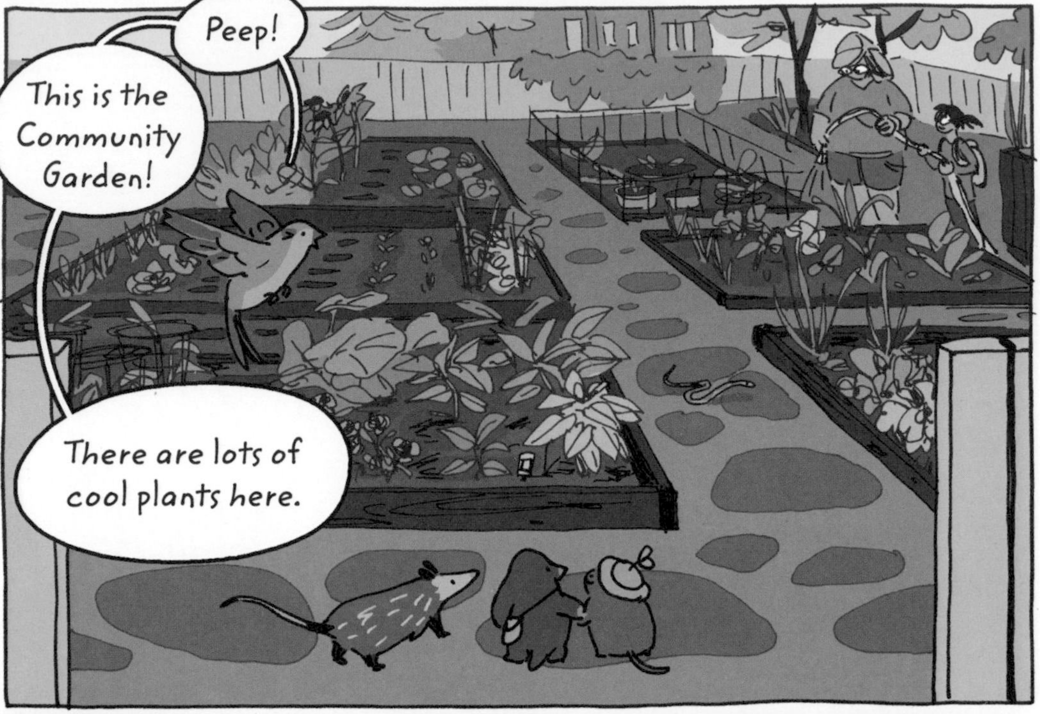
Peep!
This is the Community Garden!
There are lots of cool plants here.

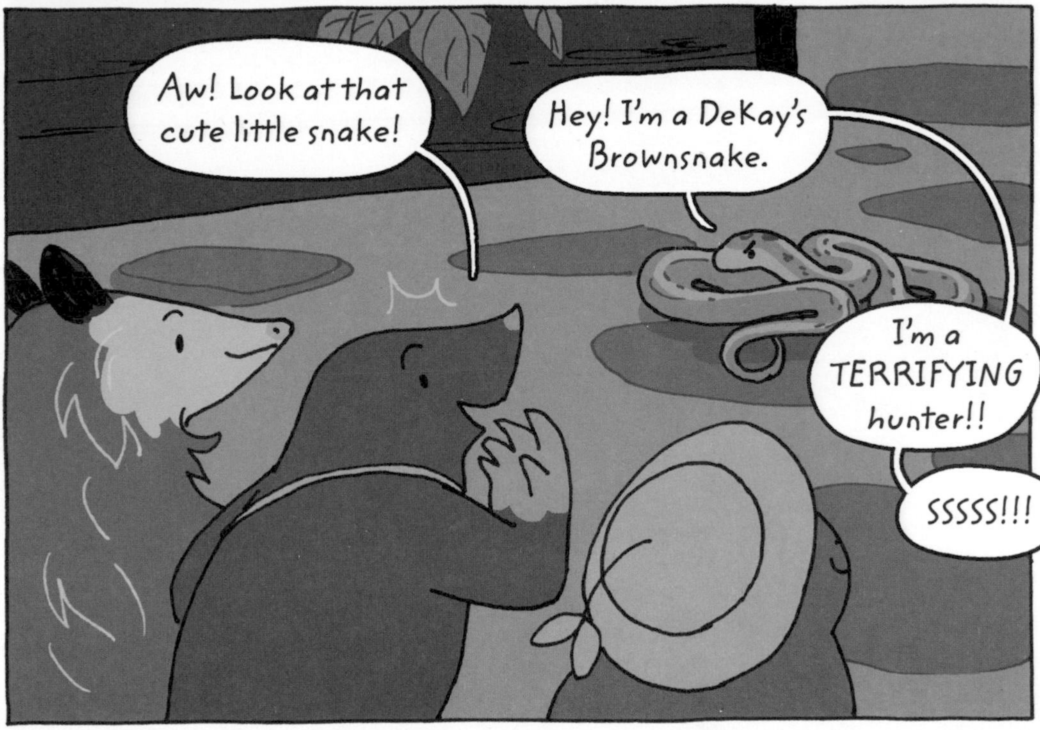
Aw! Look at that cute little snake!
Hey! I'm a DeKay's Brownsnake.
I'm a TERRIFYING hunter!!
SSSSS!!!

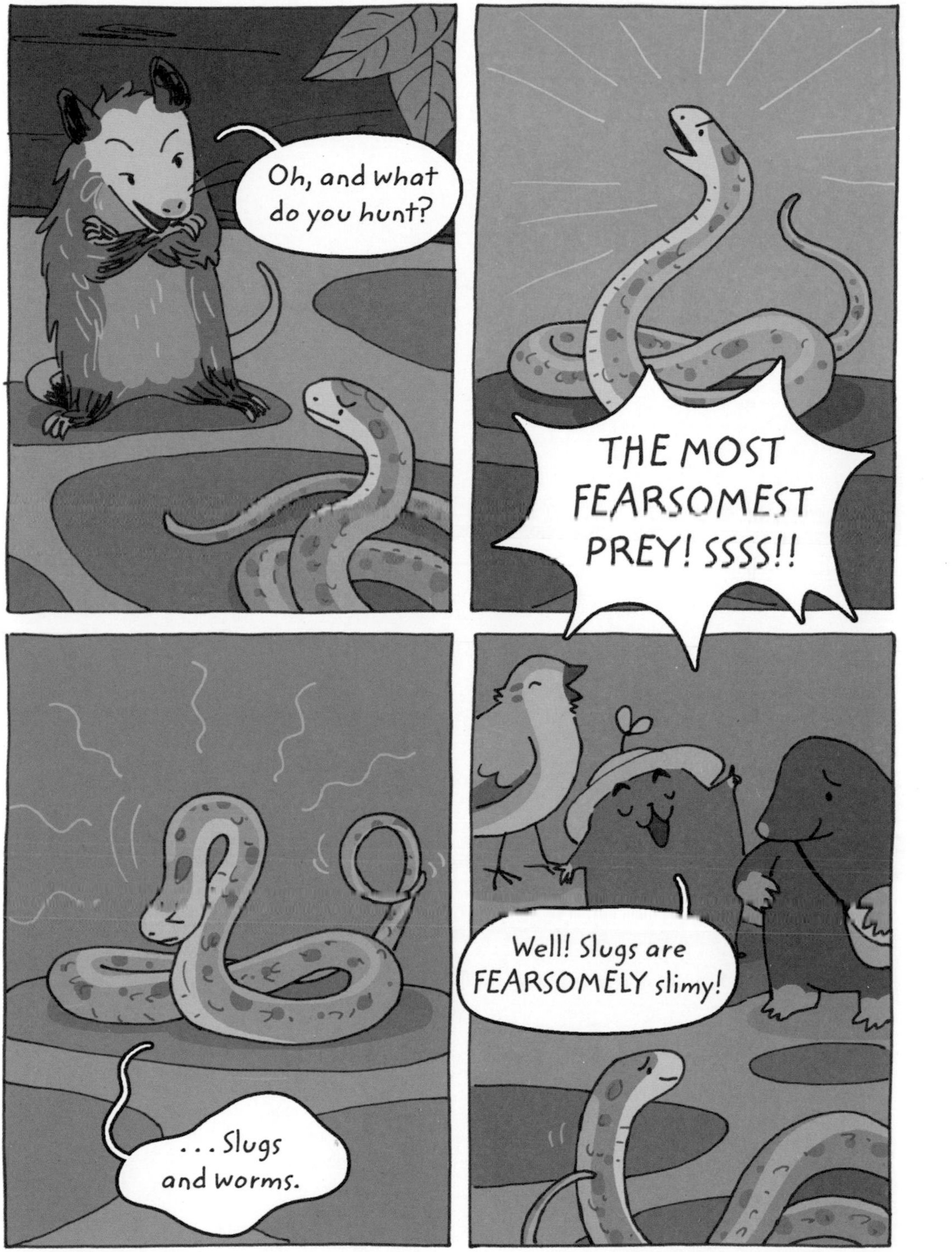
Oh, and what do you hunt?
THE MOST FEARSOMEST PREY! SSSS!!
. . . Slugs and worms.
Well! Slugs are FEARSOMELY slimy!

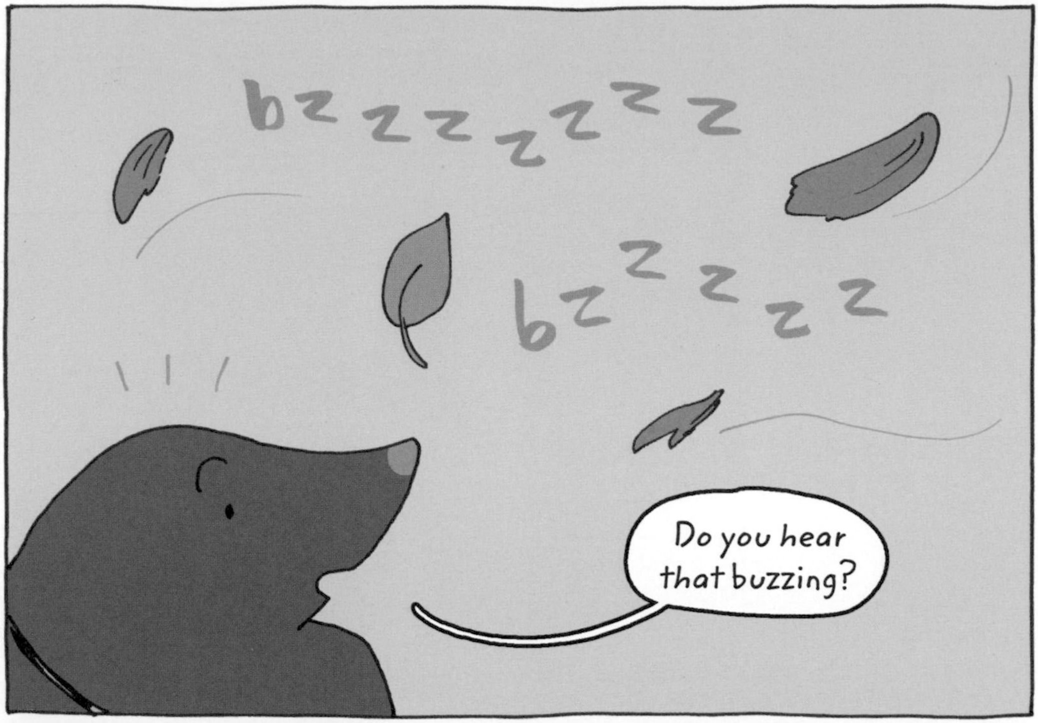
bzzzzzzz
bzzzzzz
Do you hear that buzzing?

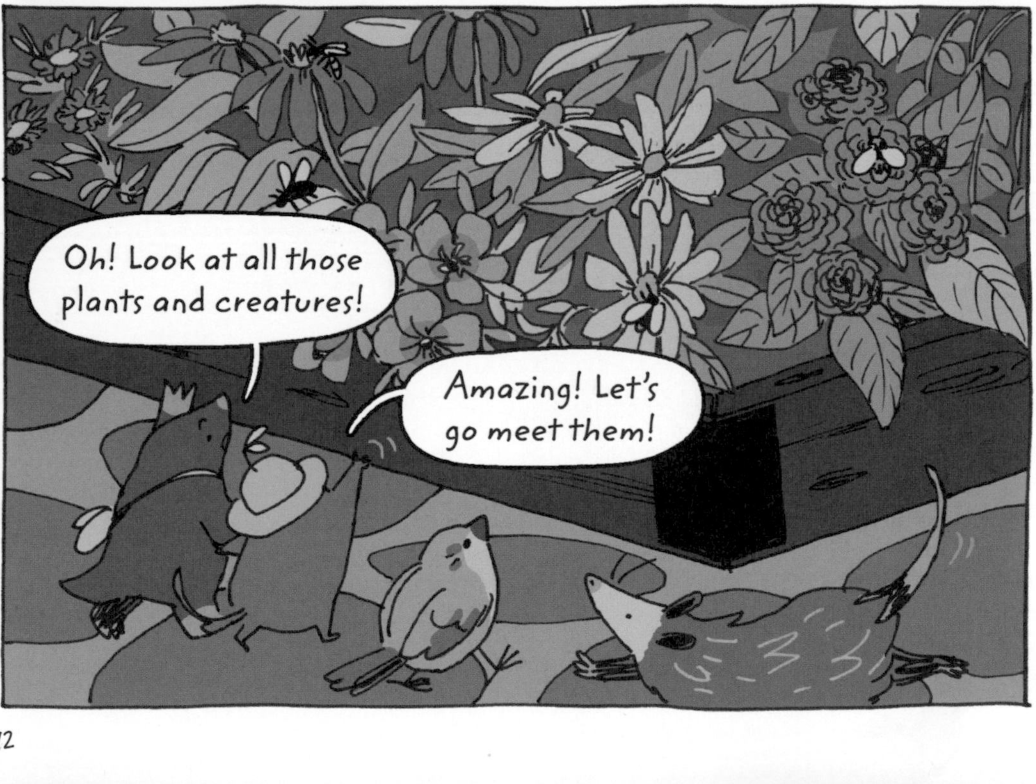
Oh! Look at all those plants and creatures!
Amazing! Let's go meet them!

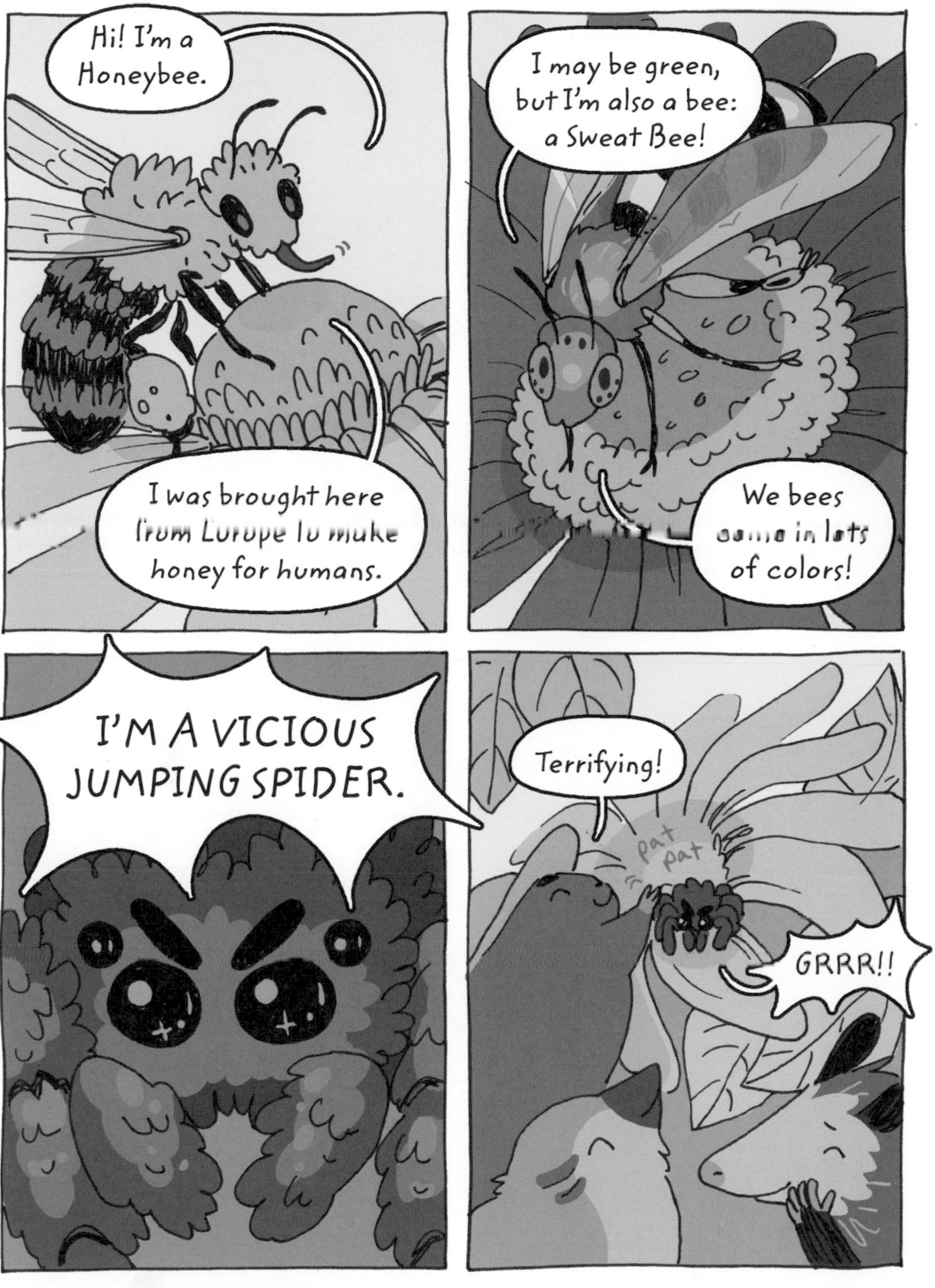
Hi! I'm a Honeybee.
I was brought here from Europe to make honey for humans.
I may be green, but I'm also a bee: a Sweat Bee!
We bees come in lots of colors!
I'M A VICIOUS JUMPING SPIDER.
Terrifying!
pat pat
GRRR!!

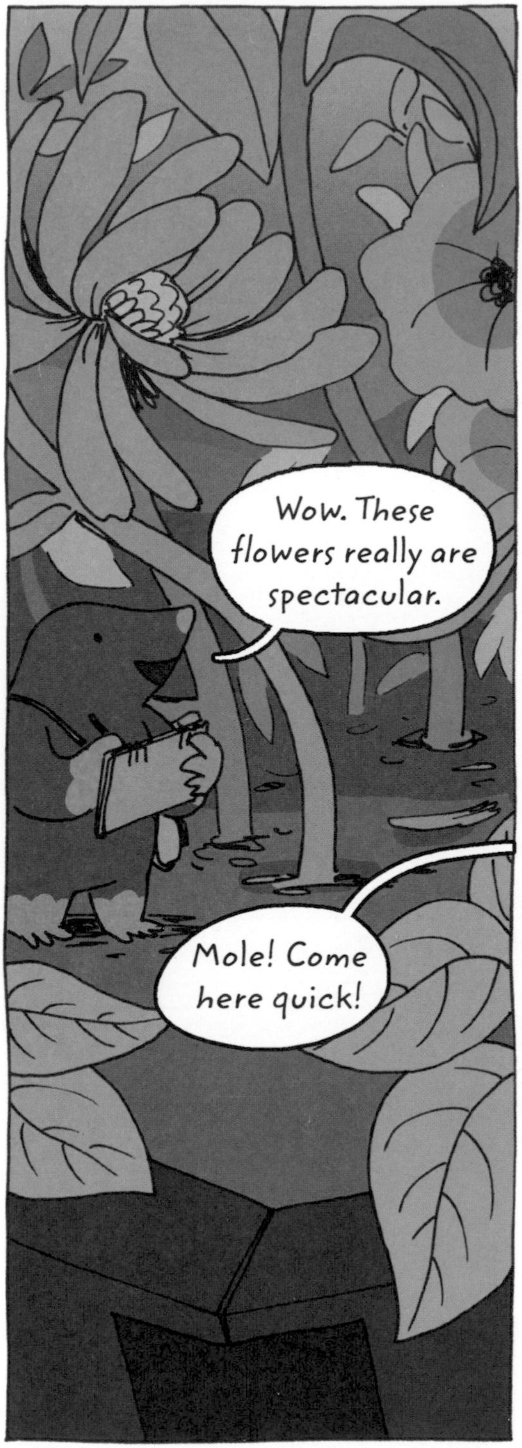
Wow. These flowers really are spectacular.
Mole! Come here quick!
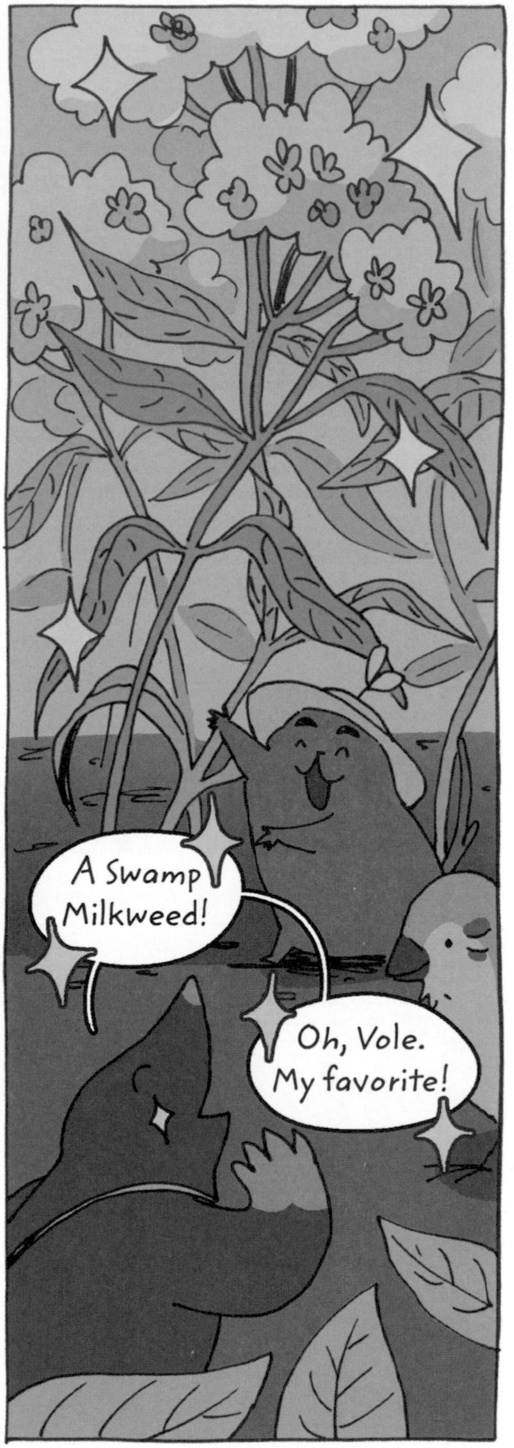
A Swamp Milkweed!
Oh, Vole. My favorite!

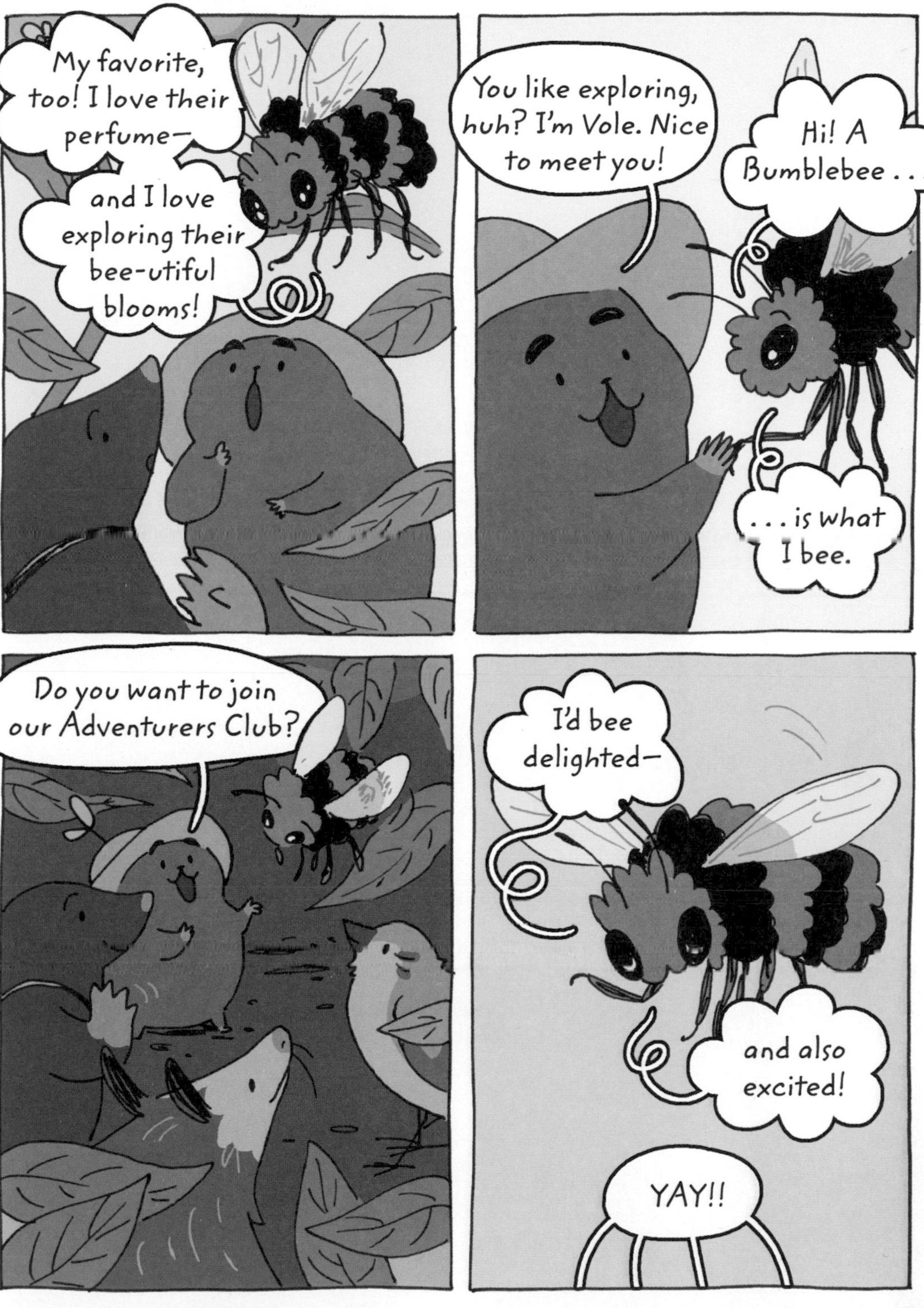
My favorite, too! I love their perfume—
and I love exploring their bee-utiful blooms!
You like exploring, huh? I'm Vole. Nice to meet you!
Hi! A Bumblebee . . .
. . . is what I bee.
Do you want to join our Adventurers Club?
I'd bee delighted—
and also excited!
YAY!!

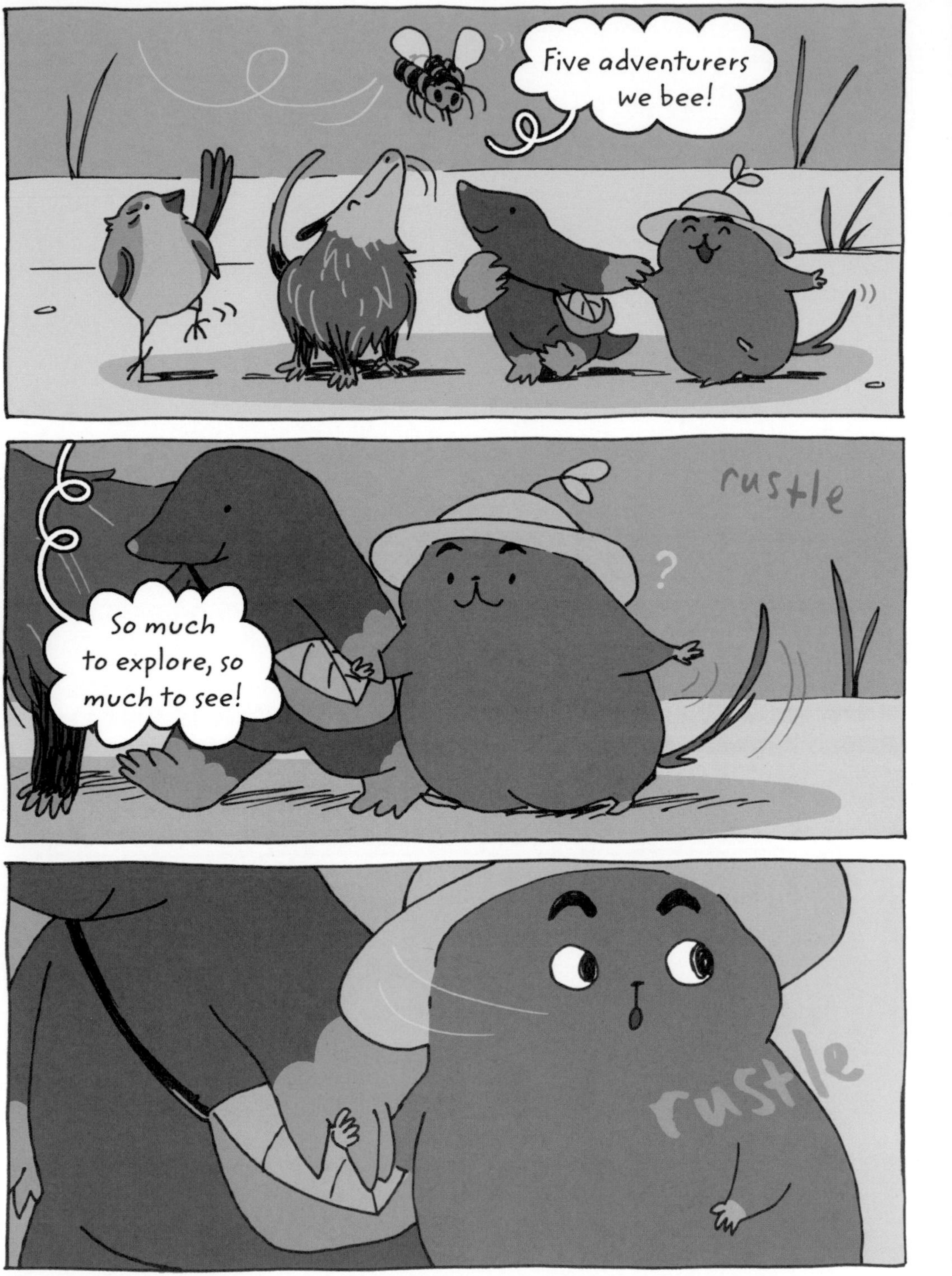
Five adventurers we bee!
rustle
So much to explore, so much to see!
?
rustle

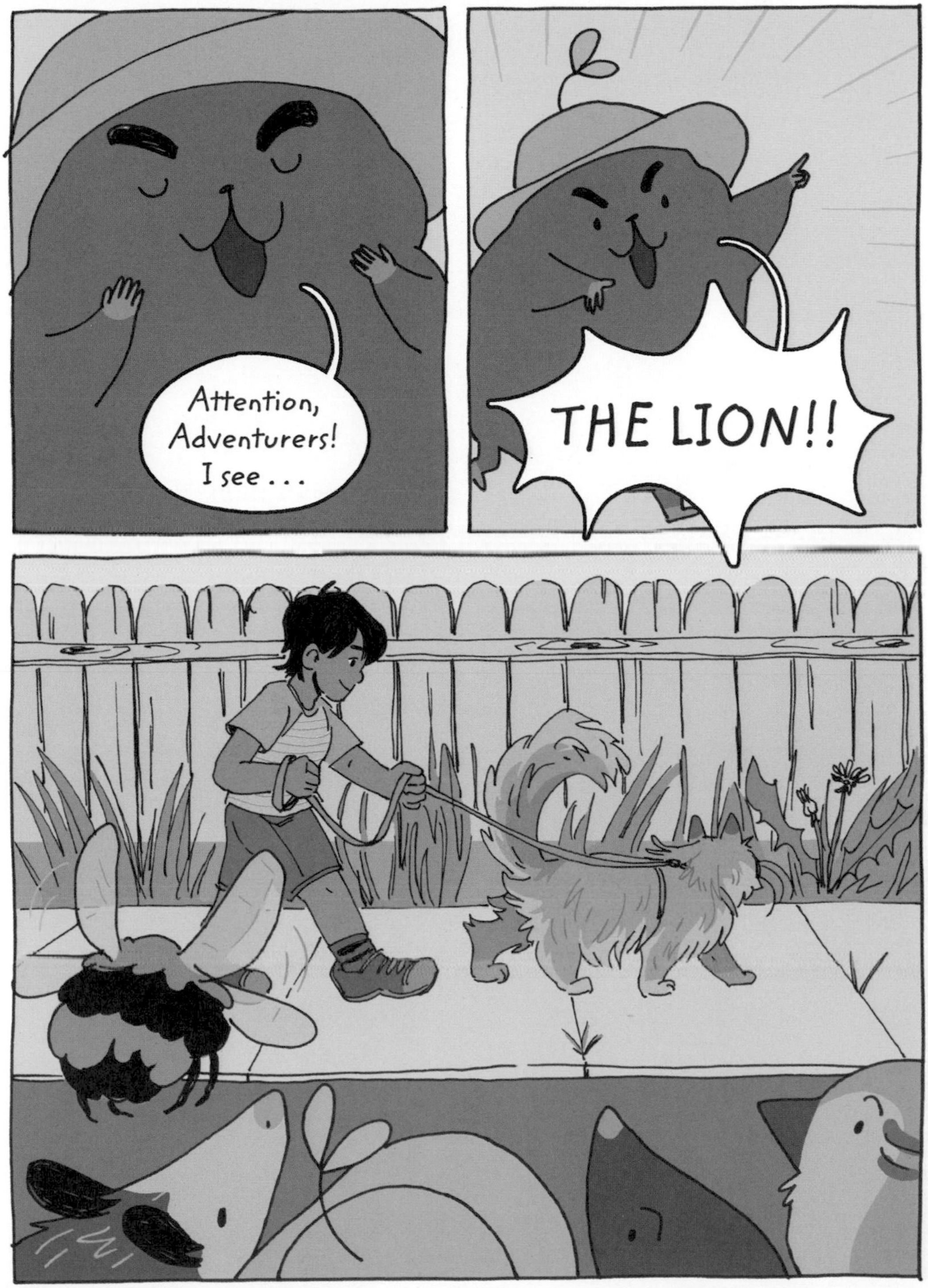

Attention, Adventurers! I see . . .
THE LION!!

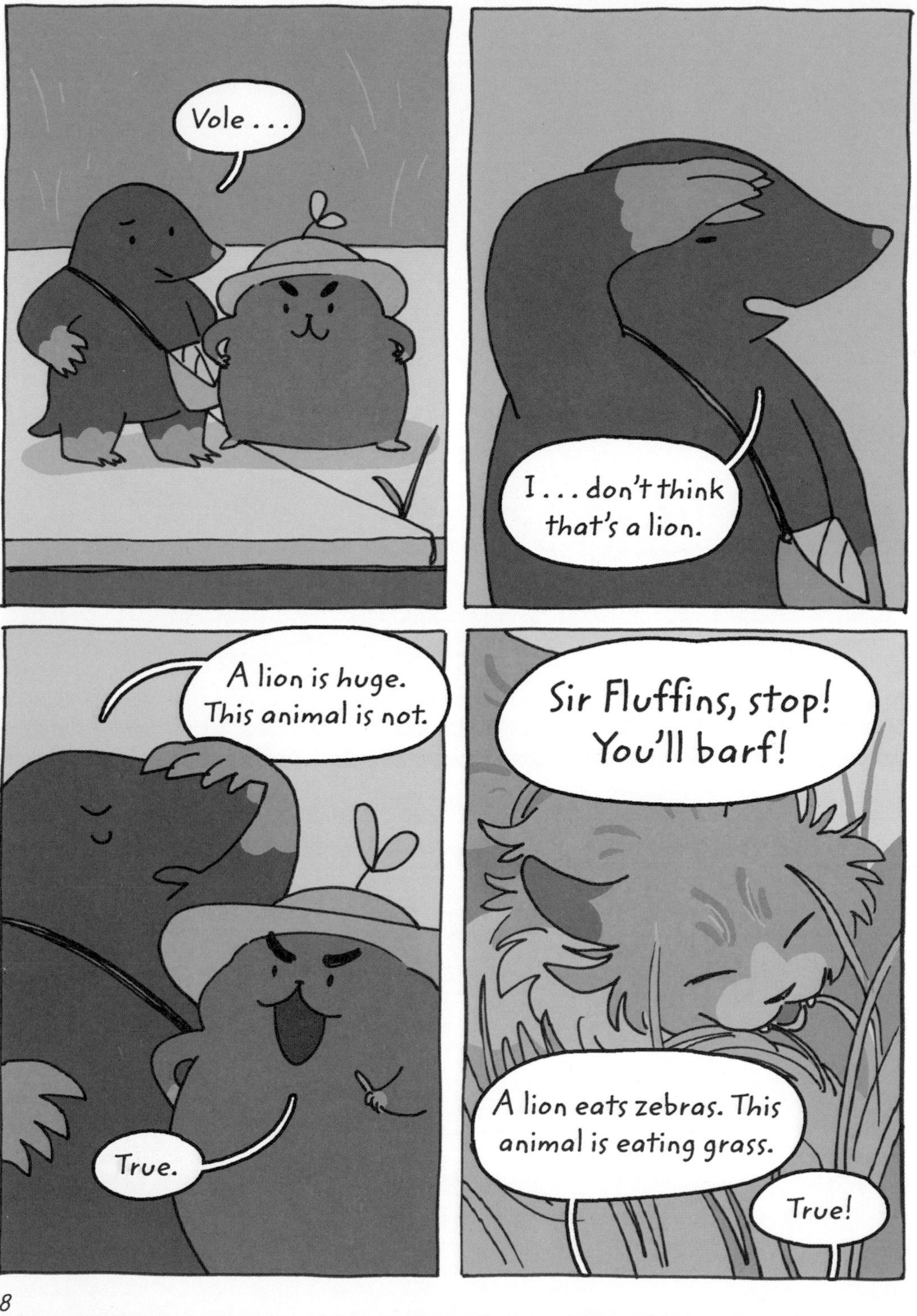
Vole . . .
I . . . don't think that's a lion.
A lion is huge. This animal is not.
True.
Sir Fluffins, stop! You'll barf!
A lion eats zebras. This animal is eating grass.
True!

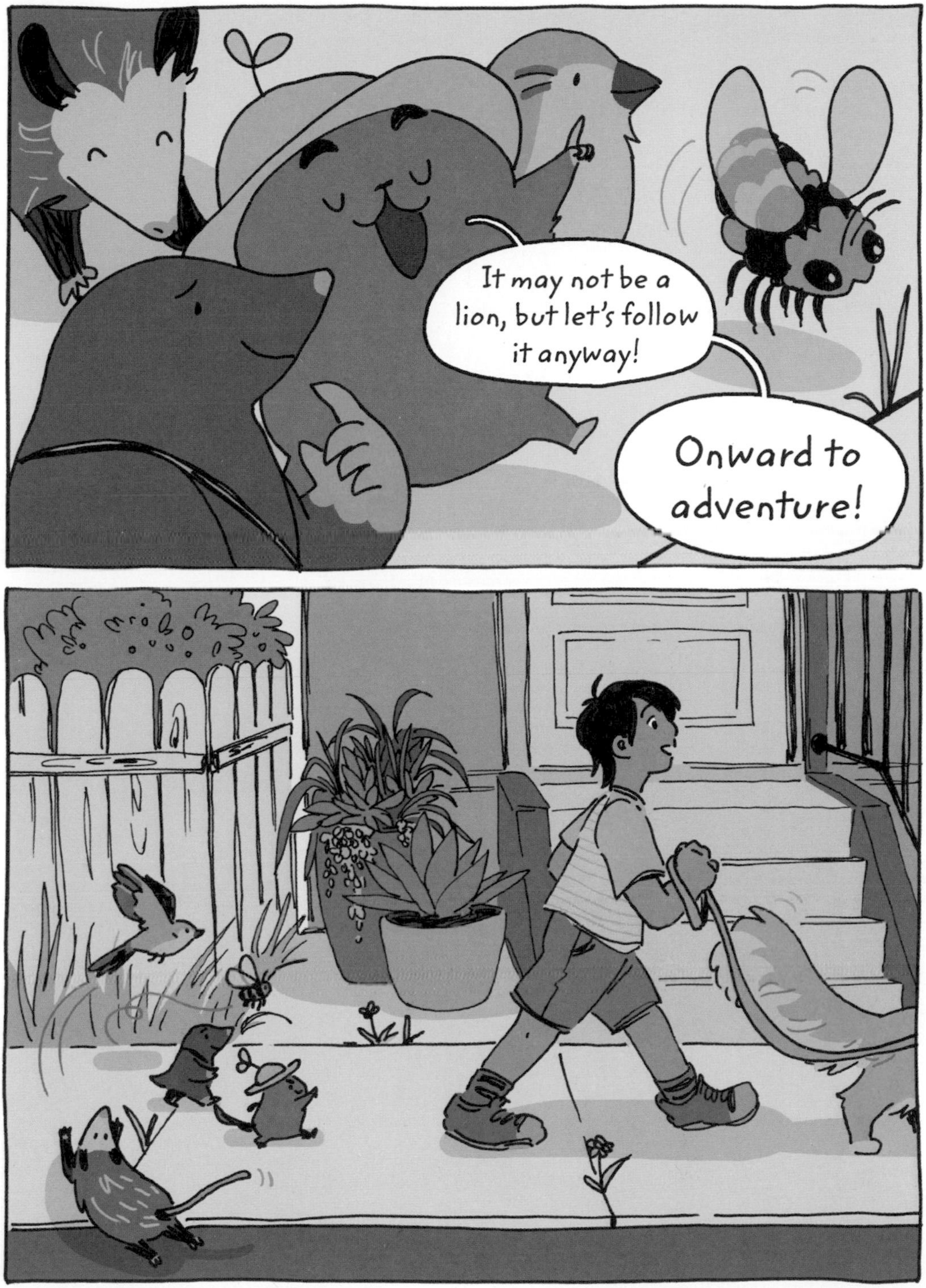
It may not be a lion, but let's follow it anyway!
Onward to adventure!

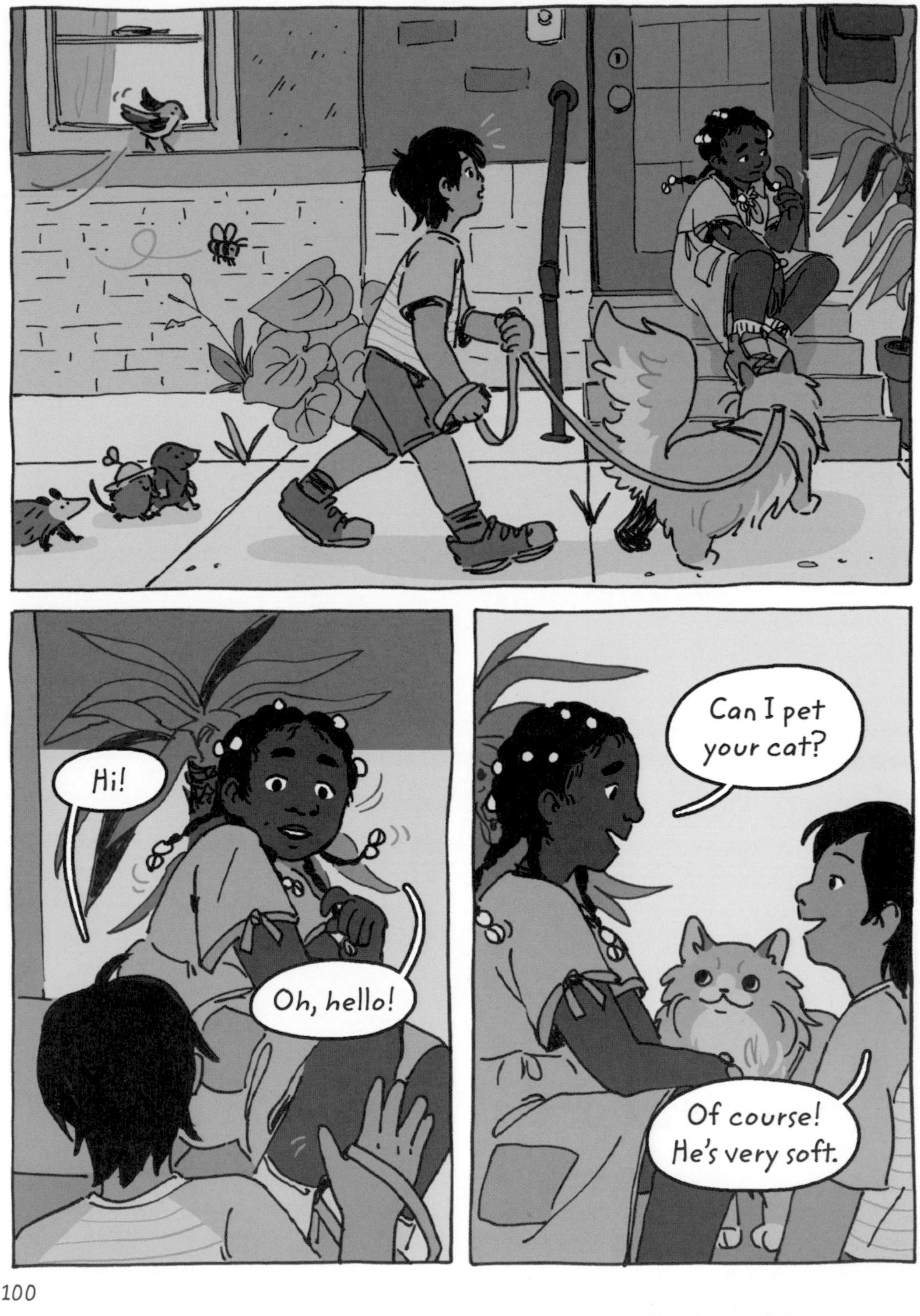
Hi!
Oh, hello!
Can I pet your cat?
Of course! He's very soft.

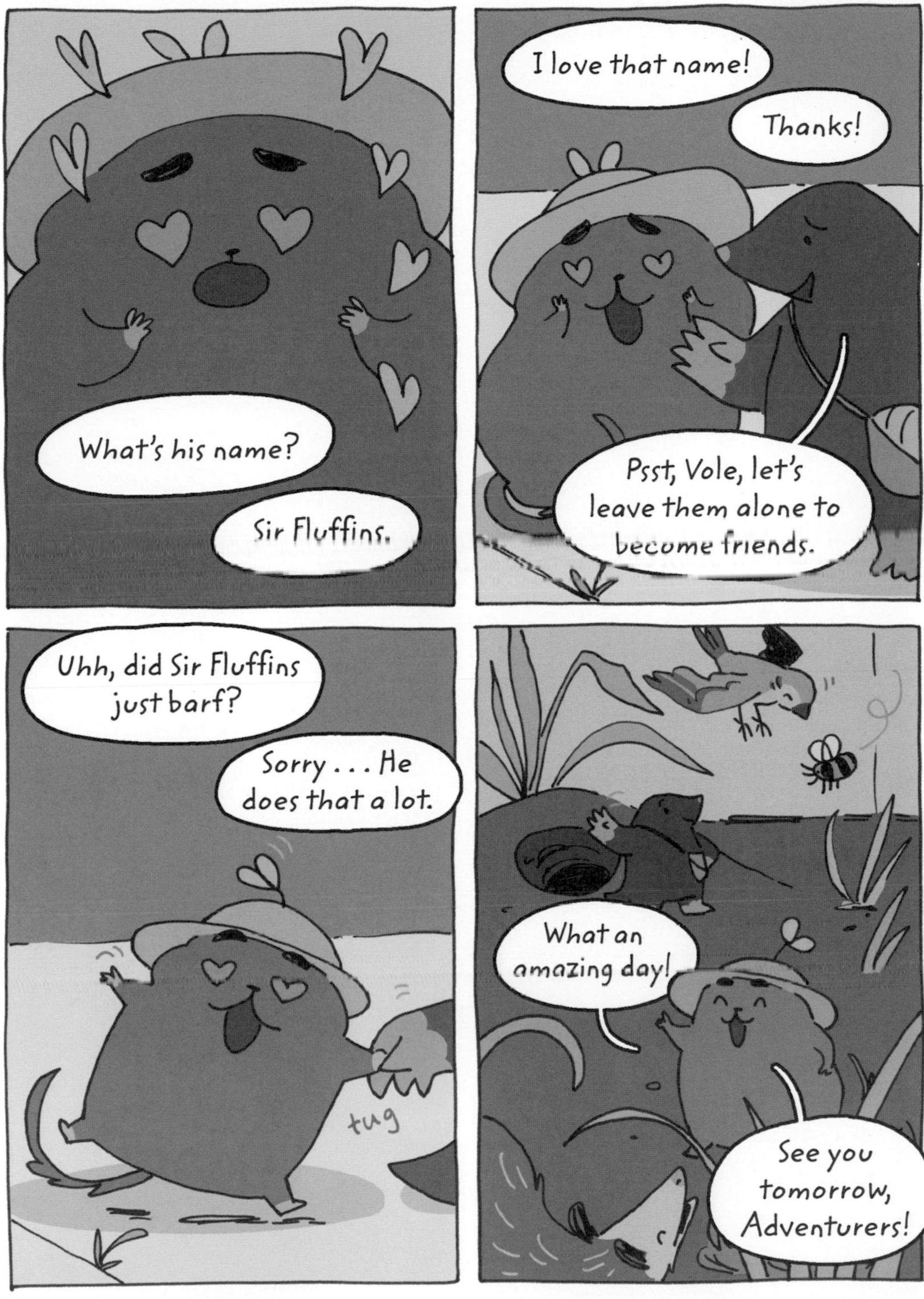
What's his name?
Sir Fluffins.
I love that name!
Thanks!
Psst, Vole, let's leave them alone to become friends.
Uhh, did Sir Fluffins just barf?
Sorry . . . He does that a lot.
tug
What an amazing day!
See you tomorrow, Adventurers!

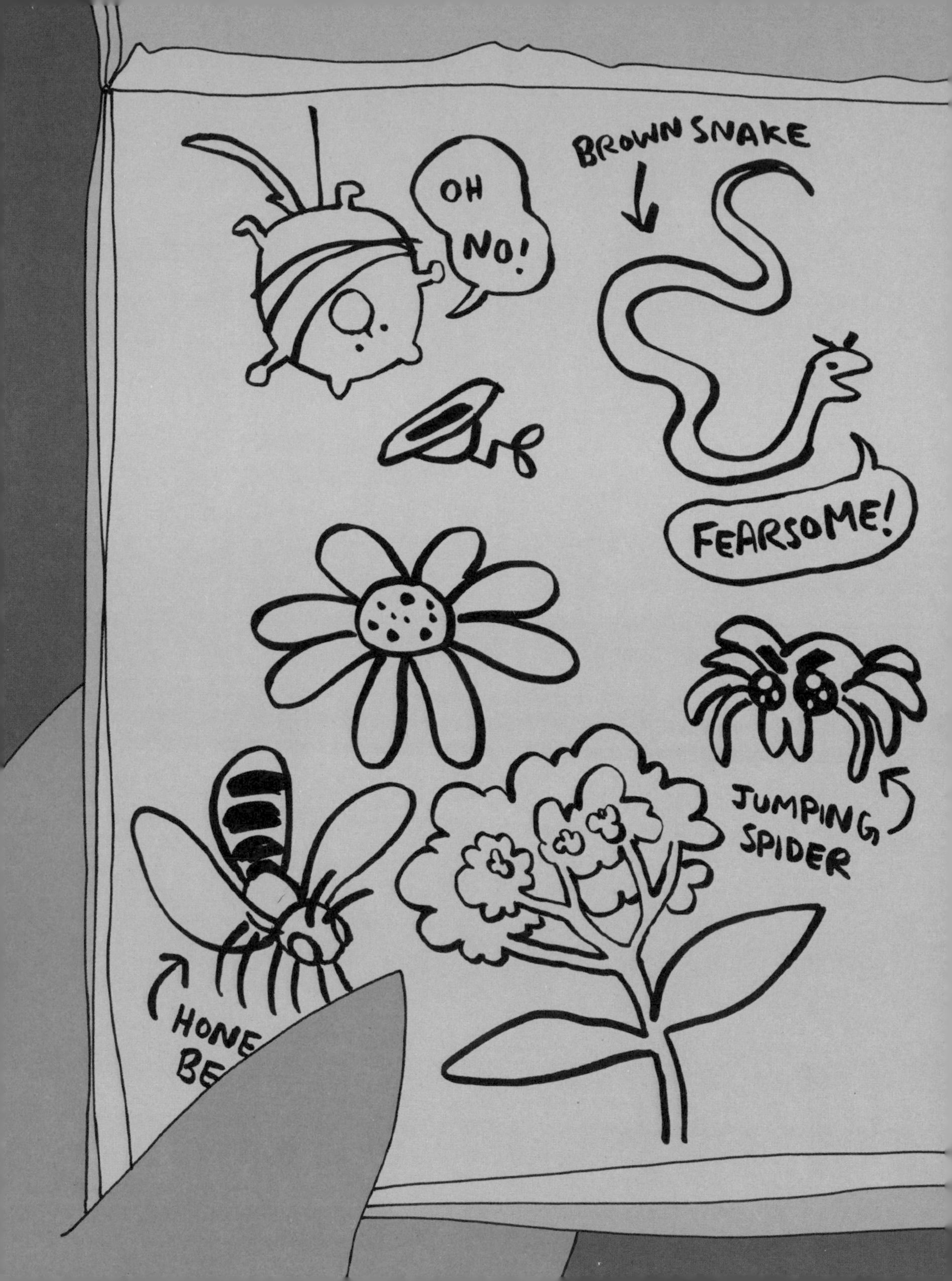
OH NO!
BROWN SNAKE
FEARSOME!
JUMPING SPIDER
HONE
BE

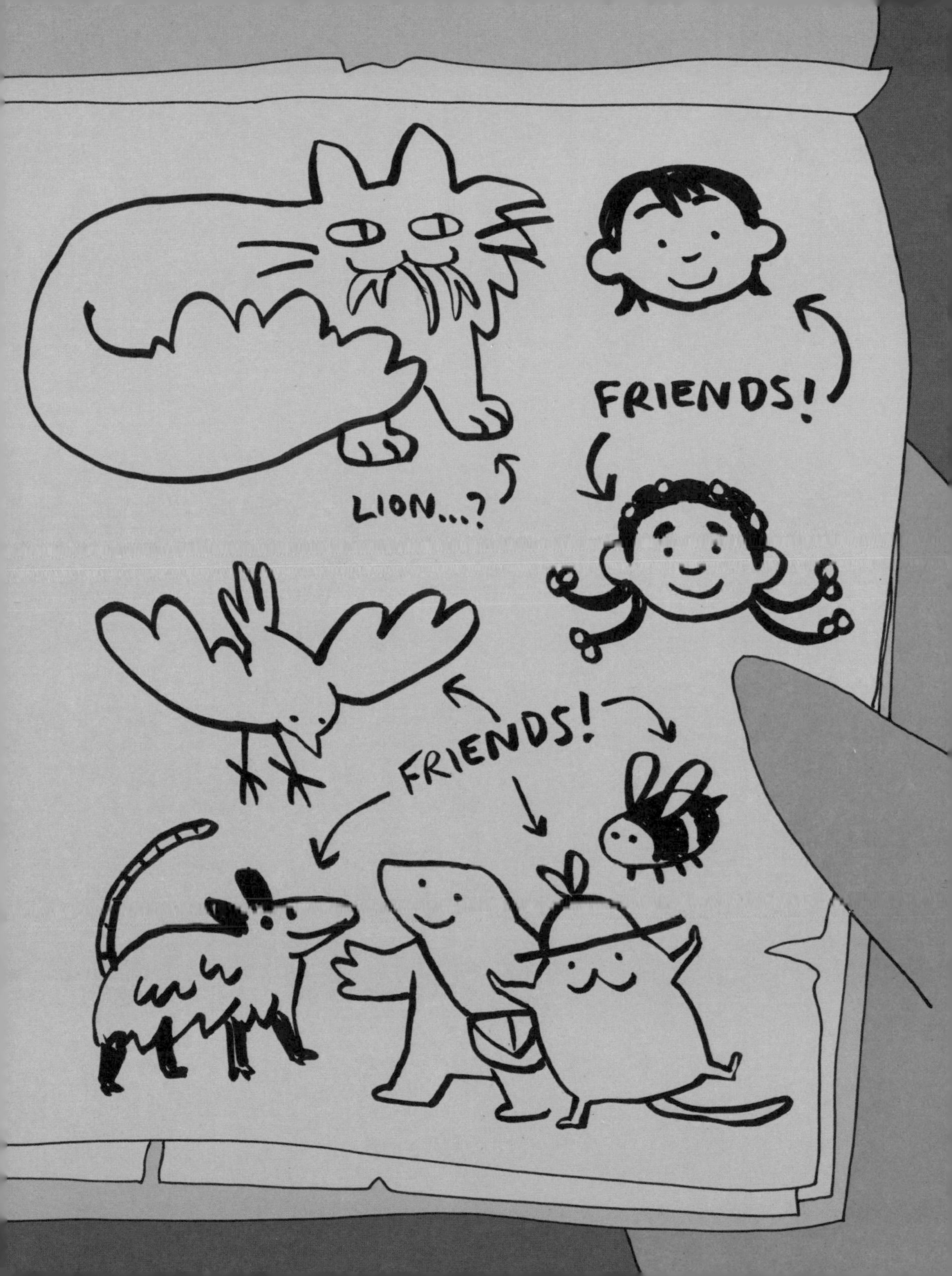

FRIENDS!
LION...?
FRIENDS!

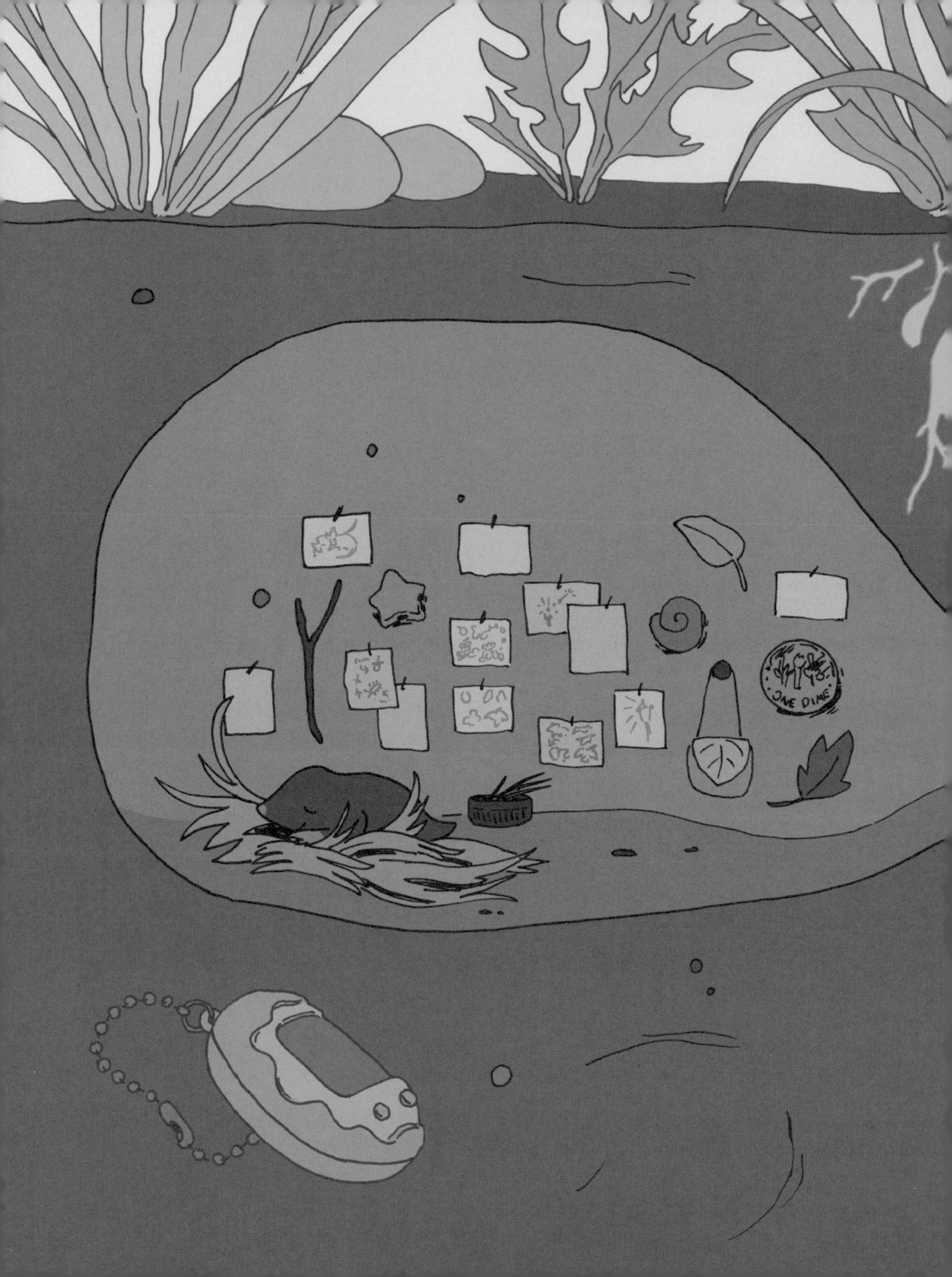
ONE DIME

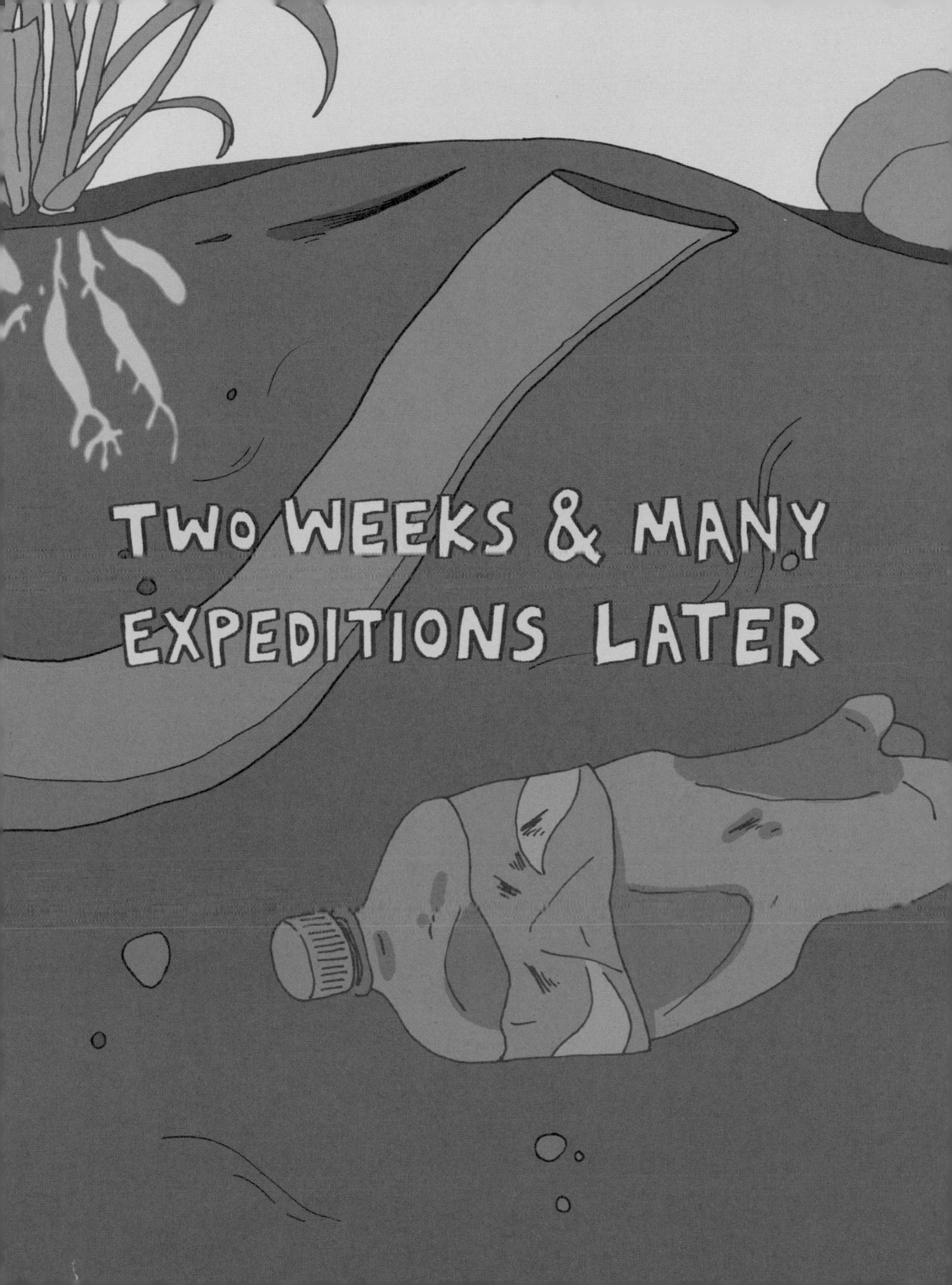
TWO WEEKS & MANY
EXPEDITIONS LATER

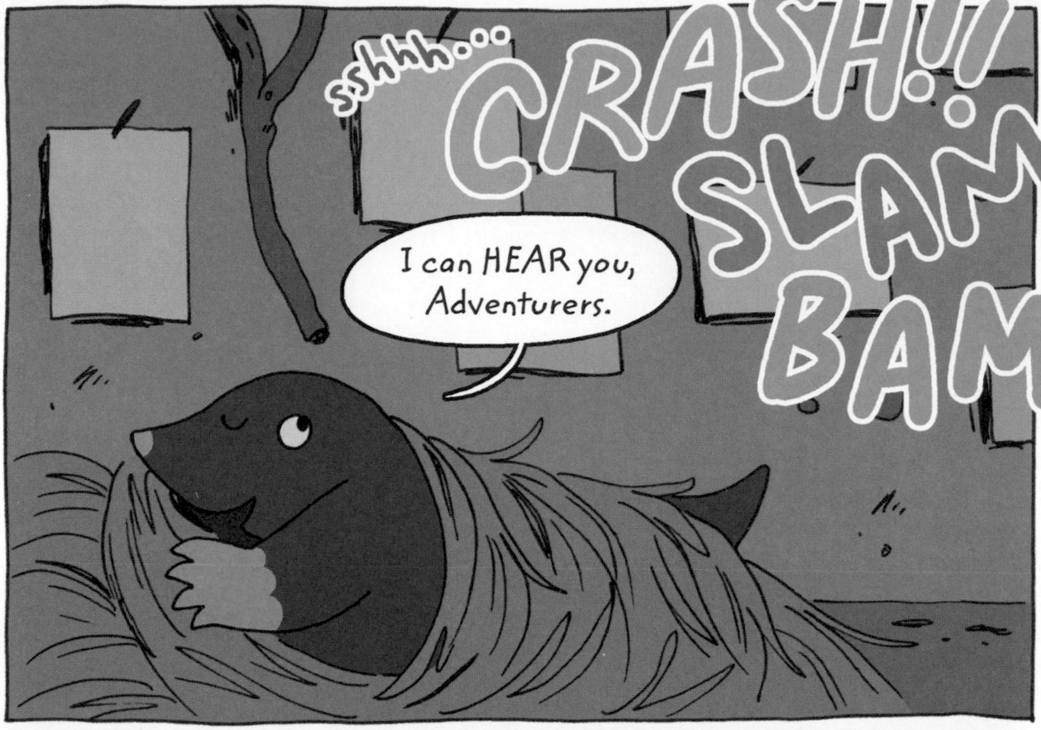
sshhh...
CRASH!!
SLAM
BAM
I can HEAR you, Adventurers.

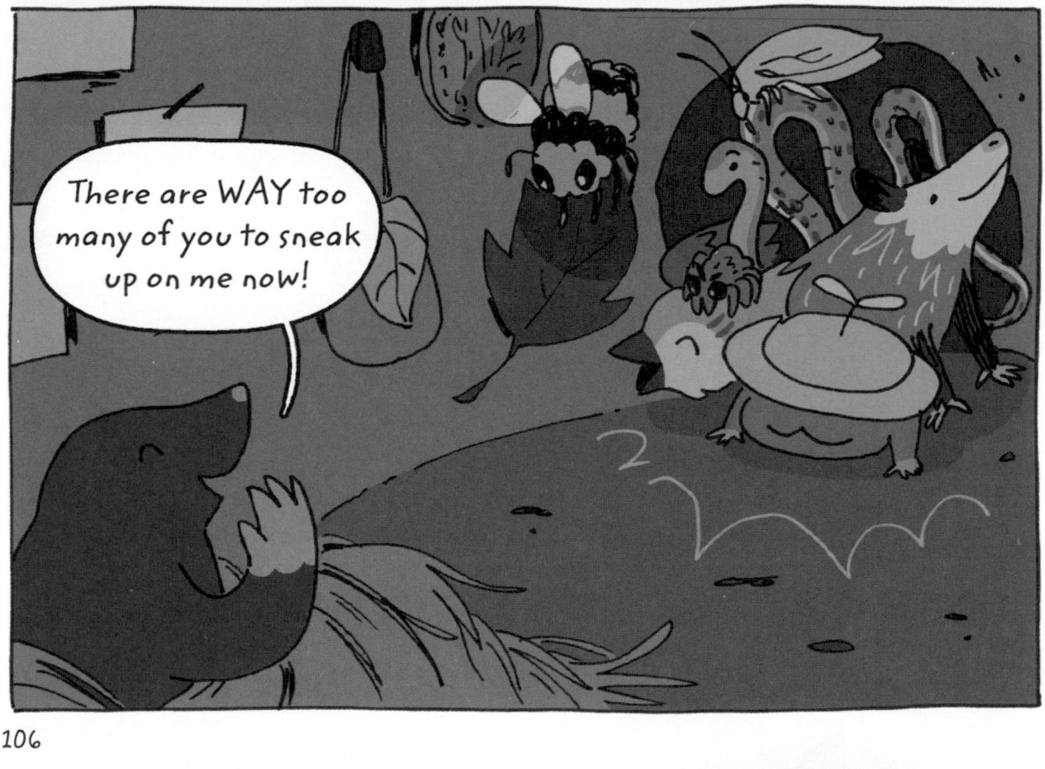
There are WAY too many of you to sneak up on me now!

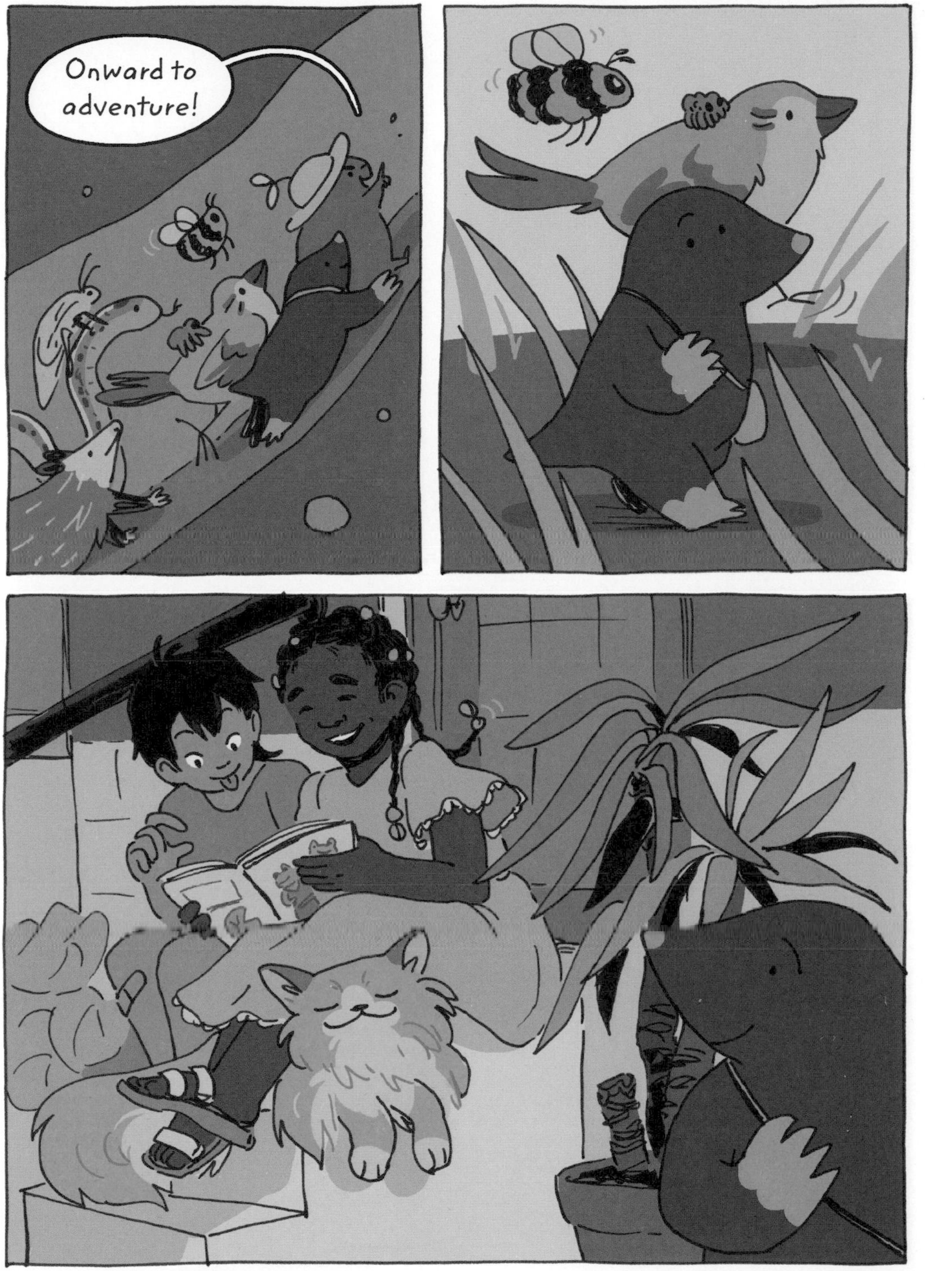
Onward to adventure!

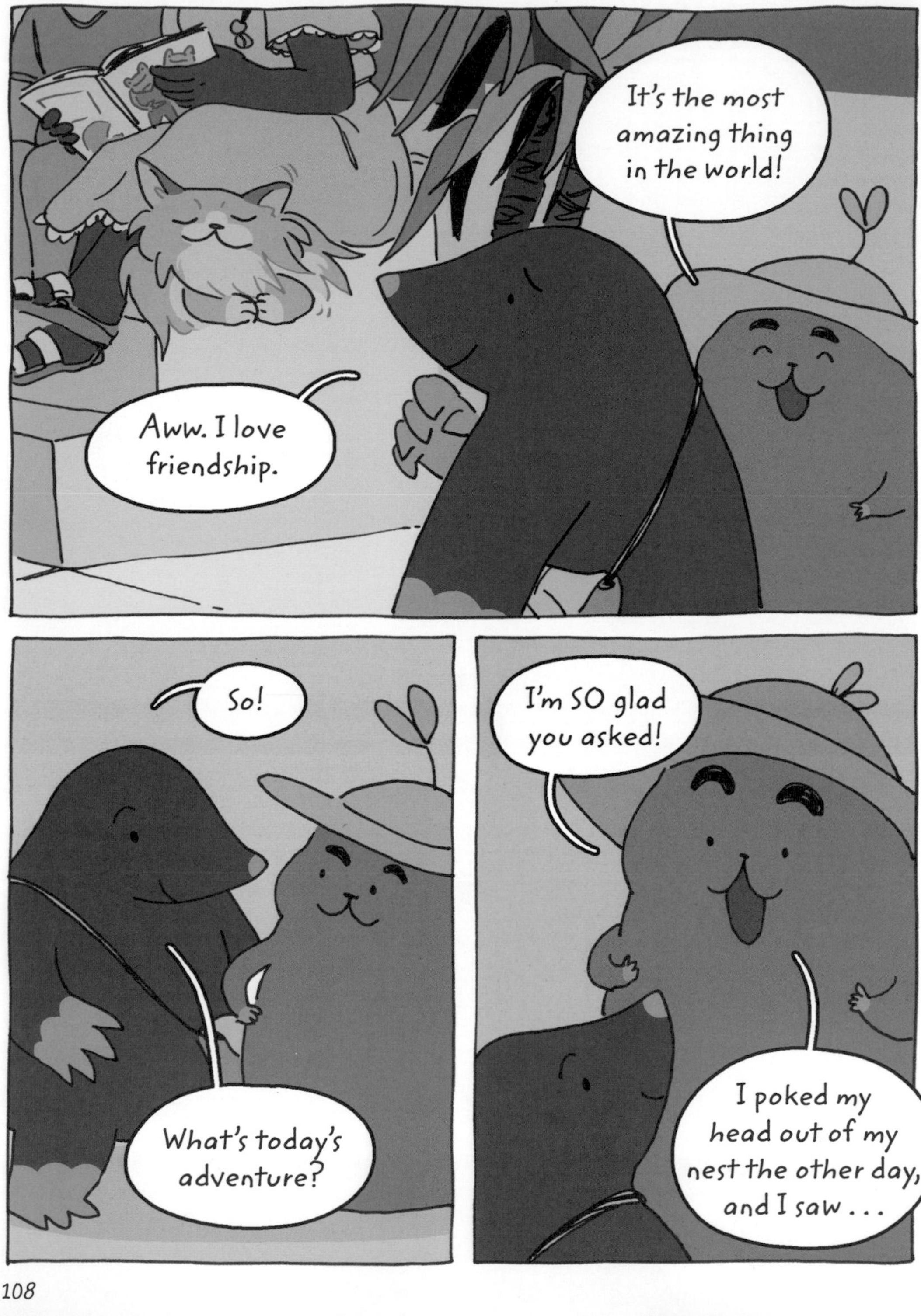
It's the most amazing thing in the world!
Aww. I love friendship.
So!
What's today's adventure?
I'm SO glad you asked!
I poked my head out of my nest the other day, and I saw . . .

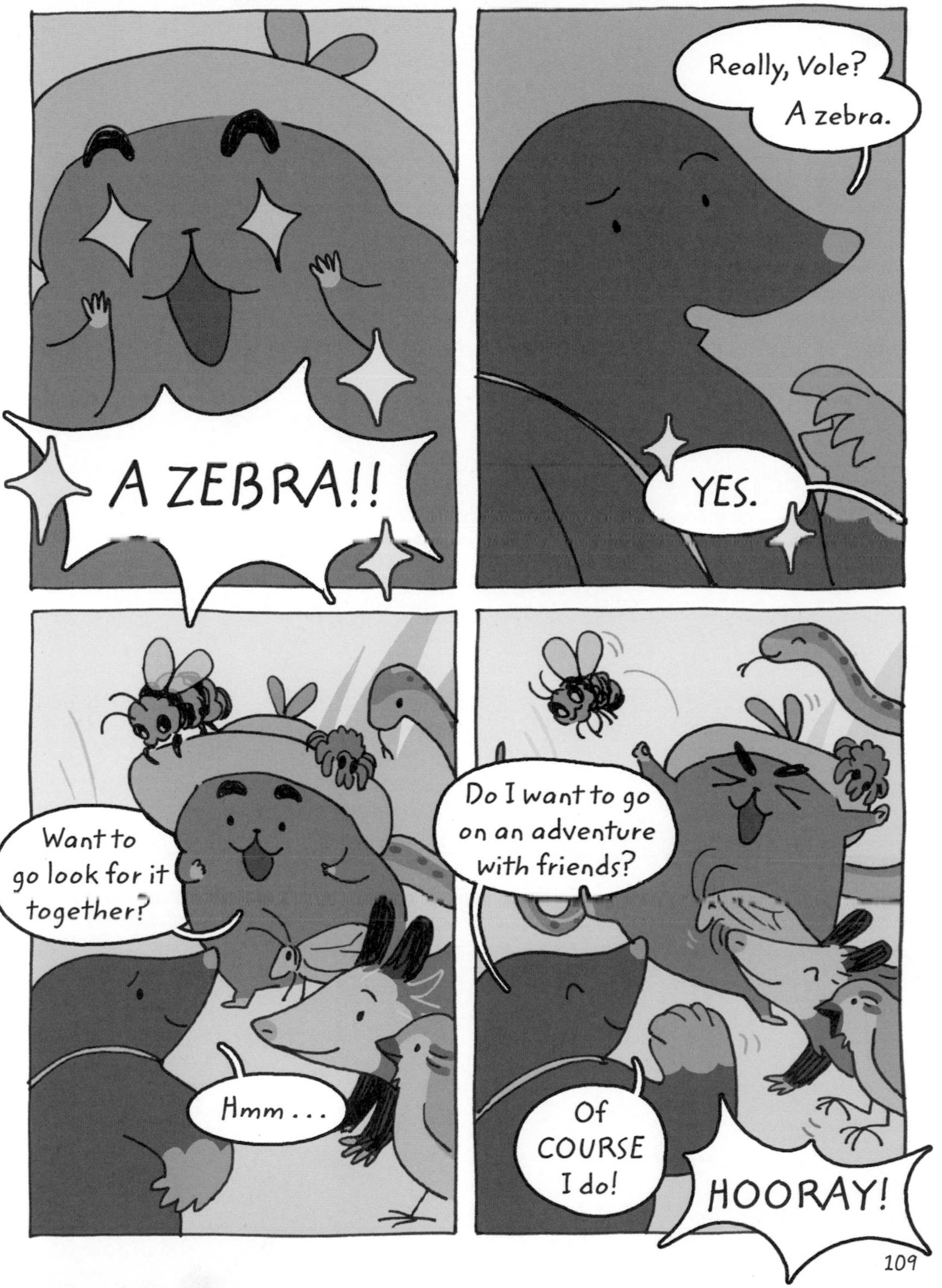
A ZEBRA!!
Really, Vole? A zebra.
YES.
Want to go look for it together?
Hmm . . .
Do I want to go on an adventure with friends?
Of COURSE I do!
HOORAY!

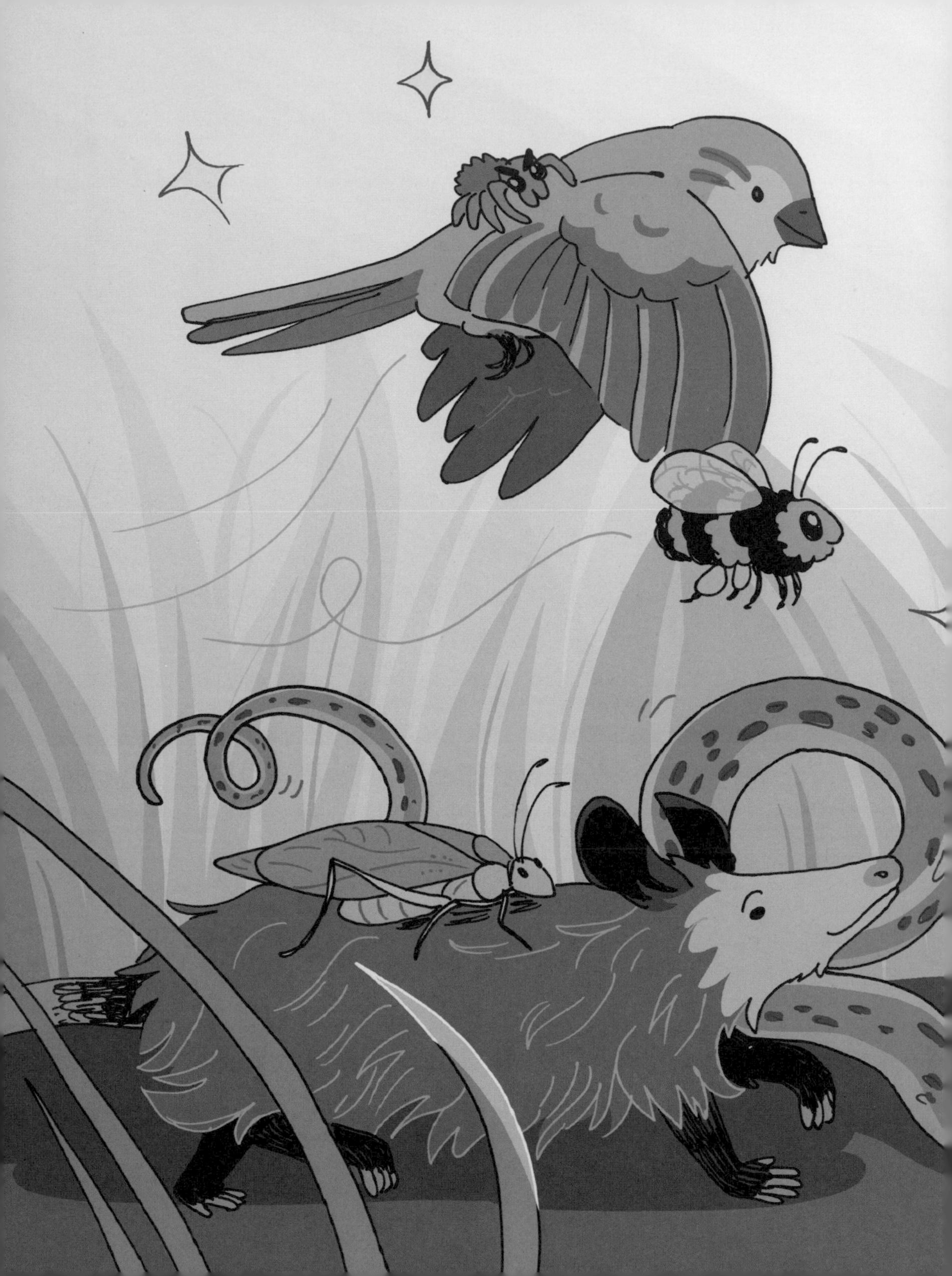

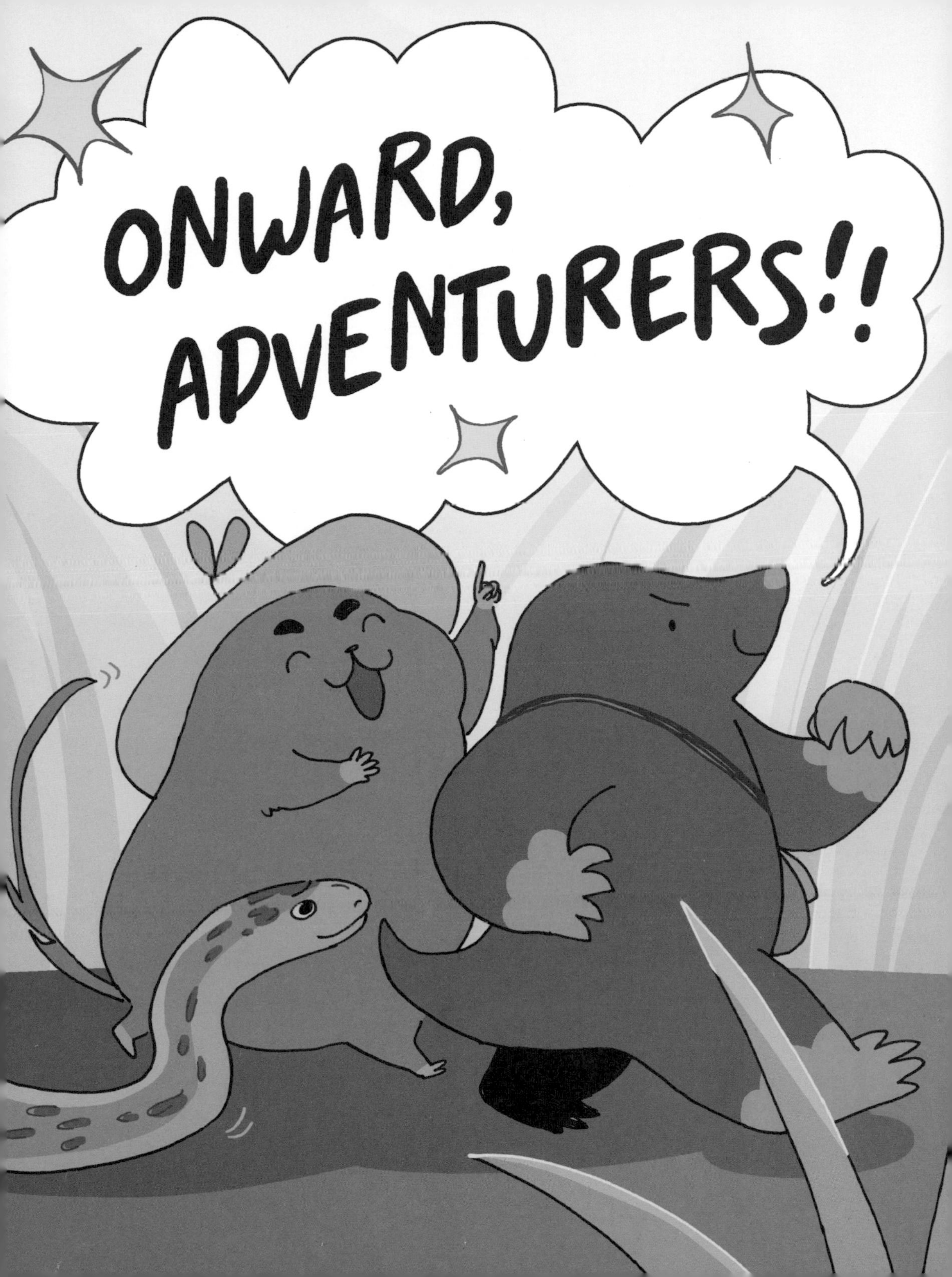
ONWARD, ADVENTURERS!!

HOW TO DRAW MOLE

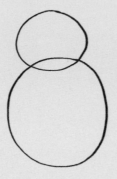

Step 1: Sketch a circle for Mole's head and a larger oval underneath for her body.

Step 2: Mole's arms and legs are rectangular. They end in triangle shapes, which make up her claws.

Step 3: Draw Mole's snout, which curves like a leaf. Use lines to connect and smooth over the shapes that make up the body.

Step 4: Add final details, like her face and bag. To finish, erase the sketch lines from the earlier steps.

HOW TO DRAW VOLE

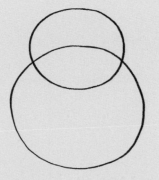

Step 1: Sketch a circle for Vole's head and a bigger one underneath for her body.

Step 2: Vole's arms and legs are triangular. Her arms end in tiny little fingers.

Step 3: Draw Vole's tail. Use lines to connect and smooth over the shapes that make up the body.

Step 4: Add final details, like her face and hat. To finish, erase the sketch lines from the earlier steps.

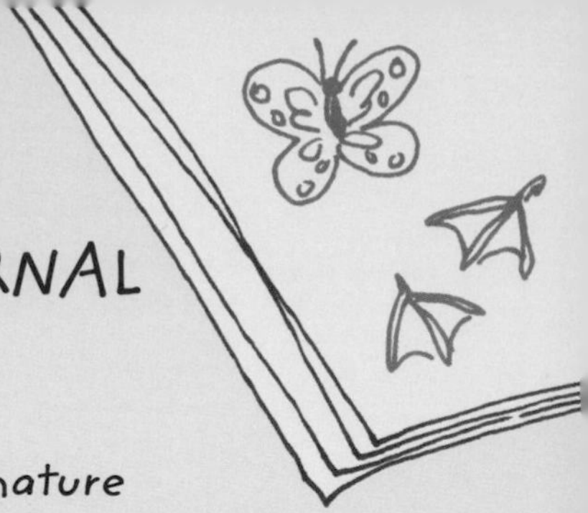

HOW TO KEEP A NATURE JOURNAL

by Mole

Whether I'm in the city or the country, I find nature everywhere. During my adventures, I record what I see in a nature journal. I'm always learning new things, and my journal helps me remember what I've discovered. Plus, sometimes I find something surprising or even a tiny bit scary. If I draw it and learn more about it, my fear turns into curiosity.

Here's how you can start a nature journal:

- Get some paper and something to write with.

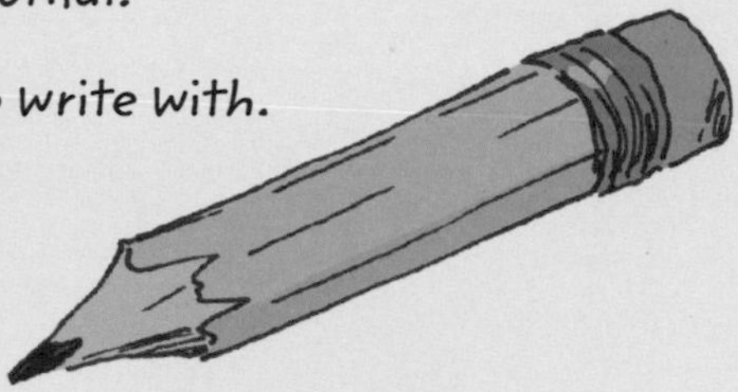

- Go outside and use your senses to explore the world. Write and draw what you find.
- Be creative! Your journal can be anything you want. You can add poems, jokes, or facts you learn. Or you can just keep a list of the things you've observed.

Fill your journal with the things you notice. If you want to, you can show it to a friend and tell them all about your adventures.

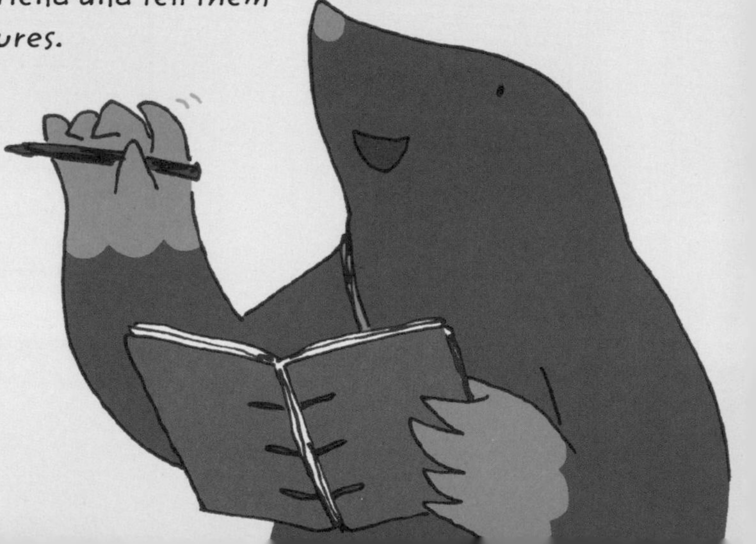

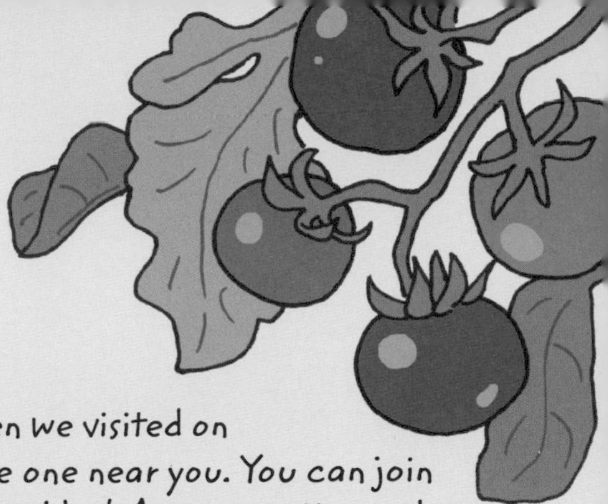

HOW TO JOIN A COMMUNITY GARDEN

by Vole

Hey, remember that community garden we visited on page 90? GUESS WHAT? There may be one near you. You can join in and grow your own flowers and vegetables! A community garden is a place where people rent a patch of ground—called a plot—to grow plants. It's a great way to meet your neighbors, grow food, and get your paws nice and dirty!

"But, Vole," you ask, "HOW do I join a community garden?" Lucky for you, I have all the answers:

- Find out who's in charge of the garden and ask them what you need to do to take part.
- Gardening takes work. Every plant is a little different! Learn more about gardening at your local library, and start with easy plants like herbs, chard, kale, and cherry tomatoes. Yum.
- Take good care of your garden!
- Don't take anybody's veggies without permission, even if they look SO TASTY. Nobody likes a tomato thief!

Oh, and make sure to share your veggies with your friends! LIKE ME!

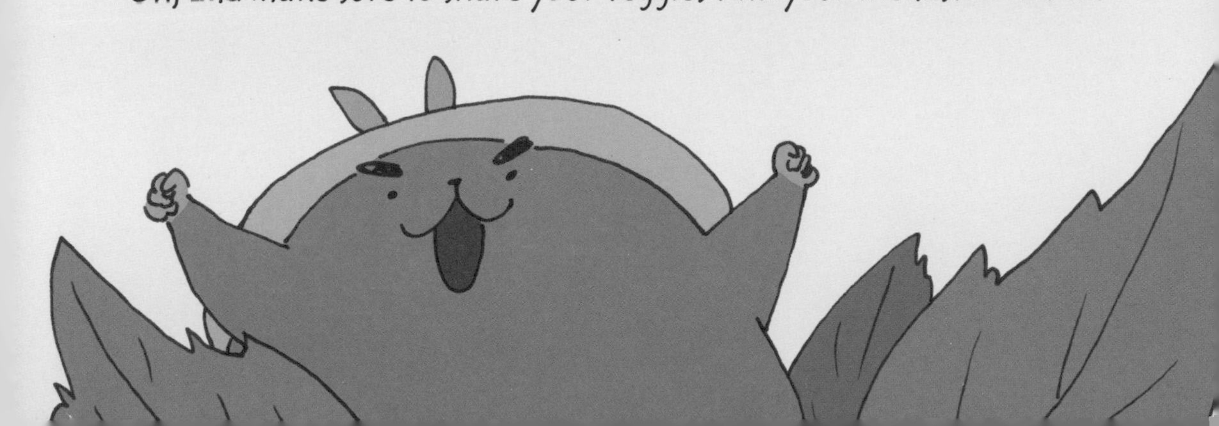

HOW TO STOP BIRDS FROM HITTING YOUR WINDOWS

by House Sparrow

Peep! Did you know windows can be dangerous for birds? We birds sometimes fly into windows and get hurt. We don't understand that they're made of hard stuff. We only see reflections of trees and the sky, or a safe place to hide on the other side of the windows. So, we think we can fly right through. But we can't! Peep!

You can make your windows safer for birds. It's easy! First, make your windows easier for us to see:

- Hang some pieces of string from the top of your windows. Or try putting window tape, window film, or stickers on the outside of the glass.
- Make sure these items are spaced two inches apart or less. Peep! Otherwise, we'll just try to fly around them!

Here are other ways to make windows safer:

- Keep bird feeders and baths one and a half feet from the window at most. (Thank you for the seeds. Peep!)
- Put screens on the outside of your windows.

Thanks for keeping us safe!

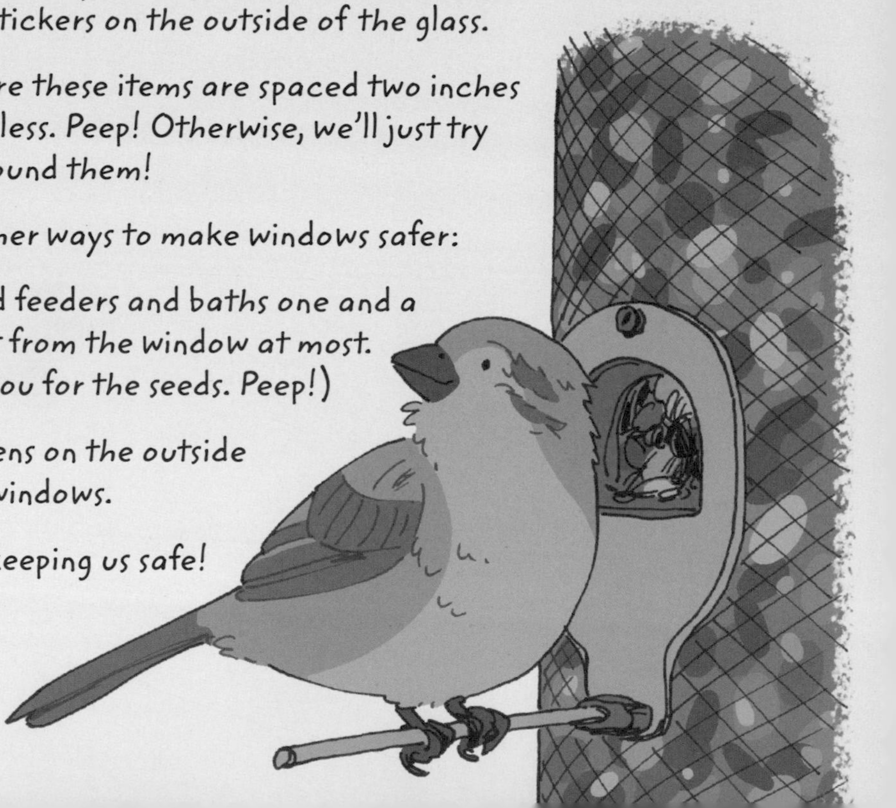

HOW TO BE THE BEST CAT OWNER EVER

by Vole

Cats make GREAT pets! But did you know that when cats and nature mix, sometimes bad things happen? Cats can eat birds and other local wildlife like me (oh no!). Sometimes they snack on bad stuff that makes them sick. Also, they can get hurt by cars or even other animals! Yikes!

It's easy to keep your cat friend safe! Here's how:

- Your kitty should stay inside your home!
- If you want to take your cat outside, try teaching it to wear a harness and a leash, like the boy in this story!
- Some people even build big backyard cages so their cats can have safe adventures. Doesn't that sound amazing?

"But, Vole," you say, "what if my cat gets bored in my house?" Here's how to bust your kitty's boredom:

- Give it some toys to play with. Try making your own!
- Make sure it has a place to scratch, and plenty of places to hide and climb and go on ADVENTURES.
- If you can, adopt a cat or dog friend for your cat! Friends are the BEST!

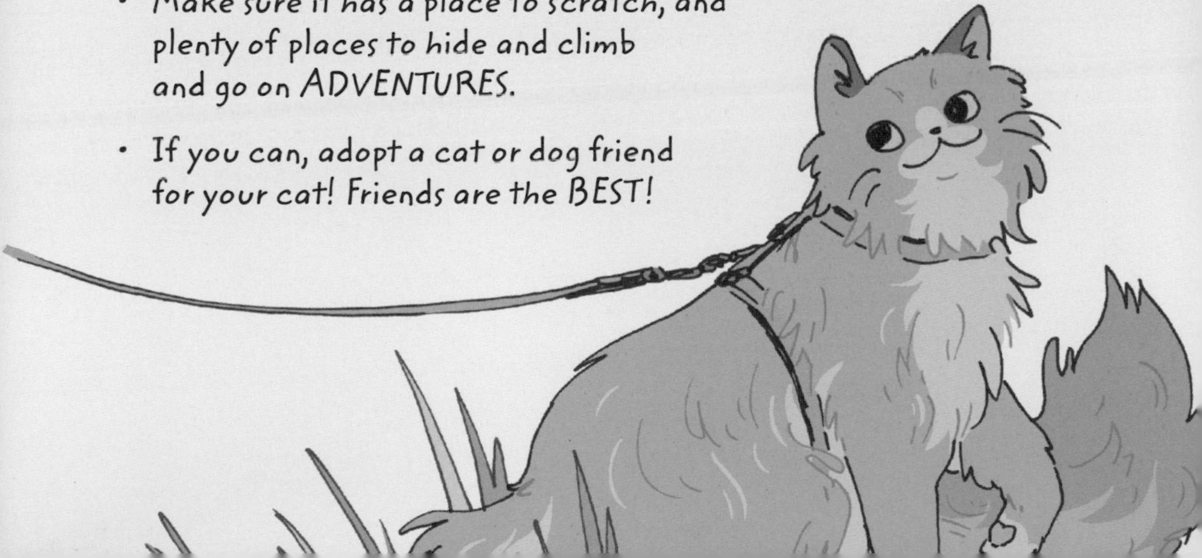

HOW TO COMPOST AT HOME
by Mole

Did you know you can turn kitchen scraps like apple cores and carrot peels into fuel for growing plants? It's called composting. Over time, tiny creatures like worms and bacteria eat your scraps and make them into plant food. Nature is great at recycling, but you need to do a few things to help this happen.

Here's how to start composting:

- Some cities have compost programs that pick up your food scraps for you. Find out if there's one in your town.

- If you have a backyard, talk to an adult about getting a big backyard bin. Composting isn't just about dumping food scraps into the bin. You have to mix the right stuff together. You and your adult need to do a bit of reading and learning.

- If you don't have a yard, you can compost indoors. Try vermicompost, a special kind of composting that involves worms. I think worms are beautiful (and delicious).

Thanks for helping nature recycle so that less stuff winds up in the trash, and thanks for making fuel that helps flowers grow.

ACKNOWLEDGMENTS

Thanks to my parents, Vincent and Catherine, for encouraging me to find nature in so many cities. Thank you to my editor, Gina Gagliano, for helping me dream up and shape this project, and to my agent, Seth Fishman, for guiding me through these bookish waters and always having my back. Special thanks to my love, always, always.

I wrote much of this book on the ancestral and unceded lands of the Massachusett people. I'd like to recognize their deep history, their suffering in the face of violence and disease brought by English invaders, and their continuing survival against all odds. Colonialism always brings ecological destruction, and it's important to acknowledge this history when we experience today's urban ecological landscape.

R.M.

Thank you to Ashanti, my wife and dearest friend, for your endless love and brilliant color expertise.
Thank you to Desolina, for your assistance on flats.
Thank you to Susan, my agent, for always believing in me.
Thank you to the Random House Graphic team, for all your work in making this book a reality.
Thank you to all my family and friends for your support and kindness.
Thank you to the medical workers, scientists, and researchers around the world who have given so much in the fight against COVID-19.

B.H.

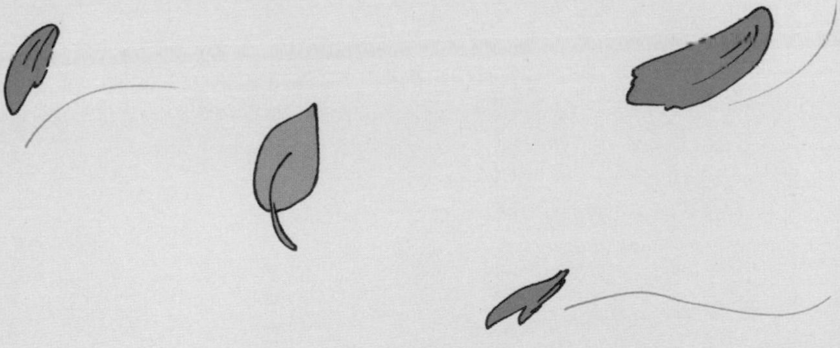

ABOUT THE CREATORS

Rosemary Mosco lives in New England, where she makes books and cartoons that connect people with the natural world. Her *Bird and Moon* nature comics (birdandmoon.com) were the subject of an award-winning museum exhibit and are collected in a book that was named an ALA Great Graphic Novel for Teens. She cowrote *The Atlas Obscura Explorer's Guide for the World's Most Adventurous Kid*, a *New York Times* bestseller. She speaks at bird-watching festivals and has written for Audubon and the PBS KIDS show *Elinor Wonders Why*. She loves pigeons more than almost any other animal.

🐦 @RosemaryMosco

Binglin Hu is a cartoonist, illustrator, and designer who loves to draw animals, people, and animal people. They make art for all ages, from kids to adults, and their work pulls inspiration from wildlife, fashion, manga, and mythology. Born and raised in icy Minnesota, Binglin now resides in Maryland, with their wife, Ashanti Fortson, and does full-time design work at the National Aquarium, which advocates for nature conservation and animal care. At this unique crossroads of art and science, Binglin has discovered a new spark for art as science communication.

🐦 @binglinhu

Ashanti Fortson is an award-winning cartoonist, illustrator, color designer, editor, and professor with a deep love for kind stories and fantastical settings. Their work explores tender and complex emotions, themes of disability and chronic illness, and life's coexisting beauty and grief. Ashanti has done coloring for other graphic novels, too: they colored *Song of the Court* by Katy Farina and did color design for the forthcoming *Brownstone* by Mar Julia and Samuel Teer. They're currently working on their debut graphic novel, *Cress & Petra*, and they teach comics and illustration on the side. They're the spider-saving sort.

🐦 @ashantifortson

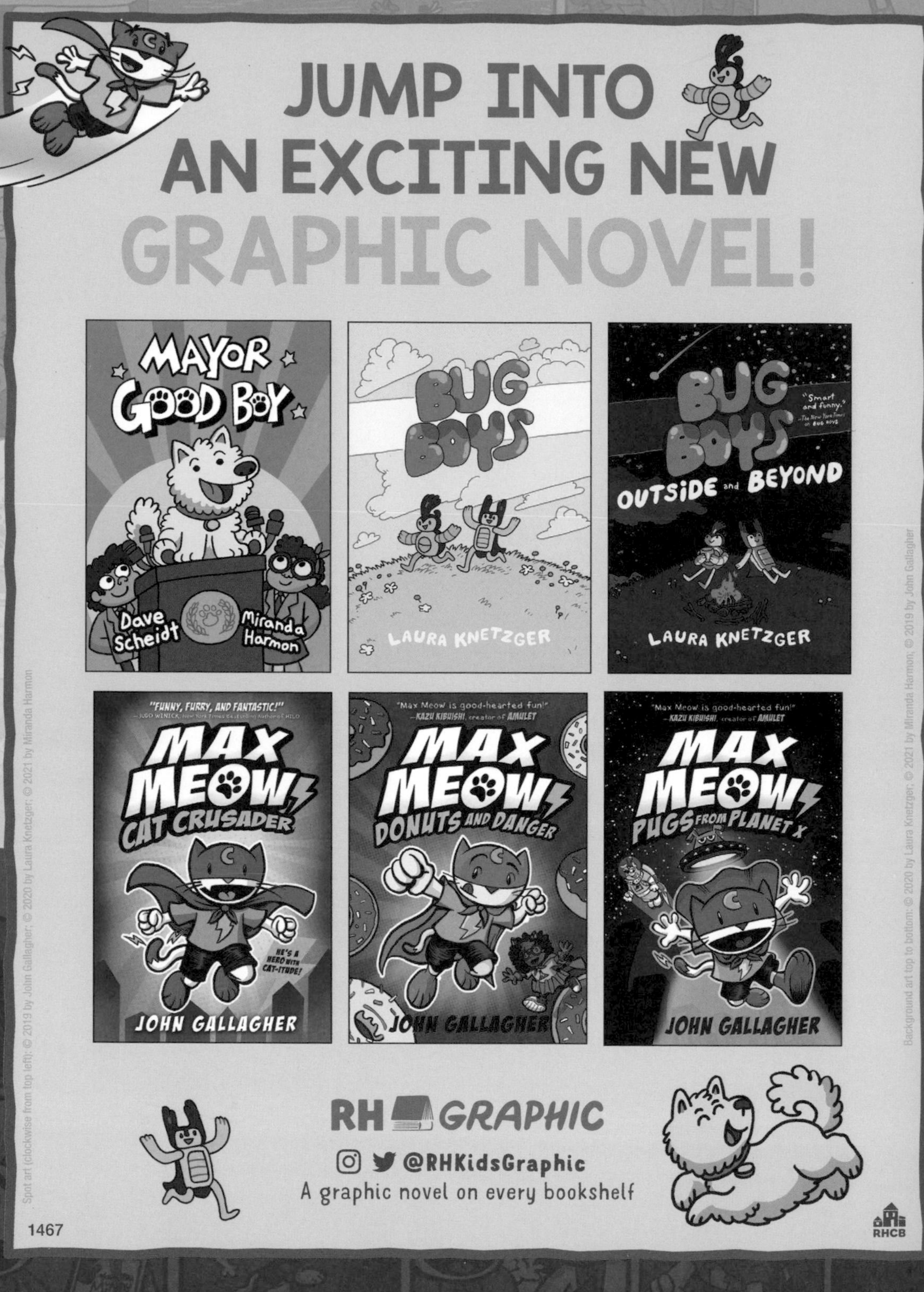
JUMP INTO
AN EXCITING NEW
GRAPHIC NOVEL!
MAYOR GOOD BOY
Dave Scheidt
Miranda Harmon
BUG BOYS
LAURA KNETZGER
BUG BOYS
OUTSIDE and BEYOND
"Smart and funny." —The New York Times on BUG BOYS
LAURA KNETZGER
"FUNNY, FURRY, AND FANTASTIC!" —JUDD WINICK, New York Times Bestselling Author of HILO
MAX MEOW
CAT CRUSADER
HE'S A HERO WITH CAT-ITUDE!
JOHN GALLAGHER
"Max Meow is good-hearted fun!" —KAZU KIBUISHI, creator of AMULET
MAX MEOW
DONUTS AND DANGER
JOHN GALLAGHER
"Max Meow is good-hearted fun!" —KAZU KIBUISHI, creator of AMULET
MAX MEOW
PUGS FROM PLANET X
JOHN GALLAGHER
RH GRAPHIC
@RHKidsGraphic
A graphic novel on every bookshelf
Spot art (clockwise from top left): © 2019 by John Gallagher; © 2020 by Laura Knetzger; © 2021 by Miranda Harmon
Background art top to bottom: © 2020 by Laura Knetzger; © 2021 by Miranda Harmon; © 2019 by John Gallagher
1467
RHCB